These Chivalrous Brothers

The Mysterious Disappearance of the 1882 Palmer Sinai Expedition

These Chivalrous Brothers

The Mysterious Disappearance of the 1882 Palmer Sinai Expedition

David Sunderland

CHRONOS BOOKS

Winchester, UK
Washington, USA

First published by Chronos Books, 2016
Chronos Books is an imprint of John Hunt Publishing Ltd., Laurel House, Station Approach, Alresford, Hants, SO24 9JH, UK
office1@jhpbooks.net
www.johnhuntpublishing.com

For distributor details and how to order please visit the 'Ordering' section on our website.

ISBN: 978 1 78535 242 3
Library of Congress Control Number: 2015946047

A CIP catalogue record for this book is available from the British Library.

Design: Stuart Davies

Printed and bound by CPI Group (UK) Ltd, Croydon, CR0 4YY, UK

CONTENTS

Spurning danger amid traitor-Egyptians,
Sheikh robbers and Bedouin bands,
Singlehanded these chivalrous brothers,
Press forward – their lives in their hands.

For England had spoken and claim'd them,
And gladly they rose at her cry,
And cheerily welcomed her summons,
'Be ready to do or to die.'

They sought not for gain or reward,
For honours, or mention, or praise,
Nor jostled for fame as men jostle,
In scheming and self-seeking days.

Then welcome your conquering Wolseley,
And crown him and feast as you will,
But spare just one thought for such heroes:
As Charrington!
Palmer!
and Gill!.

Extract from Anonymous, 'England expects every man to do his duty', *The Royal Engineers Journal,* 1 Dec. 1882.

To Maisie Metcalfe.
'Don't worry, be happy'.

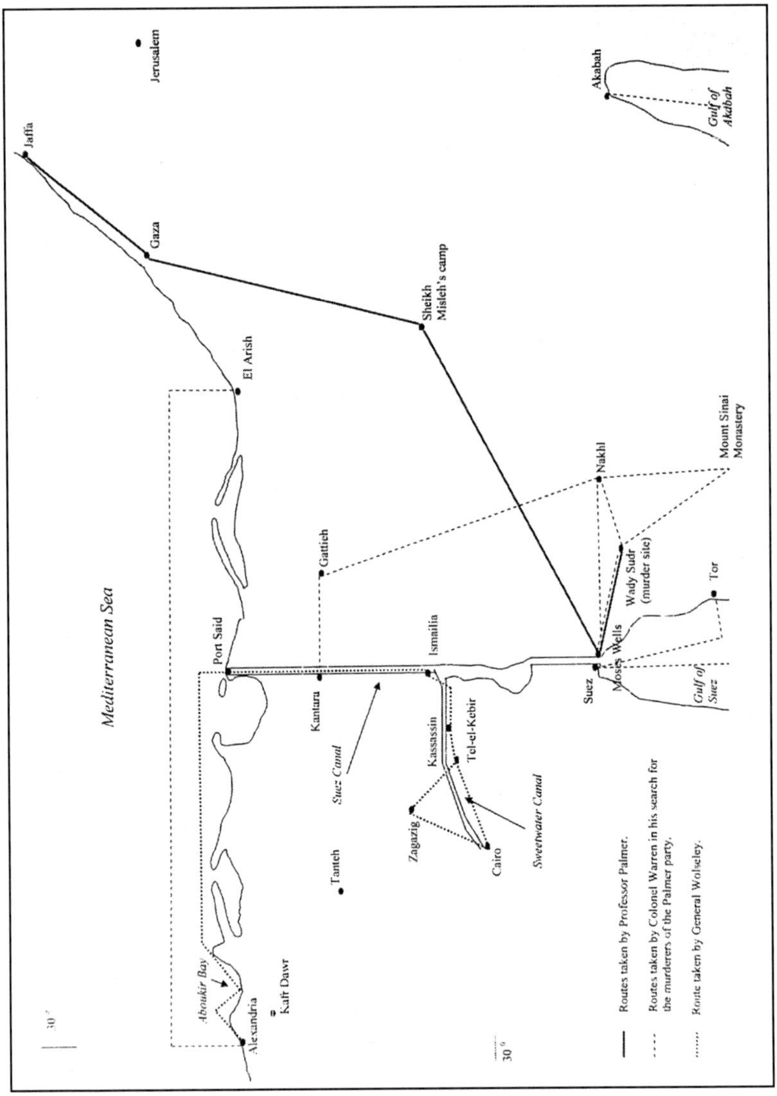
Mediterranean Sea
Jaffa
Jerusalem
Gaza
Sheikh Misleh's camp
El Arish
Akabah
Gulf of Akdbah
Nakhl
Mount Sinai Monastery
Gattieh
Wady Sudr (murder site)
Tor
Port Said
Ismailia
Kantara
Suez Canal
Suez
Moses Wells
Gulf of Suez
Kassassin
Tel-el-Kebir
Sweetwater Canal
Zagazig
Cairo
Tanteh
Aboukir Bay
Alexandria
Kafr Dawr
30°
Routes taken by Professor Palmer.
Routes taken by Colonel Warren in his search for the murderers of the Palmer party.
Route taken by General Wolseley.

Introduction

Just before sunset on August 8th 1882 HMS Cockatrice, a small paddle wheel gunboat, appeared off the shore of the Gulf of Suez. A rowing boat was lowered down its side and slowly moved towards the beach. On its arrival, six men and a teenage boy alighted. Three of the group were British, all dressed as Arabs, two were Bedouin tribesmen, one a Jew and one a Syrian. As their companions unloaded the voluminous contents of the boat, including two crates of dynamite and £3,000 in gold coin, the Englishmen talked amongst themselves. The conversation was dominated by a diminutive and slightly built middle-aged man, who had it not been for the beard that flowed to his waist, could easily have been mistaken for a child. He was Edward Henry Palmer, Cambridge University's Professor of Arabic, regarded by some as a linguistic genius and by others as an arrogant fool. By their ram-rod postures the men he addressed were obviously members of the military. The oldest, at thirty-nine, was Lieutenant William Gill. A shy melancholic individual with an upturned nose and a large drooping moustache, he was one of the richest men in Britain and had spent the previous twelve years travelling the globe. His colleague, who at over six foot five inches towered over his colleagues, was twenty-seven-year-old Lieutenant Harold Charrington, the fresh-faced second son of the owner of Charrington's brewery, England's largest producer of ale.[1]

On emptying the rowing boat, which returned to HMS Cockatrice, the older Bedouin, Meter ibu Sofieh, approached Palmer for orders. Aged over seventy, he possessed the haughty and peremptory manner one would expect of the Head Sheikh of the Lehewat tribe, one of Egypt's most important clans. Palmer instructed him to walk to Moses Wells, a small village two miles inland, where he was to inform Sulieman Zahr, a merchant, that they had arrived, and, as arranged, to send to the beach the following morning four camels and seven camel drivers. The other two men and the teenager, respectively the party's cook, Gill's servant and Sofieh's nephew, were asked to move the contents of the boat to two tents that Zahr had earlier erected at the top of the beach, where they were to spend the night. Both tasks were duly performed, and, as HMS Cockatrice majestically steamed back to Suez, the Englishmen and their attendants separately ate a hearty meal and retired to their tents.

At dawn the following morning, Zahr arrived with the camels and drivers. With him was another Bedouin, one of Sheikh Sofieh's tribesmen, who brought down three more camels. Palmer agreed to hire Zahr's beasts and drivers for six days; they would carry the party and its equipment to Sofieh's camp and then return to Moses Wells, being replaced by animals owned by the Sheikh and his own tribesmen, who would transport the Englishmen to their destination. The bargain made, Zahr's drivers began to load the hired camels. As this was taking place, another Bedouin, Salim ibu Subdeh, appeared from the direction of Moses Wells, approached Sofieh, and, overheard by one of Zahr's men, warned him against entering the desert. Britain was about to invade Egypt in support of its ruler, the Khedive, who was facing down an army rebellion, and there was a possibility that nationalistic Bedouin would attempt to murder the group. Sofieh reportedly made light of the matter. Zahr's employee who had eavesdropped the exchange, however, was more concerned and refused to leave, only changing his mind when Palmer assured him that there was no danger of an attack; he and Sofieh had recently travelled through the desert and found the local tribesmen extremely friendly. One hour later, the camels having been loaded, Zahr and Subdeh returned to Moses Wells and the Palmer Sinai Expedition left the beach bound for Sofieh's camp. Five of its members would never be seen again.

Chapter 1

The Approach of War

The Palmer mission was a small part of the British attempt to put down an Egyptian army rebellion. The revolt can be traced back to the 1860s when Khedive Ismail Pasha embarked on a mammoth spending spree. By 1875, an estimated £97 million had been expended on a war with Ethiopia and the construction of palaces, railroads, ports, the Suez and other canals and a new quarter of the city of Cairo modelled on Paris. The money was borrowed from France and Britain and the interest payments met from taxes drawn from the country's cotton industry, which was booming owing to the American Civil War and the consequent disruption of that country's cotton exports. In 1865, however, the Civil War came to an end, American cotton again entered the European market and prices and Egyptian exports fell dramatically, leading to tax shortfalls.[1]

Unable to pay the interest on his debts, the Khedive turned to the European powers for help, and, after some negotiation, it was decided that the nation's finances would be placed under the 'dual control' of Britain and France. Two 'controllers' were sent to Egypt and proceeded to raise taxes, slash army numbers and flood the civil service and the military with British and French officers, who could be trusted to act in their countries' interests. The Khedive was horrified. Aware that these initiatives were creating unrest that could threaten his own position, he reclaimed control of Egypt's fiscal and monetary policy and unilaterally reduced its interest payments. The allied powers' response was to pressure the Turkish Sultan (Egypt was a province of Turkey), to depose him, thus allowing the succession of his eldest son, the more pliant Prince Tewfiq, who accepted the re-introduction of 'dual control' and appointed a new government, the Minister of War of which cut troop numbers and introduced reforms designed to reduce Egyptian control of the army, thus reducing the likelihood of a military coup.

The opposition to the British and French effective takeover of Egyptian governance was led by an obscure middle-aged Colonel named Ahmed Arabi. The son of a village sheikh, Arabi had been conscripted into the Egyptian army at the age of fourteen and had moved rapidly through the ranks, becoming a Lieutenant Colonel at the age of just twenty. Tall and burly, he was a galvanising speaker and possessed an intimidating, faintly threatening presence. In January 1881, he and his colleagues, nicknamed 'the colonels', presented a petition to the government and the Khedive demanding the replacement of the Minister of War and the reversal of his reforms. A few hours later, they were summoned on a pretext to the War Ministry, where they were summarily arrested and court marshaled. Luckily, they had been pre-warned of their likely detention and had arranged for a battalion of troops to storm the Ministry if they did not return. Thus, as the court marshal began, the court was invaded by hundreds of soldiers. The prisoners were freed and with their men marched to the Khedive's palace, which meanwhile had been surrounded by a further battalion, and put their demands to Tewfiq in person. Informed by his advisors that there was not one soldier in the city who supported him, the Khedive had no choice but to capitulate. The Minister of War was dismissed and replaced by one of the petitioners, whose first action was to propose an increase in army numbers and pay.

Needless to say, Tewfiq's European masters were not amused. Ordered to recover the situation, Tewfiq appointed his brother-in-law Minister of War and instructed Arabi to transfer his Cairo based regiment to Alexandria thus preventing the nationalists again using military power to force through change. Arabi's response was to mount a coup d'art. On the morning of September 9th, a petition was dispatched to the Khedive informing him that at 3.30pm that afternoon all the army divisions based in Cairo would march to his palace to demand the replacement of the government. The British urged Tewfiq to make a stand. Informed by his advisors that three regiments in the city remained loyal, he immediately went to their barracks and ordered them to the palace. His courage then appeared to desert him, and, against the advice of the British Vice-Consul, Auckland Colvin, who had accompanied him, he set off for Abbassieh, three miles outside the city, to obtain the support of more troops. On arrival, however, he found that the soldiers had left for Cairo to join Arabi, and, urged on by Colvin, turned his carriage around and raced back to his royal residence.

The sight that awaited him must have been terrifying. Positioned across the square that fronted the building were between eighteen and thirty artillery guns behind which were drawn up in ranks 2,500 to 4,000 soldiers, including those belonging to one of the supposedly loyal regiments. Entering the palace by a side door, Tewfiq, accompanied by the Vice-Consul and several Egyptian and European officials, walked out of the front entrance and into the centre of the plaza. Arabi and 'the colonels' rode from the perimeter to meet him, and, as they dismounted, Colvin ordered the Khedive to instruct the rebel leader to give up his sword and disperse his troops. Replying 'We shall be killed!', Tewfiq instead agreed to discuss Arabi's demands.[2] He then scuttled back to the safety of the palace, leaving Colvin and his associates to undertake the negotiations. The rebels had won, and, over the following few hours, it was agreed that the government would be replaced by one composed of nationalists.

Despairing of the Khedive, the British and French now took matters into their own hands. A joint communiqué was sent to the new government declaring that the two countries recognized only the authority of the Khedive, who they pledged to support. In response, Arabi again raised the stakes demanding that the

Khedive form another even more nationalistic administration. Weak as ever, Tewfiq complied, making Arabi Minister of War and one of his supporters Prime Minister. For Britain and France, this was the last straw and a naval flotilla was despatched to Alexandria in the belief that its presence would force the nationalists to back down. In the event, its arrival helped to provoke a riot. Supporters of the Khedive claimed that the disturbances were incited by Arabi, whilst those who favoured the nationalist cause placed the blame on Tewfiq, arguing that he had bribed local Bedouin to instigate the violence in order to discredit his opponents. In reality, the disorder most probably ignited spontaneously. The city had long been a tinderbox. The tendency of the large European population to flaunt its wealth and privilege had created a great deal of resentment amongst the Arab community, which was intensified by the presence offshore of the British and French fleets and rumours of invasion.

The origin of the riot was a fracas at a coffee house on the Rue des Soeurs. A donkey boy, stoned on hashish, had insulted a Maltese gentleman, who had responded by giving the lad a good beating, during which his victim had pulled out a knife and stabbed him in the chest. Other Europeans at the café rushed to his assistance, and, finding him mortally wounded, turned on the boy, who they beat and kicked to death. News of the incident spread rapidly and a crowd of Egyptians gathered and eventually attacked those responsible for the boy's murder, prompting the Greek and Maltese residents of the upper floors of the café and surrounding houses to fire down on them. Several Arabs were killed and many more wounded. Alerted of the incident, the local police summoned the British Consul and the Governor of Alexandria. Assuring the throng that justice would be done, they appeared to calm tempers and departed.

Some of the crowd, however, were not convinced and began to move down Rue des Soeurs towards the Place Mehemet Ali, the city's central square, at the centre of which stood a statue of the ruler after which it had been named. At the same time, a further mob had congregated in the nearby Attarin quarter and also began to make its way to the Place Mehemet Ali. The two groups converged at approximately 5.30pm and then marched down the streets that led from the square to the harbour. As they moved to the square, they clubbed down every European they encountered, the desert Bedouins among them firing at passersby and at Westerners who were shooting at the crowd from the terraces and balconies of their houses. Those killed were stripped of their clothes and possessions and their bodies mutilated. Children were both victims and perpetrators. A young Maltese girl was clubbed to death and the shoe blacking boys that plied their trade beneath the statue of Mehemet Ali were seen gleefully beating out the brains of Europeans lying wounded around their place of work. Rather than seeking to halt the mayhem, many Egyptian soldiers and police officers joined in. Westerners who appealed to passing policemen and soldiers for protection were bayoneted on the spot; those who sought refuge in police stations were slaughtered on gaining entrance.

On heading for the harbour, the rioters came across fresh prey. Many European families had spent the day admiring the ships anchored offshore and were setting off for home. Heading in the opposite direction were men, women and children attempting to escape the violence and British and French sailors returning to their ships after a day onshore. Both groups were attacked in the most vicious fashion. A fireman saw a companion's head lopped off by a sword and a young child's body was literally slashed to pieces. Having killed all they saw, the crowd then turned and moved inland, breaking into houses and stealing the contents, and, at the Place Mehemet Ali, looted the shops and kiosks that surrounded the square. Again, the army and the police made no attempt to intervene, and, in many cases, plundered goods themselves; one soldier was seen walking down Rue des Soeurs wearing a glass chandelier as a headpiece.

Although well aware of the slaughter, both Arabi and the Commander of the British Fleet at Alexandria, Admiral Frederick Seymour, known to his friends as the 'Ocean Swell', took no action for several hours. The Egyptian army had 7,000 troops barracked on the outskirts of the city. At 4pm, the Governor of Alexandria asked their commander to deploy them to restore order. The commander declined unless a written instruction was given, and, when this was produced, refused to act unless told to do so by Arabi himself. Contacted by telegraph in Cairo, Arabi, perhaps wishing to demonstrate his power, did nothing until 6pm when he finally allowed the troops to intervene.

Admiral Seymour, who had been onshore when the rioting began, was similarly reluctant to become involved, fearing that the landing of armed marines would be interpreted as an act of war. On returning to his flagship thoroughly alarmed at what he had witnessed, he signalled to the fleet 'prepare to land armed boats', but five minutes later annulled the instruction.[3] After discussion with his captains, lasting several hours, he ordered HMS Superb to send boats to rescue those Europeans who had sought refuge in the British Consulate, but at 8pm rescinded the order on receiving a telegraph from the Governor that Arabi's troops, who were now in the city, would probably oppose the landing. A prediction that was proved to be correct when HMS Superb, not having received the telegraph cancelling Seymour's order, duly launched the rescue boats, which were fired upon before they reached the shore and were forced to turn back.

Daybreak revealed a scene of utter carnage. At least fifty Europeans lay dead, though many believe three times that number died. Most had been clubbed to death, their faces so battered that they were unrecognisable. Hundreds more were wounded, including the British Consul, who, on returning to the Consulate after calming the crowd immediately after the donkey boy's death, had been called to a meeting at the police station on the Rue des Soeurs. Within ninety yards of his destination, he was pulled from his carriage and clubbed to the ground, but managed to stumble to the police station, blood streaming down his face.

Over the following few days, the surviving Western residents of Alexandria began to depart by ship to Malta, Cyprus and Constantinople. As news of the massacre spread, they were joined by Europeans living in the interior; on June 14th 4,000 arrived at Alexandria railway station, many having ridden there on the roofs of carriages. Openly insulted in the streets, they feared for their own lives and were desperate to escape. To get them away, a mass rescue mission was launched; the British government arranged for merchant steamers to take refugees to Malta, while their French and Greek counterparts sent transport ships. Thus, two weeks after the riot, the whole of Egypt was largely denuded of Westerners, and, with their shops and businesses closed, hundreds of thousands of Egyptians found themselves unemployed and close to destitution.

In Britain, news that British subjects had been 'butchered under the very guns of the fleet' was met with shock and anger.[4] The press, opposition and even some members of the Cabinet denounced the government's timidity towards Egypt and demanded retribution. The Prime Minister's response was to seek peace, but to prepare for war. An international conference was established to allow the major powers to discuss the situation and Turkey asked to send troops to the country to restore order; a request that was peremptorily turned down. Meanwhile, in the War Office and Admiralty planning for an invasion got under way and an advance force of almost 4,000 men was despatched to Egypt under the command of General Archibald Alison.

Chapter 2

The First Palmer Mission

Lieutenant William Gill's involvement in the Palmer mission began on Saturday June 24th 1882. He and Colonel Edward Bradford were instructed by Lord Northbrook, the First Lord of the Admiralty, to collect information on the likely allegiance of the Bedouin tribes living in the area bordering the Suez Canal and to suggest ways in which the tribesmen could be encouraged to support a British campaign, and, in particular, to prevent any nationalistic attempts to block the Canal and thus prevent troops and supplies being brought into the heart of the country. The likely allegiance of the Bedouin was an unknown quantity to the British. It was accepted that they disliked Europeans. Like most Egyptians, they resented Britain's control of their country, and, furthermore, blamed foreigners for the construction of the Suez Canal, which had increased their taxes, lessened their sphere of influence and reduced the income earned from guiding pilgrims across the desert, pilgrimage traffic having moved onto steamers. On the other hand, they were suspicious of the rebels. In March 1882 the nationalist government had sought to dilute their traditional privileges of exemption from military service and corvee (forced labour) and had only backed down on the realisation that the new policies would be strenuously opposed.[1]

Edward Bradford was a buccaneering Indian army officer, who had lost his left arm after being mauled by a tiger in a local hunt, but had famously continued his great love of pig sticking by holding the reins of his horse between his teeth. Unsuited to such mundane work, he left Northbrook's task to his enthusiastic colleague, who was advised to visit a Professor Edward Palmer, the renowned Cambridge University Orientalist who had travelled through the region ten years previously. That evening

Gill called upon the Professor at his imposing house in Mecklenburgh Square, Bloomsbury. The meeting lasted barely an hour as Palmer had a later social engagement, but Gill was sufficiently impressed to suggest that they get together the following Monday.

At 10am on Monday morning, the two again met in Palmer's study and the Professor described in great detail the characteristics of the sheikhs and tribes who lived alongside the canal and advised that they could only be lured into joining the British cause if they were visited by someone they knew and trusted. Assuming that Palmer was proposing himself for this mission, Gill returned to the Admiralty for a pre-arranged meeting with Lord Northbrook, who on hearing of the Professor's great knowledge and enthusiasm decided to meet him personally, sending him an invitation to breakfast the following morning. Palmer, meanwhile, spent the afternoon with Wilfrid Scawen Blunt, another larger than life personality. A writer, poet and explorer, Blunt's main passions in life were politics, sex and horses, not necessarily in that order. During his lifetime, he campaigned tirelessly for the independence of Egypt, India and Ireland, bred Arabian stallions on his estates in England and Egypt and had a succession of affairs before marrying the granddaughter of Lord Byron. Palmer introduced himself as an ardent supporter of Arabi and claimed to have been invited by the *Standard* newspaper to travel to Alexandria to report on the current situation in Egypt. Wishing to present the nationalist cause to the British public, he asked Blunt, who was a personal friend of Arabi, for introductions to all the sheikhs who supported the rebel leader. Never having previously met or heard of this fellow traveller and not 'trust[ing] his countenance, which was far from sincere', Blunt was suspicious and refused to write introductions, but gave him 'a few names'.[2]

Next morning, Palmer presented himself at the Admiralty where he breakfasted with Northbrook, Gill, Bradford and the

Lord's secretary. As they ate, they discussed how the Suez tribes could be pacified; Palmer again advocating that someone should be sent to negotiate terms with the relevant sheikhs. After the meeting, Northbrook, Gill and Bradford conferred and agreed that Palmer's proposal was valid, but that the academic was perhaps not the right man to act as emissary. Gill and Bradford thus spent the rest of that and the following day considering alternative candidates, including the great explorer Richard Burton and the man later to be employed to search for Palmer and his companions, Colonel Charles Warren. All were rejected. Some were not available and others lacked Palmer's qualifications – he was a fluent speaker of Arabic and the dialects of the Sinai Peninsula, he had met and formed good relationships with all of the sheikhs of the region and he had no previous connections with the Admiralty, enabling the government to deny any involvement in his mission if it was discovered. On the evening of Wednesday June 29th, Palmer was thus sent an invitation to call on Northbrook at 10am the following morning.

Northbrook began the two hour meeting by asking Palmer whether he knew anyone who would be prepared to travel to Egypt at very short notice to perform the tasks he had outlined. Palmer recommended himself, partly out of patriotism, but largely because of his lifelong love of adventure and the lure of fame, honours and perhaps a permanent appointment in naval intelligence if he was successful. His offer was duly accepted and he was informed that his mission would start the very next day. After discussing his itinerary with Gill and Bradford, he met his young wife, a beautiful Polish aristocrat, for lunch, spent the afternoon clearing his diary for the foreseeable future, and, in the evening, dined with his best friend, the novelist Walter Besant, with whom he was 'for a secret agent…uncommonly and recklessly open mouthed', describing in detail the goals of his assignment and how he hoped to achieve them. The following day, he visited more of his many friends to wish them adieu, and, at 5pm, boarded the boat train to Paris.[3]

Palmer's instructions were to enter the desert at Gaza and travel to Suez, calling at the camps of every tribe and speaking to the principal sheikhs. During each conversation, he was to ascertain whether the sheikh was inclined to join the nationalist rebellion, and, if so, what sum of money would be sufficient for him to support the British, and, if necessary, to supply an invasion force with camels and to guard the Suez Canal from Arabi attack and repair its banks if they were damaged. More generally, he was to find out if the nationalist army was in communication with Turkish forces and assess whether the Bedouin would join the rebels if a jihad, a holy war on the infidel, was proclaimed. To maintain secrecy and to avoid any apparent connection between Palmer and the British military, none of these instructions were written down and two cover stories were concocted; one for European and the other for Bedouin consumption. A news item was planted in the *Times* that stated that he was about to visit Egypt on behalf of the Palestine Exploration Fund to complete a map of the Desert of Tih, which he had begun on his last visit to the region. Unfortunately, the subterfuge lacked the essential aura of authenticity – no visitor to the area would begin an expedition in the blistering heat of mid-summer – and Palmer failed to stick to the story, inventing two more of his own. He told colleagues that he was travelling to Egypt because he believed the climate would improve the chronic asthma from which he suffered and the Englishmen that he met on the journey that he was the Egypt correspondent of the *Standard* newspaper. To the sheikhs he visited, he was to be Sheikh Abdullah, the identity that he had adopted during his previous trek through the desert. Rather than a poor Syrian traveller, as previously, Abdullah was now a wealthy high ranking Syrian officer, who was acting on behalf of the Turkish government. To give this cover story validity, he was to travel to Egypt overland from Paris to Brindisi and thence by boat to

Alexandria and enter the desert from Gaza, which would allow him to claim that he had ridden from the Ottoman Empire, but would greatly increase the danger of his journey as he would be closely monitored by Turkish officials.[4]

Palmer's trip to Egypt was a pleasant affair; he met a chum from his days as an undergraduate at St John's College, Cambridge, and got to know the artist who was to cover the impending war for the *Illustrated London News*; his newfound friend drawing a fine picture of him talking to a crew member, which he hoped would eventually be published. He arrived at Alexandria on July 5th to discover the city deserted and desolate. As instructed, he boarded Admiral Seymour's yacht, where he was congratulated on his bravery in volunteering for such a hazardous task and given a revolver, a rifle, some cartridges and a pass from the Khedive, which instructed all he met to treat him with respect and to answer his questions. He then took a spin around the harbour, pronouncing the 37 gunships that packed the waters 'a grand sight' and retired to bed in his cabin.

The following day after breakfasting with Seymour and his officers on iced figs, he boarded an Austrian steamer bound for Jaffa via Port Said. The journey was horrendous. 'Jews and Syrians [were] packed like herrings, fighting, being sick, howling, poor babes and little children screaming'; the noise, the 'frightful stench', 'burning heat' and rough sea causing him to feel 'quite ill and miserable'. Going ashore at Port Said, he found the place full of 'hot stinky people…in a dreadful fright', and, re-boarding the ship, the 'burning heat' of the day made his cabin so 'frightfully stuffy and hot' that he was repeatedly sick.[5] His arrival at Jaffa was equally uncomfortable. After waiting an hour to disembark, the customs officials were uncivil, insisted on searching his luggage and attempted to confiscate his two weapons.

On emerging from the Customs House, he made his way to the home of the British consul and agent of the Church

Missionary Society, the Reverend Alexander Schapira, with whom he had arranged to stay. A Russian Jew married to a German, who had spent most of his career in Sierra Leone and Egypt, Schapira was Consul largely because he was the only permanent resident in Jaffa with some connection to Britain; he had studied at St David's College, Lampeter. Suffering from poor eyesight and with very little money, in the four years he had lived in the port he had established a chapel in the upper room of his home and three schools that educated over 200 children, most of them Moslems.[6]

During his long journey east, Palmer had unilaterally altered his instructions. Rather than travelling from tribe to tribe, he had decided to negotiate with just one chieftain: Sheikh Suileman of the Teyahah tribe. Why Palmer thought Suileman, who he had met during his first trip to the region, represented the other tribes or could be trusted is something of a mystery. He was not the hereditary sheikh of his clan, having been given the position by the Turks who several years previously had deposed his predecessor and his family and thrown them in jail in order to end a blood feud they were undertaking against other tribal chiefs. He thus had little power over his own people, many of whom supported the hereditary chieftain, and was regarded by other tribal sheikhs as a nonentity. Even if this had not been the case, he and the Teyahah made unlikely intermediaries. The tribe was infamous for stealing the camels of its neighbours and was generally held in utter contempt by other tribal leaders, and, in 1875, had attacked a British survey party. Western travellers, who had had the misfortune to come across Suileman, including Palmer himself, regarded him as a crook. The American Reverend Samuel Colcord Bartlett, who had employed the Sheikh as a guide, described his tribe as 'a band of rogues' and 'leeches' and Suileman as 'an angry child'. During Bartlett's journey, the Sheikh had countermanded his orders, threatened to attack him with a sword and tried to extract a fee even higher than the already extortionate one agreed.[7] Palmer, meanwhile, in his account of his first journey to the region recounted that Suileman had been 'absent on a plundering tour making good the reputation of his tribe' when he and his colleague had first entered Teyahah territory and that whilst accompanying them through his tribal lands he had 'tried on all occasions to cheat us' and made 'lamentable attempts to frighten us [after which] he had taken to a fawning abject demeanour that was almost as amusing as it was disgusting'.[8]

Palmer's first action once he had settled into his room was to ask Schapira to send his eldest son to the tents of Sheikh Suileman with a letter explaining his mission and requesting a meeting. Whilst waiting for a reply, he purchased provisions, had his hair cut 'quite close' in the Syrian tradition, and, on Schapira's recommendation, employed a cook, a forty-six year old Jew named Bokor Hassoun. Although Hassoun was a 'sturdy native', could shoot a revolver and spoke English and Italian, allowing Palmer to 'express my opinion without my Arab friends understanding', his recruitment is curious as few Moslems travelled with Jewish servants and it thus weakened his cover story. Suileman's reply arrived the following day. The Sheikh agreed to a meeting and Palmer thus took a carriage to Gaza; another 'dreadful' journey that comprised 'sitting upright…for eighteen hours'.[9] Originally intending to remain in the town just long enough to send a message to Suileman alerting him of his imminent arrival and to recruit a guide and escorts, he ended up staying two days. The likelihood of war had made most Arabs loath to enter the desert and messengers and escorts were in short supply. The enforced delay, however, proved fortuitous. Quite by chance, a number of tribes had camped some distance away and Palmer was able to collect information on their strengths, current camping sites and allegiances.[10]

The journey to Suileman's camp took five days. In addition to his cook, Palmer was accompanied by a guide, who was a cousin of Sheikh Suileman, and five or six Bedouin. The days took on a strangely comforting routine. The party started out each morning at 5am, stopped for two hours at noon for lunch and a nap and then rode on until sunset when they camped for the night and Palmer enjoyed his main meal, generally soup followed by roast fowl, and 'took in the twilight sitting on a carpet outside [his tent]'. Apart from a group of Bedouin belonging to the Terabin tribe, from whom he 'found out more about them…than they did about me', and two Turkish soldiers spied on the horizon, they met no one. This idyll came to an end on July 18th when 'all hell broke loose'.[11] Palmer had stopped for lunch and was just finishing his first course when twenty Bedouin charged into his camp, pulling up their camels and alighting just yards from his tent. Having heard their approach, Palmer had composed himself, and, showing no sign of fear or surprise, merely rose and greeted the two Arabs who advanced towards him. One was Sheikh Misleh, who Palmer had met during his first visit to Egypt. 'A swarthy personage of sinister look…fully conscious of his great importance', he was Suileman's elder brother.[12] The other Bedouin, a man of about seventy years of age and of 'commanding stature and haughty and peremptory manner', introduced himself as Sheikh Meter ibu Sofieh, the chief of the Lehewat tribe, which occupied the country east of Suez.[13]

Palmer invited Misleh to sit down and smoke a cigarette and was informed that Suileman had been called to Cairo, but would return in a few days time and had asked his brother to act on his behalf in the negotiations, which were to begin immediately. They did not start well. Misleh announced 'Pasha Arabi is with the Moslems, you belong to our enemies' and then remained silent, refusing to answer Palmer's questions. Gradually, however, he relaxed his position, and set out his demands. He and his brother would provide the British with 10,000 Teyahah and Terabin fighters, plus an additional 40,000 Bedouin from the other tribes, in return for £20,000 (approximately £923,000 at today's values), £500 of which was to be paid to Misleh himself, and the release from a Turkish jail in Jerusalem of the hereditary Sheikh of the Teyahah, plus all members of the chief's family. Delighted, Palmer immediately agreed to the demands, subject to their acceptance by Admiral Sir William Hewitt, Commander-in Chief of the Naval force in Alexandria, and spent the remainder of the afternoon writing a letter to his superior in which he described the proposed agreement, asked for his assent and enquired how he was to reach the British ships anchored off Suez, which was occupied by Arabi soldiers. The letter, addressed to Hewitt, was given to Sheikh Sofieh, who was asked to go to Suez, somehow get the letter to the Admiral and return with the reply.[14]

On later hearing of the agreement, those who had travelled through the region were dumbfounded by Palmer's decision to trust Misleh, who in official British papers was described as being of 'bad reputation, suspicious and brutal' and Palmer himself had depicted in his book on his earlier journey through the desert as 'an ill-looking surly ruffian' with 'a scowl of mingled cunning and distrust', who in the negotiations to fix the fee to be paid to travel through his tribal territory had attempted to 'cheat us' and had resorted to 'intimidation'.[15] The Reverend Henry Field had met Misleh earlier in 1882. The 'crafty sheikh' had expressed pro-nationalist opinions, demanded an extortionate sum for permission to pass through his lands and to obtain his services as a guide, and halfway through the trip had demanded an additional sum, threatening to abandon the party without food or water if it was not paid.[16] The Reverend Samuel Bartlett had also been forced to pay him an exorbitant sum and had found him 'a fierce fellow', who had a reputation for attacking the servants of Westerners, and, 'turning dirty white and almost speechless with rage', had almost struck a member of his own party over a minor sleight.[17] The Reverend Henry Clay Trumbell, editor of the

Sunday-School Times, meanwhile, had been assured by the 'cunning sheikh' that the Jerusalem prisoners were innocent of the charges against them, offered a £300 Arab stallion if he could persuade his Consul to help release them and warned that if they remained in jail 'the desert would not be safe for any traveller'.[18]

On the departure of Sofieh, Palmer rode to Misleh's camp to await the Admiral's response and the return of Suileman. The journey was long and tiring and only enlivened by Misleh on the final morning riding up to one of his men, who had displeased him, drawing his sword and attempting to decapitate him; luckily the intended victim slipped out of his saddle before the blade made contact. At the camp, Palmer made his tent 'quite cosy' and, over the following five days, sketched, shot partridges and wrote his journal, congratulating himself on his success and his good relationship with his newfound friends. Misleh went about his business, only leaving the camp to pursue Maareh tribesmen who had carried off camels and sheep from a browsing ground lower down the valley. Palmer exalted at the raid, as the perpetrators were supporters of Arabi and the attack 'will make my ragamuffins doubly eager to do the little job I [have] asked them [to perform]'. Lending Misleh his rifle, he wrote 'Hoorah! My Sheikh's party is twice as strong [as the Maareh]...if they catch them...there will be some murder done [tonight]'.[19]

His mood darkened when Suileman failed to return from Cairo and there was no sign of Sofieh. Aware that if his messenger had been captured by the enemy and his letter read, 'things won't be nice for me', he became so anxious that 'every time the dogs bark I think it is he [Sofieh] and jump up'. The sheikh eventually reappeared on July 26th and Palmer immediately grabbed the parcel he carried. The contents were 'a dreadful disappointment'.[20] Rather than a reply agreeing to the deal made and informing him how he was to reach the British ships moored off Suez, it merely contained some old newspapers. It later transpired that Sofieh, on reaching Moses Wells, had asked Sulieman Zahr, the camel dealer, to deliver the letter, telling him that he had never visited Suez and had no idea how to contact Admiral Hewitt. Aware that the local British Consul was onboard a ship moored off the coast, Zahr had ordered an employee to take the letter to the Consul and ask him to pass it onto the Admiral. The Consul agreed, and, in return, had given Zahr's servant some newspapers to allow the Professor to catch up on the progress of the war, which Sofieh assumed was the reply with which he was to return. Palmer, knowing nothing of this, unwilling to send another message and relive the torture of the past few days and convinced that his superiors would approve his actions, decided to inform Misleh that the agreement had been accepted and that he would return in three or four weeks with the sum demanded and proof of the release of the prisoners.

After a leaving ceremony at which both he and Misleh ate bread and salt, symbolizing that they would protect each other unto death, he set off for Suez, accompanied by his faithful cook, six Teyahah, plus Sheikh Sofieh. It was the custom for Westerners traversing the desert to be escorted by the sheikh whose tribe controlled the region to be crossed. In return for a fee, the chief acted as a guide and prevented members of his tribe attacking the party. Since Sofieh was the Sheikh of the Lehewat tribe, which controlled the area between Misleh's camp and Suez, his presence was essential.

Palmer intended to ride to Moses Wells and then catch a boat to the naval vessels anchored off Suez; the newspapers brought by Sofieh having listed the dates and times at which P & O ships called at the oasis. The journey took four days, much of it covered at night and in long rides in an attempt to avoid the Arabi forces that he suspected patrolled the desert. By the final day, he was 'dried up and burnt and thirsty and bored', possessed a 'frightful headache' and 'long[ed] for the cool smoking room at the Savile

[Club] and the even cooler drinks'; the only consolation of the trip being the close bond that he had established with Sheikh Sofieh – quoting 'Arabic poetry to the old man', he had 'quite won his heart'.[21] On arrival at Moses Wells, the Teyahah escort left and the baggage their camels carried was reloaded onto beasts rented from Sulieman Zahr and taken to the beach. Here, Palmer bade farewell to Sofieh and arranged to meet him at the oasis twelve days hence when he hoped to return to Misleh's camp to seal the deal. The old Sheikh then rode back to his tents at Wady Sudr and Palmer boarded a hired dhow, which carried him and his luggage to the ship that was to ferry him to safety.[22] Once onboard, having been up for 24 hours and not eaten for fifteen hours, he had a small meal and fell into a deep sleep. When he awoke, he was in Suez. The reception that awaited him exceeded his wildest dreams. Regarded as a returning hero, he was invited to a celebratory iced champagne party organised by the captains of the British ships. He then had a meeting with Hewitt, who had finally received his letter requesting instructions and assumed that he had made no agreement with Misleh, having received no authority to do so. Palmer, for some reason, perhaps a desire to avoid criticism and a belief that the Admiral would later countenance the deal, made no attempt to alter this impression; a mistake that would later prove fatal.

Chapter 3

The Bombardment of Alexandria

As Palmer left Gaza on his first journey into the desert, Arabi began to improve Alexandria's sea fortifications in preparation of a likely attack on the city from the English and French fleets anchored offshore. The Admiralty initially made no attempt to halt his activities as the evacuation of Europeans from Egypt was not yet complete, the Turks strongly opposed action and there was a fear that any hostile act would endanger the success of an international conference that was attempting to find a solution to the 'Egyptian problem'. Its laissez faire approach did not last long. Arabi continued to build earthworks and mount new guns, and, when ordered by Admiral Seymour to desist, denied that any work was being undertaken. On discovering a few days later that large cannons were being dragged to two of the city's most important forts, Seymour with the Admiralty's consent asked his French counterpart to support the issue of an ultimatum. Claiming that the guns posed a threat to their fleets, he proposed that they threaten to open fire on the port unless the cannons were removed. The French, secretly attempting to negotiate their own deal with Arabi that would undercut Britain's position in the country, refused to support the initiative, claiming that their parliament would not sanction what effectively amounted to an act of war. Informed by Seymour that Britain intended to unilaterally issue the ultimatum, they withdrew their entire fleet from Alexandria, disingenuously maintaining that it was needed to put down a revolt in Tunisia.[1]

Why Seymour and the British government were willing to go it alone is a conundrum; the new guns posed no danger to the fleet, which could be easily manoeuvred out of their range. Possible explanations are that the government believed that a failure to respond to the previous month's riots and massacre of British citizens would weaken Britain's reputation as the strongman of Europe, that the bombardment of the city would help topple Arabi and that the fortifications actually did pose a threat to the flotilla. Seymour, meanwhile, was under pressure to act from his officers and men, who had seen their colleagues brutally murdered in the riots, and may have been influenced by the imminent arrival of the Channel Fleet under Admiral Dowell and the disturbing possibility that the honours of the day would have to be shared if he postponed the bombardment.

The Egyptian Cabinet's response to the ultimatum was to deny that cannons were in the process of being mounted and to propose that a British deputation visit the forts to see for themselves. Declining the offer, Seymour again insisted that all the city's guns be removed. In reply, the Cabinet agreed to dismount the three cannon in the forts in which 'work may have been undertaken', but refused to order a general disarmament of the fortifications, warning that the port's military commander would respond in kind if its concession was rejected and the British opened fire.[2]

The following morning as the clock of St Catherine's church struck 7am, a single shell was fired at one of the forts in which the new guns had been installed. Several minutes later, the eight armour plated battleships of the fleet opened up and the coastal defences began to return fire. Rather than concentrating on each fort in turn, which he believed would extend the length of the bombardment, Seymour's strategy was to attack all the forts simultaneously. He thus split his ships into two groups, each of which was delegated a portion of the coast line. At first, the two squadrons steamed past their targets, each boat firing in succession before turning and making the return journey and delivering a further broadside. After two and a half hours, however, the first group of vessels, comprising HMS Superb, HMS Sultan and HMS Alexandra, began to fire from a stationary position, as, although cruising past the forts presented a moving target to the enemy and minimised the chances that they would be hit, it greatly reduced their own accuracy. HMS Sultan also changed the manner of letting off its guns; firing in succession was replaced by the careful aim and detonation of one cannon at a time.

The bombardment lasted ten hours, during which the armada expended 3,782 shells and 33,493 bullets fired from onboard Gatling guns and snipers positioned in mast heads. Theoretically, the British possessed the advantage. The forts were constructed of soft limestone, unable to withstand modern artillery; their batteries of guns were poorly positioned and had difficulty supporting each other; and the gunners were inexperienced and had little ammunition. In the event, Seymour's ships did relatively little damage. At the end of the day, the forts still stood and an observer from the American Navy believed that all could have been fully operational within a few hours had not the Egyptians surrendered. The explanation for the navy's inadequacy was two-fold. Almost half of the shells fired malfunctioned, either failing to detonate or exploding prematurely, and the accuracy of its guns was poor; many of the missiles fell short and others went over the fortifications destroying a harem, the German consulate, the city's police headquarters and several schools. Some blamed the sun into which the ships were firing during the first hour of the battle and the thick smoke that began to hang over the ocean in a heavy pall. Others held Seymour responsible. Unwilling to risk his ships being hit, he kept them at a considerable distance from the shore, increasing the range, but reducing the accuracy of their canons and limiting the effectiveness of their Gatling guns and snipers.

The battle finished at 5.15pm by which time Arabi, who had arrived early that morning, had left the city by carriage. Just five British marines had been killed and 28 wounded. The Egyptians officially lost 100 to 150 dead and had 250 to 350 casualties, though both figures are thought to be gross underestimates. The following morning, twelve shells were let off at a fort that was mistakenly thought to be still operational. The firing caused panic within the Arab population of the city, who believed the bombardment was to recommence and a British landing was imminent and began to leave in droves, followed in mid-morning by Arabi's troops. As they left, they ran into desert Bedouin converging on the port from the surrounding desert, who robbed them of their valuables and committed a number of atrocities; female members of the harem were repeatedly raped and had their jewellery stolen by having their hands and ears lopped off. The Bedouin, along with those who remained, then descended on the European quarter of the city, breaking into and plundering shops and houses. After carrying off anything portable, they set the district on fire, and, as the sun set, the whole of Alexandria was aflame.

Seymour, who at the end of the war received a Baroncy and a Parliamentary grant of £25,000, let the city burn. He claimed that he lacked sufficient men to extinguish the fires and halt the arson and that there was a danger that Arabi would massacre any landing parties. Both justifications were spurious; he had almost 6,000 marines and sailors under his command and it was known that the Egyptian troops had retired to Ramleh. The true reason for his inaction was that he only had instructions to destroy the port's fortifications and the British government feared that a landing would be viewed as a full-scale invasion.

The government finally capitulated to press demands that they save the city on the second day after the bombardment. At 10.30am, a small party of marines rowed through the decomposing bodies that clogged the harbour, and, on disembarking, viewed a scene of utter devastation; much of the European quarter had been reduced to a smouldering ruin, the houses and the surrounding streets containing the swelling corpses of those who had failed to escape the conflagration. More parties containing representatives of the other European powers were landed and their members gradually began to restore order; the British marines arrested suspected looters and arsonists, their Greek counterparts immediately shot or bayoneted them, the death toll becoming so great that Seymour was forced to restrict membership of patrols to British and American citizens. The following day, Lord Beresford, who had been appointed Chief of Police, set up martial courts; prisoners found guilty of arson and looting were forced to dig their own open grave in the Place Mehemet Ali and were then shot, those convicted of lesser crimes were flogged.

Rather than toppling Arabi, the bombardment only increased his determination to rid his country of the British. Over the following week, he called for a fatwa against all Westerners and issued a proclamation denouncing the Khedive. When Tewfiq countered by dismissing him from his post as Minister of War and attempted to rally support in the provinces, he banned all non-military cipher telegraph communications and began to aggressively lobby the two ad hoc General Assemblies that had been set up in Cairo to decide on the response to the attack on Alexandria. After much discussion, the second conclave nullified the Khedive's dismissal of Arabi and sanctioned disobedience against his rule, essentially a vote for war, though many members later claimed they had been coerced into supporting the initiative.

Given authorization to defend his country, Arabi prepared for invasion, introducing conscription and organising the collection of supplies. Assuming that the British would move inland from Alexandria, he transferred 15,000 to 30,000 troops to Kafr Dawr, four miles outside the city. The town was almost impregnable; shielded on the right and left by two shallow lakes and fronted by almost flat land that offered no protection to an advancing army, it was bisected by the Alexandria to Cairo railway, which allowed men and supplies to be rapidly brought up from the rear.

The new recruits set about digging trenches, building an earthwork large and strong enough to withstand artillery fire and damned the Mahmoudieh Canal, which ran through the town from the Nile and provided Alexandria with much of its water supply.

In London, William Gladstone, the Prime Minister, finally decided that military intervention was necessary. The reasons behind his decision are much debated. It has been suggested that he was merely fulfilling his promise to support the Khedive and wished to protect the lives of the remaining British residents of Egypt from the breakdown in law and order that his advisors assured him was about to occur. A more important motive, however, was economic self-interest. It was clear that Arabi and the nationalists would eventually overthrow the Khedive, default on Egypt's Western debts and block the Suez Canal, which would devastate the Imperial economy and could even lead to the loss of India. The closure of the canal would force merchant ships bound for Bombay to travel an additional 5,000 miles around the treacherous Cape of Good Hope, greatly increasing shipping costs, and, if there was another Indian mutiny, would delay the arrival of the British troops required to restore order. There were also strong political reasons for action. A nationalist regime could favour Russia, Britain's great enemy, and an aggressive response to the crisis would increase the popularity of the ruling Liberal government and demonstrate to other European powers that the Empire was willing to protect its interests – if necessary, by might.[3]

It was agreed that an expedition would be sent to Egypt composed of 24,000 soldiers from Britain and a further 7,000 from India; the £2.3 million cost being met by a small increase in income tax. The Commander was to be General Sir Garnet Wolseley, who had helped put down the Indian mutiny and fought in China, Canada, Africa and the Crimea. A slight man with a large ego, he had recently been satirised in Gilbert and

Sullivan's *Pirates of the Penzance* as 'the very model of a modern Major General'.[4] Attempts to launch a joint invasion with France and Turkey failed. The French Parliament refused to provide the necessary funds, fearing that the resultant dispersal of its forces would leave the country exposed to German aggression. Turkey agreed to send troops, but only if Britain withdrew its army from Egypt once they arrived. Convinced that the Turks could not defeat the nationalists alone and suspecting that they would switch sides once British forces had left, the British Cabinet refused the offer unless the Sultan publicly denounced Arabi as a rebel. By the time he agreed to issue a proclamation to this effect, the war had been won.

As Wolseley's army headed for Egypt, the advance force of British troops sent by Gladstone the previous month to prepare the ground for possible military action arrived in Alexandria. After their commander, General Archibald Alison, had given advice to Seymour on possible improvements to the defences of the city, they set out to capture Ramleh, a town five miles down the coast, where Wolseley intended to base his forces. Largely comprising a collection of sumptuous villas with exotic gardens to which wealthy European residents retreated during the summer months, the resort possessed two assets; built on rising ground, it provided a good view of the Egyptian stronghold of Kafr Dawr and it was connected to Alexandria by rail (via a branch line to the Cairo railway), allowing troops and supplies to be rapidly transported to and from the port. Moreover, its occupation would enable the British to halt any attempt by Arabi to move troops between Kafr Dawr and the forts scattered around Abourkir Bay, a short distance further down the coast.

Alison's plan for the capture of the resort was to send a small force of 250 men to blow up the Cairo railway at a point close to Kafr Dawr, thus creating a distraction that would draw fighters away from Ramleh and prevent Arabi using the line to move troops from his stronghold during any future assault on Alexandria. The men would then march to Ramleh, where with Alison and the rest of the force, who were to travel there by train, they would mount an attack. In the event, the men sent to the railway junction ran into a detachment of Egyptian cavalry and the resulting fire fight left two horsemen dead and delayed their arrival at Ramleh. The destruction of the line also appears not to have attracted large numbers of troops away from the town, as Alison's attack met relatively strong resistance. Nonetheless, after a short battle lasting around an hour, the resort was duly captured and over the following few days was fortified.

Having occupied Ramleh, Alison set about making a general nuisance of himself. A locomotive was armour plated, and, each morning, was sent up the railway line to Kafr Dawr pulling three carriages filled with soldiers on which were mounted an array of weaponry, including machine and Gatling guns and two pieces of artillery. A short distance from the enemy's defences, the troops would disembark, advance on foot and invariably meet Arabi patrols with whom they would engage, supported by fire from the train. Detachments also launched night time attacks, and, on one occasion, a pair of officers equipped with a raft, on which were mounted two Gatling guns, attempted a waterborne assault across one of the lakes that adjoined Kafr Dawr. The forays went well until Alison over-reached himself and organised a major assault on the railway junction of Millaha, where the Egyptians had set up an outpost. A thousand troops were brought up the line by the armoured train while a further four companies marched along the banks of the Mahmoudieh Canal that ran bedsides the railway. Unfortunately, their advance became known to the enemy and 2,000 troops, cavalry and artillery were rapidly moved from Kafr Dawr to Millaha. The ensuing battle lasted several hours and only ended at nightfall when Alison ordered his men back to Ramleh. Four soldiers had been killed and 27 wounded, but more damagingly the withdrawal was seen by Arabi as a retreat and clear proof that his fighters could easily overcome the might of the British army.

Chapter 4

Preparations for the Second Palmer Expedition

The declaration of war and the possibility that the invasion could be launched from the Suez Canal rather than from Alexandria made it even more crucial that the local Bedouin remained neutral, and, if possible, assisted the British through the supply of camels and the protection of the Canal and its repair if it was damaged. On his arrival in Suez, Edward Palmer was thus instructed to write an account of his trip to the desert and to recommend further action that would gain tribal support. The report was a curious piece of work and largely comprised a list of the tribes of the region, their chief sheikhs and the location of their summer camps, much of which was well known and some inaccurate. Palmer claimed to have obtained the information from interviews with the sheikhs of the tribes discussed, a total of 27 chiefs, and from a party of Terabin Bedouins that he had met soon after leaving Gaza. The agreement with Misleh was not mentioned. Instead, he asserted that if given £20,000 to £25,000 he could gain the support of 50,000 Bedouin fighters and would call a meeting of all the sheikhs at which the pact would be formalised within two weeks. He also proposed that the tribes recruited be given equipment and materials that would allow them to protect and repair the canal and that a gunboat be stationed at Gaza to safeguard its Christian residents. No reference was made of the release of the sheikhs imprisoned in Jerusalem, information that he presumably considered too sensitive to be recorded and was passed onto his superiors verbally along with a request that the Bedouins recruited be supplied with rifles.

The report was sent to Lieutenant William Gill, who had

arrived at Port Said five days previously with Khalil Attick, the Syrian attendant who had accompanied him on a previous mission. 'Tearing…[his] …hair' that he was not on active service, Gill had asked to be attached to Wolseley's invasion force.[1] His wish was only partly granted. He was sent to Egypt, but given an intelligence role, and, as cover, the impressive title Deputy Assistant Adjutant General and Quarter Master General. Leaving England on July 21st , he spent a few days in Alexandria, which he found 'in hideous ruins' and as deserted as Pompeii, and then went onto Port Said. Here, he attempted to discover the likely prospects of a British occupation of the town and of Ismailia, writing up his findings in a report, planned the defence of the port's water supply and obtained from the Khedive himself a list of the principal sheikhs living in the region adjoining the Suez Canal.[2]

His official view of Palmer's report was positive. He believed £20,000 to £25,000 was a reasonable price to pay for 50,000 men and that the release of the jailed sheikhs could be achieved by the British Consul in Jerusalem or unnamed individuals at Beirut or Constantinople bribing Turkish officials. As for the rifles and equipment required, to avoid any connection with the British these would have to be bought in a number of small purchases spread over time in either Tripoli or Barbary. Palmer's recommendations thus received his full backing and he telegraphed the report, plus his endorsement, to Lord Northbrook, who sent his decision that the proposals should be put into immediate effect back to Admiral Hewitt. Privately, he had grave doubts about the report's 'rose coloured' contents, as later did Colonel Charles Warren and the explorer Richard Burton, who both went in search of the missing party. Gill believed Palmer had failed to contact all the principal sheikhs living in the region – there were significant disparities between Palmer's and the Khedive's list of chiefs – and was unconvinced that all the tribes would be susceptible to bribery. Warren and Burton, meanwhile, questioned the claim that the tribes could provide the British with 50,000 fighters as Palmer himself twelve years previously had estimated the entire population of the region to be just 4,000. Warren estimated the actual number available to be 5,000 and Burton that it was 'in the hundreds'.[3]

To cloak his true activities and as a reward for his bravery, Palmer was appointed Interpreter in Chief to Her Majesty's Forces. Regarding himself an 'awful swell', he bragged to his wife that he was 'one of the chief officers of the expedition' and had forty 'servants, clerks and interpreters at my beck and call'.[4] As part of his new post, he was asked to perform two tasks; to accompany the 500 Royal Marines who were to capture Suez on August 2nd and to purchase camels for the Indian contingent of the invasion force. The assault on Suez met no opposition; the occupying Arabi soldiers fled on seeing the British heading for the harbour. Palmer, who later boasted that he was on the first boat to land, reassured the local notables that they would not be harmed and became involved in persuading the Acting Governor to give up the £50,000 that the rebels had left in the Governor's safe. His organisation of transport was less successful. A Towarah sheikh refused to enter the desert and buy camels on his behalf owing to the danger involved and he thus turned to Sulieman Zahr at Moses Wells, who supplied eleven animals, one of which he returned. A further Suez merchant, to whom the Professor appears to have divulged details of his first mission and who offered to source 400 beasts for a fee of £40, was also employed, but then mysteriously disappeared.

The new mission was authorised by Hewitt on August 4th and due to begin on Augusts 7th.. Palmer was to meet the principal sheikhs of the region, purchase their allegiance for £20,000, and, in return, require them to patrol the canal, repair any damage inflicted by Arabi and to supply 1,500 (later reduced to 750) camels for Wolseley's army. To demonstrate to the chiefs that he was acting in an official capacity, he was to be accompanied by a

British military officer. His cover story, given to the press and to be used if he was captured, was that he was entering the desert only to buy camels, a surprisingly poor subterfuge as both those who had travelled through Egypt and any hostile Bedouins would have been well aware that the European manner of acquiring camels was to order them from a dealer and then await delivery.[5]

Elated that the operation was to go ahead, Palmer began to make plans, which he relayed in a series of letters to his friend Walter Besant. A message was sent to Sheikh Misleh arranging to meet him at Nakhl, a town 100 miles east of Suez, from where they would travel to Misleh's camp. Given that the Governor of Nakhl was known to be one of Arabi's most ardent supporters and the town could only be reached via a well-used route on which nationalist sympathisers were likely to be encountered, this was another poor decision; presumably made to conceal the fact that the meeting was to be with Misleh rather than the assumed large gathering of tribal chiefs. A letter was also dispatched to Sheikh Sofieh, whose tribal area Palmer stated extended to Nakhl, to come to Suez by August 6th with twenty armed men and 92 camels for the Indian invasion force and eight to carry the party's baggage. Strangely, even though he was aware that the Sheikh, like most of his compatriots, was illiterate, he did not give the courier a verbal message. The collection and transfer of the £20,000 to Suez and the release of the imprisoned sheikhs was left to respectively the Admiralty and the Foreign Office. Admiral Hoskins had already withdrawn £10,000 from the Anglo-Egyptian Bank at Port Said, and, on August 4th, drew a further £10,000; both withdrawals being 'for special purposes' and in gold sovereigns. The money was then moved to the ship HMS Penelope and brought down the Canal to Suez by Gill and another naval officer, who, 'not sorry to get rid of it', passed it to the Paymaster of HMS Euryalus. At the same time, the Foreign Office put pressure on the Turks to release the sheikhs in jail in

Jerusalem, and, soon afterwards, all received their freedom.[6]

Of the seven officers who volunteered to join the mission to Nakhl, the one chosen by Palmer was Harold Charrington, Hewitt's Flag-Lieutenant, in effect the Admiral's secretary and personal assistant. The second son of Spencer Charrington, the owner of the brewery that bore the family name and later the MP for Mile End, he had enlisted in the Royal Navy as a Cadet at the age of thirteen, and, after serving on five ships in the Pacific, attended the Royal Naval College at Greenwich and then undertook further training in Portsmouth. Joining Admiral Beauchamp Seymour's flagship patrolling the Mediterranean and then the English Channel, he had became a full Lieutenant in 1880 and had subsequently served in the Baltic, Ireland and India. Not the brightest of men and with no experience of Arabia, Palmer perhaps hoped that he would fail to realise that the meeting with Misleh was bereft of sheikhs.[7]

Whilst Palmer was planning his own mission, William Gill was becoming involved in another naval intelligence operation – the cutting of the telegraph line that linked nationalist Cairo with the Turks in Constantinople by blowing up approximately one mile of pylons. The British were obliged to inform the Turkish Sultan of their military plans and there was a fear that this information would be immediately passed to the rebels. Destroying the telegraph line would stop such an exchange of information, as well as preventing Arabi from requesting help from the Turks. The cable was originally to be sliced in late July, but the plan had to be abandoned when the French refused to countenance the action and Ferdinand de Lesseps, part owner of the Suez Canal, made it clear that any act of war on behalf of the British would prompt him to close the waterway.[8] In early August, with military action likely to occur within weeks, the scheme was reactivated and its organisation allocated to Gill.

In order to determine the location of the cut, Gill decided to confer with a Mr Pickard, a telegraph engineer in the pay of the

British who had obtained a position in the Egyptian telegraphy service. As Pickard was onboard HMS Orion, anchored off the Canal port of Ismailia, which stood halfway between Port Said and Suez, Gill decided to accompany the officer carrying the £20,000 in gold to Suez, thus increasing its security, and to stop off at Ismailia. He arrived at 8pm just in time for dinner with the Orion's Captain, who updated him on Arabi deployments along the Canal and proposed bribing the new nationalist governor of Ismailia to switch sides. Pickard, a non-military man and of a lower social status than either Gill or the Captain, was not invited to dine, but when he appeared, provided much useful information. He disclosed that there were three possible locations for the cut; only one of which was likely to be successful. Destroying the line near the town of El Arish would be dangerous; the Governor was another fervid follower of Arabi and his fort held a large Turkish force. There was therefore a high risk that the British would be caught in the act, and, even if the project was successful, the pylons would be rapidly re-erected. A cut outside Kantara, a town on the bank of the Suez Canal, would also be quickly patched up and would breach the neutrality of the waterway. The only viable site therefore was in the environs of Gaza. The Bedouin of the area were less pro-nationalist than elsewhere and could be persuaded to prevent the repair of the line.

Having determined the location of the cut, Gill next had to decide who would carry out the deed. Three men were considered. Pickard dearly wanted to perform the task, arguing that he could use a claimed friendship with the Governor of Gaza to the mission's advantage. Gill was unconvinced. A more likely prospect was Charles Clark, the Director of Telegraph at Zagazig, who was on friendly terms with one of the Gaza sheikhs. Clark was duly contacted, but rejected the assignment; he had a family and he foresaw disaster. That left, the third possibility – Edward Palmer. On arriving at Suez, Gill had a meeting with Admiral

Hewitt, now based at the opulent Suez Hotel, and then went to see the Professor in his rooms. After giving him verbal authority to use the £20,000 to 'buy' the Bedouin, he suggested that he cut the wire at Gaza before proceeding to the meeting at Nakhl. Palmer was enthusiastic, but a discussion of the distances involved clearly demonstrated that such a detour could cause him to miss 'the great meeting of sheikhs…which might do incalculable injury'.[9] Gill was thus left with no feasible candidate, and, straining at the leash to see action, he proposed himself; he had some experience of the Bedouin, could speak Arabic and whilst at Gaza could collect intelligence. After some consideration, Hewitt agreed and it was decided that he and his Syrian attendant would travel with Palmer's party, allowing them to benefit from the protection provided by Sheikh Sofieh and his escort, until it neared Nakhl when they would head off on their own.

In the two days between Gill's meeting with Palmer and their departure for Nakhl and Gaza, their mission underwent a number of changes. The most important modification was that Palmer was instructed to pay the sheikhs £3,000, worth approximately £138,000 today, for their support and the provision of camels and to promise them a further £17,000 if they were required to defend the Canal. The explanation given by the Admiralty was that it could not authorise a large £20,000 outlay until it had consulted with General Wolseley, who was making the journey to Egypt by sea on account of his health and had not yet arrived. The true reason was that the intelligence branch no longer believed that the nationalists would attack the Canal and was confident that it would soon be in British hands. It had discovered through the interception of telegraph messages that its part-owner, Ferdinand de Lesseps, had given Arabi his word that he would not permit the landing of British troops in the Canal zone and that the rebel leader had consequently rescinded a scheme to block the thoroughfare.[10] The money was also needed elsewhere. Expecting the final battle of the war to occur at Tel-el-Kebir, Wolseley intended to pay the Bedouin living in the area £32,000 in return for their allegiance. In the event, this plan again went awry; the Arabi officers to whom the money was given via the President of the Chamber of Notables only passed a small amount to the Bedouin, keeping the majority for themselves.[11]

A further setback was the non-appearance of Sheikh Sofieh, which prevented their August 7th departure. With little else to occupy their time, Gill and Charrington spent the day cruising up and down the Canal, noting the deployment of Arabi troops along its banks, and Palmer boarded HMS Euryalus to borrow six swords and belts from its officers, which he intended to present to Sheikh Misleh as a sign of his good intent. Sofieh eventually arrived in late afternoon. He had received Palmer's letter, but unable to read, was unaware that it required him to arrive at Suez by August 6th with an escort and 100 camels. Assuming that it was a request to accompany Palmer to Misleh's camp, he, his teenage nephew and one of his tribesmen, who he took along in case he was attacked by rebel soldiers, rode to Moses Wells, where he asked Suileman Zahr to read him the note. Lacking the time to return to his tents for the armed men and camels, he asked Zahr to arrange his passage to Suez, and, the following day, accompanied by the dealer's son and his nephew, caught the P & O boat to the port. Oddly, Palmer displayed no concern that he had not fulfilled his orders. Neither did he require the sheikh to sign a document making him responsible for the safety of the party or agree the payment of a fee, standard practice when arranging to travel through a chief's territory. Instead, he presented him to Admiral Hewitt and the local British Consul at the Suez Hotel. Impressed to meet one of the great sheikhs of the desert, the Admiral thanked him for joining the British cause, and, in appreciation, presented him with one of the Naval swords Palmer had acquired earlier in the day. Immensely grateful,

Sofieh gave the sword to Zahr's son for safe keeping, as he feared the party might be attacked in the desert and the weapon stolen; a premonition that was to prove remarkably prescient.

Sofieh's failure to bring armed men and camels created more problems for the mission. Given its nature, the amount of money carried and the number of Arabi soldiers patrolling the desert, an escort was essential. Palmer, however, decided to make the journey with no protection, even though he could easily have employed guards from the residents of Suez. Moreover, the party carried just two guns – a revolver and a rifle. A decision that the Reverend Samuel Bartlett, who had travelled through the region in peacetime, found inconceivable; weapons both allowed travellers to defend themselves and deterred attack 'show[ing] what we could do if we would'.[12] When the lack of an escort was later raised in the House of Commons, the Admiralty claimed that Palmer had no apprehension of the danger he faced; a statement that was palpably untrue. He had expressed his anxieties about his first mission to his friend Walter Besant before he had even left London and the letters and journal that he wrote during his stay at Misleh's camp and at Suez are full of fears that he would be captured and killed by either Turkish or nationalist forces. He had also been warned by Zahr, the camel dealer, that the desert was infested with nationalist troops and Richard Burton, who went in search of the missing party, heard rumours that the Admiralty had explicitly warned him that if captured he and his colleagues would be treated as spies and shot.[13]

To overcome the lack of camels and camel drivers, Palmer decided to hire beasts and their attendants at Moses Wells, and, instead of travelling direct to Nakhl, to make a detour to Sheikh Sofieh's camp at Wady Sudr. Here, the party's luggage would be transferred to Sofieh's camels and the hired men and beasts sent back to Moses Wells. Such a procedure would save the cost of renting the camels/drivers for the whole journey to and from

Nakhl and Gaza, make both available for the invasion force and satisfy Sofieh's demands that the party use his animals; it being the custom for Westerners to hire the animals and drivers of the sheikh that controlled the desert through which they were to pass. This was another odd decision. The detour was unnecessary – the cost of the mission was of little importance; only a small amount of money would be saved; if, as Palmer believed, Sheikh Misleh would provide all the camels the invasion force sought, there was no need to return the hired animals; and there is no evidence that Sofieh would have objected to the abandonment of the custom of renting the ruling sheikh's beasts. Furthermore, the detour threatened the success of the expedition – it would lengthen the journey and increase its danger and could delay both Palmer's arrival at Nakhl and the destruction of the telegraph line.

The party finally left Suez on the afternoon of August 8th. In the morning, Palmer sent a message to Suileman Zahr, Moses Wells' camel trader, informing him that he and some companions would arrive later that evening and asking him to erect tents on the beach, where they would spend the night, and the following morning to bring down four camels and seven camel drivers. He then went to collect the £3,000 in gold sovereigns from the Paymaster of the ship HMS Euryalus; the money had been divided into sums of £1,000, each of which had been placed in a cotton sack, the three sacks then being deposited in a canvas bag. Oddly, given the weight of the cash and the secrecy of the mission, he did not immediately return to headquarters, but spent the next few hours wandering around Suez making last minute purchases. Several witnesses recalled seeing him and noting with some surprise that he was carrying a large and heavy bag of money. At some point, he also met a Mr Hammond, a captain employed by the P & O shipping company, to whom he lent £100 of his own money, a considerable sum, receiving in return an IOU. On his return, he, Gill and Charrington ate a hearty lunch after which they supervised the loading of their baggage onto HMS Cockatrice, which was to take them to Moses Wells, and bid farewell to Admiral Seymour, promising to return within the week. They then rounded up Sofieh, his nephew and their two servants, boarded the HMS Cockatrice and sailed to their fate.

Chapter 5

Professor Edward Palmer

Those who attended social occasions arranged by the members of the Savile Club, one of London's premier gentlemen's clubs, in the 1870s would have come across Professor Edward Palmer, known to his friends as 'the Palmer'. Once seen, he was not easily forgotten. A small pale man, little more than five foot tall, he possessed an unusually large head atop a painfully thin and slightly stooping body. His face was that of an ancient prophet; above curiously large, limpid protruding eyes was a high and ample forehead, below was a hooked nose and a thick long silky brown beard that flowed down his chest. Although known to wear a suit, he was more usually attired in Arab dress, his thinning hair hidden by an oriental fez. On most occasions, he would be discovered 'working the room', exchanging a few words with friends before rapidly moving onto other acquaintances. If he judged a stranger to be of some future use, he would 'mould [them] like dough'.[1] He would introduce himself and offer a compliment. He would then ask about their interests and views, all of which he would invariably share. Some personal details about himself would follow – his facility with languages, his great treks through the deserts of Egypt etc – all relayed with great humility and self depreciation. Whilst speaking, he would give the person his complete attention, staring intently at them. He would speak softly and quietly, forcing them to concentrate on what he said. His body language and the words he used would match their own, and, occasionally, he would place his hand with its long thin feminine fingers on their forearm for emphasis. Before parting, he would offer them his help – an introduction to a friend, the research of an interesting expression etc. At subsequent meetings, more favours would be offered and eventually he would make a request of his own.[2]

Those who did not attend soirées did not escape his clutches. If of use, they would receive a note praising a book or article they had written or congratulating them on a post they had attained. To ensure a reply, he would pose a question, and, when he received a response, would write a further letter full of compliments and queries. Favours and gifts would then be offered and requested. The American writer Charles Leland, for example, in January 1874 received a letter from Palmer congratulating him on his book *The English Gypsy* and claiming that he had heard Romany, the gypsy language, spoken in Palestine. A few hours later, another note arrived, containing two or three Romany words that Palmer believed should be included in the next edition of *The English Gypsy*. More letters followed in which Leland was invited to attend a college dinner and offered a copy of Palmer's latest book, a supply of Indian ink and countless introductions to friends and acquaintances. Each letter suggested that they work together – on a Romany-English dictionary, on a periodical on gypsies and the Romany language, on the foundation of a society composed of those interested in gypsy lore and on a translation of Romany ballads. As each project was rejected, a new one was proposed until Leland finally capitulated.[3]

If the person became a friend, he (and it was always 'he', the Professor was uncomfortable in the company of women) would be invited to private parties where a different Palmer would be revealed. He would be 'bubbling over with mirth'; he was never morose, carrying with him at all times 'a pleasant atmosphere of cheerfulness'. As the hours passed and the drink flowed, perched on a chair with his legs tucked beneath him, he would tell droll anecdotes of his life and travels, many of which were so fantastical that they were difficult to believe, and criticise those he despised but were not present in the most outrageous manner, describing them as skunks, blackguards, humbugs, cads and curs and mimicking their voices and expressions. Gradually, he would dominate the event. He would perform card and conjuring tricks, recite verse, draw caricatures of fellow guests, and, as a finale, sing his favourite Arab lullaby in his high sweet voice whilst accompanying himself on a tambourine or mandolin.[4]

Edward Palmer was born in Cambridge in 1840. The account of his early life relayed to friends was as follows. He was the son of the owner of a private school – 'a man of considerable acquirements and a strong taste for art'. Shortly after his birth, his father had died, followed by his mother and he had been adopted by a wealthy unmarried aunt, who educated him privately and then at the prestigious Perse Grammar School. In his spare time, he had read poetry, and learnt Arabic from the Arab servant of a friend of his aunt's and Romany from travelling tinkers, paying for lessons with pocket money.

The reality was somewhat different. His twenty-year-old father, William Henry, certainly ran an academy, but it was not the large institution conjured up in Palmer's reminiscences. William Henry and his wife lived in Green Street, Cambridge with his mother, sister and one of his brother's children; significantly the household employed no servants. The school comprised a room in the house and his pupils never numbered more than half a dozen. He died when Palmer was two years old of tuberculosis, a disease closely linked to overcrowding and malnutrition, which at this time was responsible for almost one in four deaths. Soon afterwards, his wife expired from the same condition.[5]

Palmer continued to live with his grandmother and aunt, but in even more straightened circumstances. With the loss of the family's only source of income, his grandmother, then in her late fifties, was forced to take a job as a college servant and to rent out the rooms formerly occupied by her son and daughter-in-law and the 'academy' to two students attending Cambridge University.

In 1850, the household was joined by his widowed uncle, Charles Palmer, and his two cousins. A self-employed tailor who had rented out a spare room to undergraduates, Charles Palmer's business had recently failed and he had been forced to sell his own home to pay his debts. Although his arrival forced Palmer to share a bedroom with his cousins, his contribution to the family income enabled him to attend an academy similar to that run by his late father, and, at the age of ten, Perse Grammar School. During his time at this prestigious place of learning, he made good progress in Latin, Greek and Divinity, but otherwise did not distinguish himself; his former masters failing to recall him on hearing of his disappearance.[6]

He remained at Perse School for just three years. In 1853, his grandmother and uncle died, the latter in a traffic accident, leaving him and his two cousins to be brought up by his unmarried aunt. Unable to survive on rental income alone, she sold the Green Street property and purchased part of the Hoop Hotel, a former coaching inn on Bridge Street, Cambridge that had fallen on hard times with the arrival of the railway. Palmer was withdrawn from school, on the grounds of ill health, and with his two cousins helped to run the hotel. That in his spare time, he became fluent in Romany seems improbable.[7] It is unlikely that his aunt would have allowed him to associate with gypsies, who were viewed with great suspicion, and in later years Palmer admitted to Charles Leland that he picked up only 'a slight knowledge of Romany…when a boy'.[8] As for Arabic, he perhaps heard the language spoken by one of the Hotel's guests.

Palmer left Cambridge at the age of sixteen to become a junior dock clerk in a firm of wine merchants in East Cheap, adjacent to St Pauls Cathedral. Here, he later claimed, he bloomed. He spent most nights at the theatre, becoming great friends with Henry Irving then a bit-part player, but later to become the greatest actor of his generation, and the fire eater Signor Buonocorre, known to all as the 'Fire King'. After a performance, he would dine at an Italian or French restaurant, where he learnt both languages within a few weeks by listening and conversing with fellow customers and waiters, becoming fluent in every Italian dialect. At weekends, he dabbled in photography, taking pictures of his new-found friends, carved wooden figures and practiced hypnotism. After reading a book on the subject, he found that he could place an individual in a trance within minutes; a skill that proved useful when he came across a young woman who had been involved in an accident and whose pain miraculously disappeared when he put her under his spell. His only negative experience in the great metropolis was when a pickpocket attempted to snatch his watch. Our young hero, however, taught the 'bounder' a well-deserved lesson; 'while the thief kicked, Palmer with the grip of a bulldog, was pounding his man's head and grinding his unlucky nose upon the edge of the curb stone, insomuch that when he had worked his term and came out of prison his own friends failed to recognise [him]'.[9]

Whether these recollections are a true reflection of reality is a mute point; it would appear that many were exaggerations or inventions. His small wage as a clerk and his long working hours would not have permitted nightly trips to the theatre or the expensive hobby of photography, and his friendships with Irving and the 'Fire King' were probably no more than passing acquaintanceships, perhaps from theatre stalls; the soon-to-be great actor was largely based in Edinburgh during these years. As regards his astounding fluency in French and Italian, this probably comprised a working knowledge of the languages picked up in cafes, but largely from his visits to the docks where he supervised the unloading of continental wines.[10]

Palmer's cosmopolitan life came to an end after three years. The stated reason was that he contracted tuberculosis and returned home to Cambridge to die; his employer on their last meeting assuring him that he was 'the very best clerk' the firm had ever employed.[11] Other possible explanations are that he was sacked or had simply tired of the mundane nature of the job. His recovery from the fatal disease was nothing short of miraculous. In later years, he recounted how he had died, only to be brought back to life by a God determined to preserve a life that promised so much. His 'death' was the result of the administration by an herbalist of lobelia, a herb used to cure a variety of breathing problems, muscle pain and syphilis. On ingesting the drug, he was seized with a violent attack of vomiting. A doctor was called and Palmer 'felt a dreadful cold spreading over me...By my bedside stood my aunt, poor soul, crying. I saw the doctor feeling a pulseless wrist, watch in hand; the cold dews of death were on my forehead; the cold hand of death was on my limbs...[I] could see and hear, but not speak, not even when the doctor let my hand fall upon the pillow and said solemnly "He is gone!"'.[12] A diagnosis that proved somewhat premature. The patient recovered, and, within weeks, had returned to perfect health,

Over the following two years, Palmer worked part-time for his aunt and attempted to become a professional actor and writer. His interest in acting arose from watching performances of the Cambridge University Amateur Dramatic Club, based at the Hoop Hotel from 1855. Palmer joined an amateur group, and appeared in three plays, all performed at the Cambridge Theatre. Discovering 'that he could act better than most of [his fellow performers], perhaps better than any', he boasted that he had been asked to join a Lyme Regis theatre troupe, only to have the offer withdrawn when he missed the train taking him to his first performance. His writing career suffered a similar fate. After creating a farce entitled 'A volunteer in difficulties', which he persuaded his amateur dramatics group to present, he turned his hand to burlesques and poetry.[13] A poem entitled 'Ye hole in ye wall' with illustrations by the author and a friend was published in 1860, but achieved poor sales despite an uplifting first verse:

'Oh ! 'tis a glorious thing to stand
On the shore and gaze on the deep blue sea,
And feel the innermost soul expand
With the joyous sense of liberty'.[14]

Having failed as a thespian and a writer, Palmer turned his attention to linguistics, aiming to become an interpreter, book translator or teacher. Believing that the greatest career opportunities would come from a knowledge of Hindustani, he inveighed himself into the presence of Syed Abdullah, who taught candidates for the Indian civil service exam. Having worked for the Punjab government and the East India Company as an interpreter, Abdullah had initially come to Cambridge 'to sniff out his chances of a projected University readership in Hindustani'. Discovering that such a post would only be open to Anglicans, he stayed in the city for a further twenty years before returning to India to take up the post of Deputy Inspector of Schools and suffer an early death, at the age of fifty, from cholera. Palmer joined his class, became his close friend and was eventually employed as his assistant, teaching the rudiments of the language. Having mastered Hindustani – so thoroughly that 'he might have been supposed to have lived all his days on the banks of the Ganges' – he next turned his attention to Persian, Urdu and Arabic. Through Abdullah, he met a wealthy Indian, who in his spare time taught him all three languages, and Nawab Dawlah, the son of the late Rajah of Oudh, who having lost his throne, lived in England in exile. Impressed by this attractive Englishman's apparent enthusiasm for Indian culture, the Nawab employed two instructors to teach him and even allowed him to stay at his Cambridge house. Others who donated their time to improving his vocabulary were three Cambridge University Moslem students, his friend 'Hassun the Syrian' and Professor Mir Aulad Ah of Trinity College, Dublin, with whom the young scholar corresponded.[15]

Needless to say, Palmer soon tired of teaching and embraced a new ambition: to study for an undergraduate degree in Classics at Cambridge University, which he believed would allow him to enter the diplomatic service. Two obstacles stood in his way: he lacked sufficient funds to support himself for three years and he possessed less than three years of secondary education. He let neither stop him achieving his goal. Through Abdullah, he became acquainted with George Skinner, the Chaplain of Kings College and expert in Hebrew. Suddenly discovering an urge to learn the language, Palmer persuaded Skinner to help him in this task and soon the two men were firm friends. Skinner, in turn, introduced him to two classics lecturers and Fellows of St John's College, Cambridge, the Rev. Albert Calvert and Mr Newbury, who suggested that he make himself known to Theodore Preston, the holder of the Lord Almoner's Readership in Arabic. Palmer sent Preston a letter enclosing some Arabic verses he had translated and claiming that he had taught himself the language 'unassisted...by any native teacher'. Although he congratulated him on his achievement, Preston offered him no help and Calvert and Newbury thus took events into their own hands and recommended Palmer as a prospective scholarship student to Isaac Todhunter, the Senior Fellow of their College. Todhunter asked Palmer to call upon him and was so impressed by the young man, who brought with him a copy of his translated verses that he immediately agreed to admit him to St John's. It was also decided that he would apply for a sizarship, by which he would be helped financially in return for performing some role for the University. With the help of Calvert, he began to revise for the sizarship exam, studying for the first time in ten years Classics and Mathematics, and was awarded the grant three months later.[16]

Palmer's undergraduate career was a mixture of industry and pleasure. Unfortunately, his hard work was not directed towards his studies. In return for his sizarship, he was given the job of cataloguing the Arabic, Persian and Turkish manuscripts lodged in the University Library and at Kings and Trinity Colleges. As the grant was insufficient to cover the whole of his living costs, he also took on other paid tasks. He continued to teach, acted as an interpreter to Nawab Dawlah when he visited Paris and returned to writing. As well as penning articles in Urdu and Persian for two Indian newspapers, he published two books: the translation of the poem that had so impressed Preston and Todhunter and an English version of a Persian manuscript on Oriental mysticism that he discovered whilst cataloguing.[17]

As a relief from the rigours of his various jobs, he enthusiastically threw himself into the life of a student. He attended countless parties, edited the college magazine, formed the Original Burlesque Club, a society whose members wrote and performed satiric plays, and became involved in various high jinks, once climbing scaffolding to the top of the newly constructed St John's Chapel Tower and swinging from a batten, and at a cricket match, humorously felling the wicket keeper as he swung at a ball, his victim being carried off the field on a stretcher. He also adopted more unusual past times. He continued to practice hypnotism, curing his fellow undergraduates of migraines and hiccup attacks. Indeed, such was his local fame that he later claimed that Addenbroke's Hospital had asked him to take part in an experiment to test the anaesthetic powers of hypnotism and that the Chief Surgeon was dumbfounded when the young girl he proceeded to place in a trance underwent a finger amputation without the slightest trace of pain.[18]

To mesmerism, he added conjuring, specialising in sleight-of-hand and the balls and cups trick; thought reading, informing his friends, often incorrectly, of their innermost beliefs and desires; and spiritualism. In his desire to communicate with the dead, he was far from alone. Spiritualism was immensely popular during this period attracting those coping with personal bereavement and Christians whose faith had begun to fade under the onslaught of science and who saw the phenomenon as either material proof of an afterlife and incontrovertible grounds for belief or an alternative way of viewing the world. Palmer initially used a ouija board to contact the deceased. He then began to hold séances in his rooms during which he became possessed by spirits, writhing on the floor as they entered his body, and passed on comforting messages from the demised relatives of those present.[19]

Inevitably, his work commitments, active social life, inadequate secondary education and utter disinterest in Classics stymied his studies. Fearing that he would fail his degree and worrying about his finances, in 1865 he appears to have suffered a minor nervous breakdown. Whilst greeting a friend in his rooms, he suddenly fell onto the sofa and bent himself into an arch – balancing his body on the back of his head and his heals. There he lay until a doctor was called and he was persuaded to regain his normal posture. Over the following weeks, he repeatedly took up this strange position, became 'low-spirited', suffered from migraines and sleeplessness and began to drink to excess – becoming so drunk that he could 'neither walk nor stand'.[20]

Over time, he recovered. His aunt and cousin, William Palmer, lent him money and the College authorities awarded him a small scholarship. He also found solace in Islam, spending two hours per day loudly reciting the Koran, much to the annoyance of those who shared his College staircase, and two months after his 'breakdown' fell in love. The object of his affections was Laura Hanbury Davis, 'a singularly beautiful girl, fair and with a lovely complexion', whose 'crowning glory' was her long blonde hair. Palmer first met Laura, then fourteen years of age, in late October 1865 when he and a fellow undergraduate visited the home of Samual Page Widnall, a farmer who lived with his wife Elizabeth at the Old Vicarage at Grantchester, later the home of the poet Rupert Brooke and the thriller writer Jeffery

Archer. Widnall was a friend of a distant relative and of a fellow undergraduate at St John's College, and, like Palmer, had an eclectic range of interests. Within the grounds of his home, he had built 'The Ruin', a mock dilapidated medieval castle, the upper floors of which housed his photography studio and an occasional theatre and the lower rooms his carpentry and metal workshops and a printing press, on which he produced his own books on local history. Laura was the daughter of his wife's sister and was largely brought up by the Widnalls, who were childless. Her father, Thomas Archibald Davis, a notoriously poor businessman, often had little money and the Widnall's home was close to the school she attended.[21]

To the Widnalls and her parents, she and Palmer appeared to have a much older brother/younger sister relationship. Palmer helped her to write poetry and often accompanied her and her myriad relatives to concerts and theatre productions in Cambridge. They were thus astounded when, a few days before her fifteenth birthday and a mere seven months after their first meeting, Palmer proposed marriage. Her father refused to allow the engagement, but aware that his daughter was besotted with this very strange man, permitted him to continue to call upon her.[22]

Palmer graduated in April 1867 with a third class honours degree, avoiding an outright fail only because of his 'proficiency in Persian and other oriental languages'.[23] On hearing the news, he immediately again proposed to Laura, marking the glorious occasion with a less than glorious poem, which began:

> I felt the flood-gates open fly,
> And poured my secret in her ear,
> And paused awhile for her reply.
> With hope, though somewhat mixed with fear.[24]

Surprisingly, her father gave them permission to eventually

marry; having been declared bankrupt the previous year he was perhaps happy to be relieved of the financial burden of a daughter. However, he suggested that the marriage be delayed until Laura, then sixteen years of age, was older and her intended groom was in possession of a regular income. With that incentive and as ambitious as ever, Palmer began to search for employment. Convinced that his degree class failed to reflect his true brilliance, he began to gather a collection of testimonials from friends and contacts, including Syed Abdullah, Abdullah's uncle and Nawab Dawlah. These praised his character and language abilities, often in florid language eerily reminiscence of the parodies Palmer himself wrote to amuse his friends. To Abdullah's uncle, for example, the young scholar was 'the ornament of his school and creed who sits on the throne of reputation and honour, reclining upon the pillows of fame [having] dived into the ocean of perfection after the fairest of pearls'.[25]

Although the testimonials did not succeed in obtaining him the post of Interpreter at the British Embassy in Persia, a position he applied for soon after graduating, they did impress the Master of St John's College, where a Fellowship in Oriental Languages had recently become vacant. Having been made aware of Palmer's linguistic skills by the Rev. Albert Calvert and Professor Todhunter and wishing the position to be filled by an alumni of the College, he asked Edward Byles Cowell, Professor of Sanskrit, to examine the young scholar in Hindustani and Persian. More than impressed by his abilities, Cowell wrote a glowing report of the interview and Palmer was awarded the Fellowship, which paid a small income and provided free bed and board.

He stayed in the post for just one year. Bored with teaching and longing for adventure, in 1868 he joined a survey of Sinai organised by the Palestine Exploration Fund. The Fund had been founded three years earlier and had two goals; one public and one hidden. Its public purpose was to prove the literal truth of the Old Testament through a study of the archaeology and geography of Palestine. Since the publication of Charles Darwin's *Origin of the Species*, faith in the accuracy of the Bible had waned and the Fund sought to use scientific methods to prove the legitimacy of the texts. Its second concealed goal was to allow the War Office to secretly collect information and create maps of the region to be used by the military if a local uprising threatened British interests, such as the Suez Canal, or another continental power attempted to grab control of the area. All of the Fund's expeditions were partly manned by Royal Engineers, who provided the necessary equipment, and combined biblical investigation with mapping and the collection of intelligence.

The public aim of the Sinai survey was to establish the veracity of the biblical narrative of the Exodus, the escape of Moses and the Israelites from Egypt. The physical features described in the texts, and, in particular, Mount Sinai would be matched with actual locales, the veracity of biblical place names investigated through the questioning of local Bedouin and the inscriptions on ancient monuments translated in case they contained references to the Exodus. Its concealed purpose was to create a one-inch-to-two-mile map of the region, take photographs of the terrain and collect information on water supplies and the local Arab population. Intelligence that would prove useful if the newly opened Suez Canal had ever to be defended.[26]

The survey had a troubled history. It was originally to have been led by Captain Henry Spencer Palmer and the main theological work undertaken by Rev. Piere Butler, who had visited the region in 1853 and proposed that it should be studied in greater detail. Captain Charles Wilson, the leader of an ordnance survey of Jerusalem for the Fund, then expressed an interest in becoming involved and Butler died. The eventual expedition was thus jointly commanded by Wilson and Captain

Henry Spencer Palmer and Butler's role performed by Rev. George Williams of King's College, Cambridge, the author of a book on Jerusalem and Reverend F. W. Holland, who had been travelling in Sinai at the time of Butler's death. They were accompanied by five other Royal Engineers, a naturalist and Palmer, whose role was to discover the present and ancient names of villages and other places of interest from local residents, to observe and record Bedouin customs, to translate and log ancient inscriptions and to assist in the topographic survey. He was recruited largely because the few other Arab speakers in England had turned down the job and he brought with him a grant from Cambridge University's Worts Travelling Scholarship Fund, established to finance all forms of academic research, which removed the need to pay him a salary. He was also young, claimed to be fit, and, like Holland and Williams, was an alumni of Cambridge University.[27]

The party arrived in Egypt in October 1868. Palmer was elated to find himself travelling through country he had only previously read about. Wilson was less pleased. The young academic's insistence that he was physically fit was found to be an exaggeration; to Holland he was 'a fragile creature who looked as if he would not last a month'. In the first few weeks, he was unable to endure long marches, and, during the climb of Mount Jebel Katarina, his only wish was 'to lie down and perish'. Gradually, however, he became more robust, and, at the end of the expedition, bragged that he was the fittest member of the party. His difficulties with the physical challenges of the mission were matched by problems in fulfilling his duties. He found the local Bedouin to be inherently untrustworthy, making up place names, or, if asked to verify a name, invariably doing so, even if it was the first time they had heard it uttered. The inscriptions on the ancient monuments, meanwhile, were discovered to be relatively modern, and, after a few weeks, Palmer no longer even bothered noting them down.[28]

The survey was completed in eight months and was generally regarded a great success. The area had been thoroughly mapped, the routes and encampments of the Israelites and the location of the parting of the Red Sea had been identified and Mount Jebel Musa shown to be the biblical Mount Sinai. Palmer reluctantly returned to Cambridge to 'teach boys the Persian alphabet'. Determined to escape academia, he presented himself as a candidate for the position of India Office Librarian, and, on his rejection, applied for admittance to the Middle Temple with the eventual intention of practicing law in India. The acceptance of his application coincided with news that the Palestine Exploration Fund was organising a further expedition to the country north of Sinai, known as the Desert of Tih, through which the Israelites had wandered after their exodus from Egypt. It was proposed that the two members of the mission would map the area, attempt to verify the presence of the Israelites through the identification of sites described in the Bible (in particular Kadesh, the location of their main encampment) and then travel to Moab to search for pieces of stonework containing ancient inscriptions similar to the fragment, known as the 'Moabite stone', discovered a few years previously.[29]

On hearing of the expedition, Palmer immediately volunteered to be its leader. Since he already had experience of the desert, no one else offered their services and he could partly finance the cost of the journey via a grant from Cambridge University's Travelling Bachelors Fund, his offer was accepted. As his companion, the Fund chose twenty-four-year-old Charles Trywhitt Drake, who could also obtain an award from the Bachelors Fund and was willing to partly finance the trip from his own resources. He was also an accomplished photographer and painter, had 'some acquaintance with Arabic' and was a good 'all round naturalist'. Unlike Palmer, he was a giant of a man, well over six feet tall, intensely religious and came from a privileged background; the son of a Colonel in the Horse Guards and educated at Rugby and Wellington Colleges and Trinity College, Cambridge. Suffering from asthma, he had been forced to leave University at the end of his third term and had spent the following three winters in countries with climates less injurious to his health. In 1866 and 1867, he was to be found in Morocco and north west Africa, where he hunted, practiced ornithology and collected natural history specimens, and, in 1868, he travelled to Egypt. Here, he had met the members of the Sinai survey just as they were returning home and had spent some weeks in the desert visiting places of interest.[30]

In an attempt to aggrandize their achievements, on their return from the Desert of Tih, Palmer emphasised the basic nature of the expedition, which he claimed had multiplied its dangers and reduced its chances of success. Owing to a lack of funds, he and his companion had made the entire journey on foot with just four camels to carry their luggage and no escort, guides or servants. In fact, the mission was not as minimalist as he claimed. For part of the trip, the two men employed both a servant and a guide, and, at other times, the four camel drivers acted as guides and escorts. Its basic nature was also unavoidable given the Desert of Tih's lack of springs, water being obtained by the digging of pits in dry water courses, and actually increased their safety. The small entourage made them less conspicuous and less likely to be attacked.[31]

After receiving basic instruction on surveying from Wilson and provided with £300 in gold coin to cover expenses, Palmer and Drake left Suez on December 16th. They planned to travel to the fort town of Nakhl, and, from there, through the Desert of Tih to Jerusalem and then onto Moab. The trip to Nakhl took two weeks. In addition to mapping the region, the two men visited the convent on Mount Musa, where they examined ancient manuscripts, and some ruins at Erweis el Ebeirig, which Palmer confidently declared had been an Israelite encampment. At Nakhl, they discharged their camel drivers and recruited new drivers from Sheikh Misleh, whose tribal lands they were to cross. Although they had completed less than a fifth of their trip, Palmer wrote to Walter Besant, Secretary of the Palestine Exploration Fund, pleading for more funds. Misleh had demanded an extortionate fee, and, after the trip to Moab, Palmer wished to return to Jerusalem to examine various interesting inscriptions.[32]

The 600 mile journey from Nakhl to Jerusalem again went according to plan. Working fourteen to sixteen hours per day, Palmer and Drake continued to survey the region and came across and examined stone circles thought to have been used for sacrificial purposes; a cave that had been home to a Christian hermit, who had painted crosses on its walls; signs of early Israelite cultivation in the form of drainage systems and the remains of a reservoir and aqueduct; and the ruins of two fortresses and three towns. They also identified (wrongly as it turned out) Kadesh as Ain Gadis, where they discovered numerous once-inhabited caves and a cavern that had been used as a Christian chapel. Arriving in Jerusalem to find an additional £100 awaiting them, Palmer again wrote to Besant requesting further funds, claiming that their future expenses were likely to be higher than anticipated.[33]

The journey to Moab was less satisfactory. Approaching the ruins of El' Abdeh, they were stopped by thirteen 'ruffians', who refused to let them pass unless a payment was made, and, on discovering that no money was forthcoming, threw stones and fired a gun 'in bravado'. After a lengthy standoff, an entry charge of eight shillings was agreed and they were allowed to measure and photograph the deserted fort. A few weeks later, their guide threatened to abandon them unless he received an additional £25, which was duly paid, and then betrayed them to a gang of robbers. Surrounded by fierce heavily armed fighters, Palmer claimed he drew a letter from his fiancé from his pocket, declared that it stated that he was travelling under the protection of the

Turkish Sultan and exclaimed 'Down on your knees, you dogs and kiss the handwriting of the Sultan' and 'down went the whole three hundred of them on their faces, utterly subdued'. Arriving at Moab, they spent three weeks combing the region for inscriptions, but failed to find any written in an ancient script.[34]

Their expedition over, Palmer and Drake returned to Jerusalem. Palmer reported the guide who had betrayed them to the Turkish Governor, transcribed the inscriptions on the walls of the Dome of the Rock and wrote to Besant asking to be recompensed for the additional expenses he had incurred during the trip to Moab and in Jerusalem. Although no further funds were forthcoming and he was supposedly close to penury, on completing his work in the city he accompanied Drake to Damascus and Beirut, before travelling home via Constantinople and Vienna. In Damascus, the two men climbed Mount Hermon and visited several mosques, from which Palmer stole several ancient Persian manuscripts, one of which he later gave to his friend Charles Leland. They also dined with the Turkish Governor of Jerusalem, who presented them with a very special gift – a sack containing the head of the dishonest guide – and met Richard Burton, the great explorer and translator of *The Arabian Nights*. Burton, then the British Consul of Damascus, came across Palmer and Drake when he visited his summer residence at Bliidan, a small village to the north west of Damascus. A small tent had been erected on his front lawn, out of which emerged two men 'sunburnt, hard as nails [and] in the finest travelling condition'. Although the meeting was not as serendipitous as he assumed, Burton got on well with the valiant explorers and they accompanied him and his wife on a 'jolly' three week trip to the Libanus mountains. After visiting the ruins of Ba'albak, which one night Palmer and Burton illuminated with magnesium flares, the party galloped to Ayn Ata, where they camped, spending the following few days visiting the snow wreathed summits of the Libanus and attempting to determine their disputed altitudes. On the outskirts of Lebanon's great cedar forest, they parted; Burton later writing 'I cannot say which of the four [of us] felt the parting most'.[35]

Palmer and Drake went their separate ways at Beirut, after they had inspected copies of inscriptions in a mysterious ancient language that had recently been discovered on stones in Northern Syria. They were never to see each other again. Drake made his way back to England via Greece and Turkey and the following winter was again employed by the Palestine Exploration Fund to travel to Northern Syria in search of the stones bearing the intriguing inscriptions. Before starting on the expedition, he called in on Burton and his wife in Damascus and all three visited the volcanic region to the east of the city and the Syrian highlands, where at Nazareth they found themselves caught up in a riot and were stoned. He then proceeded on his official mission, taking photographs and copies of a number of engravings, before returning to the Burtons to help them leave Damascus; Burton having become 'unpopular with the Moslems' and recalled to England. The following winter, he joined the Fund's Western Palestine Survey on the illness of one of its members. It was to be his last great adventure. After almost two years working in the Jordan valley, he contracted typhoid and was taken to Jerusalem where he died; he was just twenty-eight.[36]

On his return to Cambridge, Palmer began to prepare for his bar exams and resumed his teaching and writing careers. After contributing to the Palestine Exploration Fund report on the Sinai survey, he co-authored with Walter Besant a short book on the history of Jerusalem and wrote a popular monograph on his two expeditions entitled *The Desert of the Exodus*, in which he typically exaggerated some of his findings. He also got the opportunity to repay Richard Burton for his recent kindness. Soon after his return to Damascus, Burton blamed the local Jewish community for inciting the massacre of Christians in the city ten years previously, claiming that they were motivated by a wish to buy property destroyed in the disturbances at knock down prices. His remarks prompted leading Damascus Jews to demand his removal, calls that were championed by Sir Moses Montefiore, a leading banker and financier, and, ironically, a supporter of the Palestine Exploration Fund. On learning of their friend's plight, Palmer and Drake wrote an inflammatory letter to the *Times* in which they claimed that Jews had incited attacks on Christians the previous year by chalking crosses 'in the most conspicuous places', and, during the former massacre, had provided those responsible, 'hot and weary with the slaughter of Christians', with refreshing glasses of lemonade and had offered the 'terror-stricken' victims sanctuary in their homes 'and then brought in the Turks to murder them'. The letter resulted in an increasingly bitter correspondence with Montefiore, who unsuccessfully demanded that Palmer and Drake either provide evidence of their accusations or withdraw them.[37]

Palmer's post-expedition goal was to become a barrister and then embark on a glittering legal career in India. However, as so often occurs in life, fate intervened and he found himself on a quite different path. In 1871, the Cambridge University Thomas Adams Chair of Arabic became vacant when its incumbent unexpectedly died. Palmer duly applied, convinced that he would be awarded the post. He was undoubtedly one of the best speakers of Arabic in the world, had published a number of books, possessed the support of Edward Byles Cowell, Professor of Sanskrit, and was the only applicant with a Cambridge University degree.[38]

The position was awarded to William Wright, the Assistant Keeper of Arabic Manuscripts at the British Museum. Palmer was appalled and immediately claimed that the appointment had been fixed by the Master of Queens College, George Phillips, who had forced the college heads on the appointment committee to vote for Wright. On the morning of the election, Palmer asserted that he had been given a card that had been sent to all the Committee members on which was written 'Dr Wright will be voted for tomorrow'. Moreover, he accused Phillips of making a deal with his preferred candidate, promising him that he would be made a Fellow of Queen's College on taking up the post and thus receive two salaries.

Both charges were vehemently denied by Phillips and by other Cambridge academics. Wright had received only eight of the fourteen possible votes and was far better qualified than Palmer. He had held the post of Professor of Arabic at University College, London and Trinity College, Dublin, published a large number of well received books and articles and his specialisms were particularly useful to the University. By comparison, Palmer possessed a third class degree in Classics, had spent less than three years as a full-time academic and had published nothing of note. He was also regarded by many as an arrogant mountebank and by others as slightly mad. As regards Wright's Fellowship, he was already an Honorary Fellow of Queens College and the decision to make him a Fellow was taken without his knowledge and after he had obtained the Chair.[39]

Palmer regarded the appointment as a gross injustice and an insult to his reputation as scholar and would no doubt have left the University had not a few months later the Lord Almoner's Readership of Arabic become available on Theodore Preston's retirement. Unlike the Thomas Adams Chair, the appointment lay not in the hands of college heads, but with the Queen's Almoner, who was responsible for the distribution of alms to the poor. In 1871, the Almoner was Gerald Wellesley, the Dean of Windsor, who offered the position to Palmer after receiving a deluge of recommendations from the young academic's friends. Although the post had a relatively low status and offered a stipend of only £40 per year, Palmer immediately accepted. Many regarded the Readership to be the equivalent of a Chair and the regulations enabled him to retain his Fellowship. Elated at becoming a 'professor' and finally having an adequate income, he asked Laura Davis's father permission to marry his daughter, now a respectable twenty years of age. Thomas Davis, aware of his prospective son-in-law's strange relationship with the truth, granted him his wish, but demanded evidence of the appointment, subsequently postponing the wedding when this failed to materialise owing to an administrative oversight. Finally, however, on 11th November 1871, the happy couple wed, and, after a brief honeymoon, rented a small house in Brookside on the southern edge of Cambridge. One year later their first child, Ethel, was born, followed thirteen months later by a second daughter, Laura.[40]

For the next seven years, Palmer worked as an academic, and, in his spare time, pursued a number of other careers. His academic work largely comprised lecturing. Although his Readership did not require him to teach, the relatively low combined income he obtained from the post and his Fellowship left him with little alternative. He bitterly resented the 'wasted' hours spent in the classroom and the requirement that he live in Cambridge during term time and was convinced that he was underpaid and overworked. In reality, his teaching load, three courses of lectures on Arabic, Persian and Hindustani, was similar to that of colleagues, who were also bound by the residence regulation. Moreover, though his salary of £250 pa was £50 less than that of a Professor, the University had authorized that he receive an additional payment for each student taught, which brought his total teaching pay to the Professorial level.

To further augment his income, he undertook a series of other jobs. He acted as an interpreter for visiting foreign dignitaries and coached candidates for the India Office exam, achieving an exemplary pass rate, perhaps because he now both helped to set and mark the exam papers. Each week, he produced articles in Urdu and Persian for a number of Indian and Persian newspapers and began to write for English journals such as the *Saturday Review*, the *Athenaeum* and the *Academy*. During

University vacations, he was a lawyer. Called to the bar in 1874, he attended county assizes in Cambridge, Bedford, Huntingdon, Norwich and Ipswich and specialised in criminal law; his greatest victory being the acquittal of a notorious thief, who was caught with his pockets stuffed with stolen articles. He also continued with his literary career producing an impressive nine monographs in a mere nine years and editing the St John's College periodical, *Momus*, and a series of books on the grammar of the principal Asiatic and European languages, though he appears to have made few changes to the proofs sent to him.[41]

His books comprised non-fiction, translations and poetry. The non-fiction works included an Arabic grammar and a Persian dictionary, written despite his oft-expressed belief that grammar was unimportant in the learning of languages; *A History of the Jewish Nation*, in which his virulent anti-Semitism is thankfully not apparent; and a biography of Caliph Haroun al Raschid, the hero of the *Arabian Nights*. His most important translation was of the Koran, which appeared in 1880 and reflected his continued interest in Islam, 'a valuable instrument for good…progress and civilisation', that now extended to the attendance of prayer meetings at which he occasionally preached. In addition he translated a number of Arabic and Persian poems in an anthology entitled the *Song of the Reed*; the poetry of Behā-ed-Dīn Zoheir, an Arab poet who died in 1258; and, with an Icelandic co-author, the lyrical songs of the Finnish poet Johann Ludvig Runeberg. His verse was mostly published in journals, though in 1874 he contributed poems to a collection entitled *English Gypsy Songs*, obtaining the ideas for the rhymes from an old gypsy acquaintance who he 'squeez[ed] as dry as an old orange'.[42]

Most of his books were rapidly researched and written, often dictated to his wife or a secretary, and lacked academic rigour and contained numerous errors. Remarkably, all received enthusiastic reviews and achieved excellent sales, the first edition of *English Gypsy Songs* selling out in just four weeks. Good reviews were obtained by 'nobbl[ing]' newspapers, either by encouraging editors on which he was on good terms to employ his friends to write notices or encouraging his chums to put themselves forward as possible reviewers, particularly for the *Saturday* or the *Athenaeum*, whose opinions were often repeated in lesser known journals. To ensure that the critiques met his high standards, he sent the authors lists of 'tips', itemising the aspects of the work to be praised, or asked to read the finished articles, which he often 'improved'. If no friends were available and the editor was amenable, he simply wrote the review himself without a by-line; a practice he believed to be eminently ethical, as he always gave his honest assessment of the work.[43]

High sales were attained partly through the superlative reviews and partly by other means. Palmer sent out at his own expense advertisement circulars that encouraged the recipients to purchase his books, he and his wife wrote personal letters to friends and acquaintances 'beg[ging] for subscriptions' and he sought to get his monographs to people of influence who would recommend them to others. To encourage Queen Victoria to read *English Gypsy Songs,* he included a poem about her Majesty, which he ensured was 'loyal, grateful, devoted, humble, pious, magnificent, sublime', and sent copies of the collection to both the Lord Almoner and her equerry, with a request to pass them onto their employer. To gain the attention of Alfred Tennyson, he included a Romany version of one of the great man's poems, sent him a proof copy of the book and asked whether it could be dedicated to him. Other methods of maximising sales included 'log-rolling', he and his friends referring to a soon-to-be-published monograph in newspaper and journal articles, and, in the case of *A History of Jerusalem,* encouraging his friend and co-author Walter Besant, the Secretary of the Palestine Exploration Fund, to order 300 copies on behalf of the Fund for resale to its subscribers.[44]

Palmer's enormous workload was matched by his hectic

social and private life. He was an enthusiastic freemason, though in private he ridiculed the movement; a member of the Savile Club, regularly attending its Saturday lunches with such luminaries as Robert Louis Stevenson and Edmund Gosse; and a founder of the Rabelais Club. The latter comprised a small number of admirers of the French renaissance poet Francois Rabelais who regularly dined together and exchanged their own pastiches of the Master's works. Fellow members of the society included the novelists Henry James, Thomas Hardy and George du Maurier and the actor Henry Irving. For relaxation, he improved his linguistic skills, once claiming that he could speak every European language and dialect; sketched, drawing amusing caricatures of friends; supposedly occasionally helped the Cambridge police solve local crimes; and participated in a range of outdoor activities, including fishing and bird watching. He was particularly fond of theatre visits and long lazy holidays in the fens, Cornwall and Wales accompanied by close male friends such as Walter Besant, John Radclyff Pretyman, the son of the Dean of Lincoln, the American humorist and Romany expert Charles Leland and the geologist Thomas Bonney. He also learnt ventriloquism, became a proficient escapologist, having a special box built in which he would be locked, bound head to toe, from which he would escape a few minutes later, and continued to amaze friends and colleagues with his card tricks and séances.[45]

As his income increased, his séances became more elaborate. A typical meeting would begin with the participants sitting around a specially constructed table on the top of which was a lever positioned between two words – 'Yes' and 'No'. Questions would be asked of a spirit, who would answer by moving the pointer to the appropriate response. The room would then descend into darkness and Palmer, bound to prevent any trickery, would conjure up fresh apparitions, which would throw books, turn around pictures and cause an accordion to play. When the lights were brought up, the ceiling above the still-bound 'professor' would be found to contain a charcoal message with special meaning for one of those present. As a finale, Palmer would himself become possessed, draw a portrait of the spectre that inhabited him, either whilst blindfolded or staring blankly into the distance, and relay further tidings and warnings from 'the land of the dead' in a voice and accent not his own.[46]

The séances involved numerous elaborate tricks devised by Palmer and his friend Gordon Wigan, a fellow barrister, the part-inventor of the cable car and the son of the actor-manager Alfred Wigan, famed for organising the first Royal Command Performance. The lever on the table was moved by electricity; Palmer placed an electric battery in the basement of his house, brought wires up through his drawing room floor and moved the pointer via a metal plate attached to the sole of his boot, breaking the current at will. When the lights dimmed, Wigan dressed in a black jumpsuit and his face covered in shoe polish would creep into the room and throw books, turn pictures and either write the ceiling message with a piece of charcoal on a rod or use a broom to brush away white chalk covering a pre-written communiqué. Palmer, meanwhile, would play a miniature mouth organ secreted in his mouth, the sound of which was similar to that of an accordion. As for the spirit voices and portraits, Palmer was an accomplished mimic, and, after hours of practice, had leant to draw whilst blindfolded.[47]

As their interest in spiritualism and fame grew, Palmer and Wigan began to attend séances conducted by professional mediums, which they delighted in disrupting, and to hold séances in the homes of friends and acquaintances, for which they charged a fee. They also invented a magic trick used by a number of professional magicians and developed their own act that they performed for friends and at charity events. Using a mixture of memory and pre-arranged verbal signals, they played chess games whilst sitting at separate chess boards in separate rooms and a blindfolded Palmer, prompted by Wigan, identified articles produced by members of the audience. When his friend was not available, Palmer became Professor Herman Frikell, 'Wizard of the East…illusionist and prestidigitateurinordinary to his Imperial Majesty the Shah of Persia'. The advertisement for his show promising 'magic and mystery' 'never hitherto attempted by any living professor of the art', including the 'wondrous experiment of the luminous hat…Cockalorum or the human hen, Excalibur or the enchanted sword…[and] the unprecedented and astonishing feat of extracting a live person from an ordinary box locked and corded by the audience'.[48]

In December 1878, Palmer's life changed forever. Two years earlier, in June 1875, his wife and two daughters left Cambridge for Paris. The main reason for the move was that Laura was found to be suffering from consumption and it was thought that the milder French climate would help to relieve the symptoms of the condition. She and Palmer had also recently rented a house in Newnham, Cambridge, which did not 'suit her', and there is a possibility that having married early and now seeing little of her husband, who spent most of his life working or with friends, she wished to live apart from him. Palmer sold their furniture, moved into his rooms at St John's College, and, in July, joined his wife and family for a two week holiday.[49]

Nine months later, Laura and the children came back to Cambridge, living with the mother of Palmer's friend John Radclyff Pretyman, and then moved to the Queen's Hotel, Aberystwyth, owned by her husband's cousin, William Palmer. The autumn of 1876 was spent on the Isle of Wight, where she discovered she was pregnant. After a month staying with friends in Surbiton, she returned to Paris, where her consumption worsened, before travelling to Aberystwyth to give birth to a frail and sickly son. The birth caused her to become 'very weak and sick' and Palmer was informed that her tuberculosis was now terminal. His response was to tell no one of the prognosis, including his wife. He remained 'happy and cheerful' and continued to work and socialise as normal. Laura was moved to Bath for treatment at its spa and then to Bournemouth, a popular place of recuperation for consumptives, whose promenades were crowded with bath chairs 'carrying…those who are about to pass away'. Here, her son died, and, four months later, she herself breathed her last breath, her husband by her side. Palmer was devastated. His own health gave way and he sent his children to Cornwall to live with Captain Henry Spencer Palmer, joint leader of the 1869 Sinai survey, spurning the offer of help from the Widnalls, whose opposition to his engagement and marriage still rankled. On their departure, he retreated to Paris, spending his days in the city's libraries and his evenings obsessively practicing card tricks, covering the walls of his hotel room with mirrors in a futile attempt to achieve perfection.[50]

Seven months after Laura's death, he remarried. His bride was twenty-two-year-old Auguste Marghereta Elisabeth Von Langa, 'a large and noble woman' seventeen years his junior and the daughter of a Polish count, who had played an active part in the 1863/4 Polish uprising against Russian rule. On the defeat of the patriots, narrowingly escaping execution and stripped of his estate, Auguste's father had fled to Leipzig and then to Hamburg, where he and his family lived modestly off his investments. Seeing little future in Germany, his daughter moved to London to teach German, using songs and drawings to help her students learn the language. Introduced to her at a soiree, Palmer, the great linguistic, booked a number of lessons and was soon bewitched. Although he claimed he married because 'my children were not improving without a lady's care', presumably to assuage the social opprobrium of marrying so soon after his first wife's death, the letters he wrote to Auguste whilst in Egypt clearly show that he loved her dearly. After living in lodgings in Cambridge, the couple moved to a house in Belsize Park, a relatively prosperous part of London, where they were joined by Palmer's daughters from his first marriage and Auguste's brother, an art student. A year after their marriage, he was the proud father of a son, and, twelve months later, of another boy. Family life, however, was not happy. Auguste's relationship with his two daughters was fraught; the girls no doubt resented her usurpation of their late mother's role and Auguste perhaps saw them as living reminders to her husband of his previous wife. Whatever the reason, much to the horror of their maternal grandparents, she persuaded Palmer to pack the two girls off to Germany, where they were to be brought up by her own parents.[51]

The death of his first wife and his remarriage were accompanied by another major change in his life. Early in 1881, he walked out of his career as an academic. His decision to quit was prompted by a wish to make a new start and his hatred of academia. He no longer obtained any satisfaction from teaching and the three courses of lectures he taught per year had begun to affect his physical and mental health; 'my normal condition is one of fatigue' he wrote 'and my only feat of imagination one gigantic oath'. He also felt 'cabined, cribbed, confined' by the petty politics of the University and his imagined grievances against his employers continued to fester and grow. Not only had he been unfairly deprived of the Thomas Adams Chair of Arabic, given an unusually heavy teaching load and a relatively low salary, but in 1875 Professor's Wright's stipend was raised, whilst his remained unchanged.[52]

His new career was journalism, though until he became established he continued to teach privately and to examine for the India Office. His first foray down the 'street of shame' was less than propitious. Answering an *Evening Standard* advert for a reporter, he was given a three month trial at the end of which he was 'let go'. His writing style was thought overly academic and he had little knowledge of or interest in politics, an important requirement of the post. Nonetheless, he was given occasional freelance work, which he gradually increased in his own inimitable manner. He began to deliver his copy personally during the late evening and so became friendly with the editors on night duty; cracking the 'merriest of jokes' and brimming with tall stories, 'his very entry into the dingy premises in Shoe Lane was like that of a glint of sunlight'. Soon, he began to pop in regularly for 'a little chat', and, if 'something happened…a murder, a railway or mining accident or some sudden disaster' and no other journalist was available, he would be asked to write about it. After a few months, he had became a regularly contributor, arriving at the paper at 3pm in the afternoon, and, if there was work, not leaving until 2am in the morning. In addition to covering evening news stories, he wrote articles on relatively obscure topics, able to research and write such pieces rapidly, and began to specialise in the politics of Turkey and Italy and the activities of the London School Board.[53]

To augment the income he obtained from teaching, examining and journalism, he also took on other writing work, which he completed during the morning and early afternoon in between visits to the Savile Club and friends. He edited with Besant the Palestine Exploration Fund's monograph *The Survey of Western Palestine*, revised a translation of the New Testament for the British and Foreign Bible Society, compiled a basic Hindustani, Persian and Arabic dictionary and wrote two *Encyclopaedia Britannica* entries on card tricks and the Persian mystic and poet Hafiz. Prospering, in April 1881 he moved his family to up-market Bloomsbury, taking a house in Mecklenburgh Square, which is where, on the morning of June 24th, Lieutenant William Gill called upon him with his intriguing queries regarding the Bedouin tribes east of Suez.[54]

Chapter 6

The Admiralty Search: Pickard, Foote and Warren

Four days after the Palmer party had left Suez one of the camel drivers who had accompanied the Englishmen into the desert galloped into Moses Wells. He claimed that two days earlier the party had divided. Palmer, his two companions and Sheikh Sofieh and his nephew had ridden on ahead, leaving the drivers and the camels carrying the baggage to follow on behind at their own pace. The next morning, as the cameleers were preparing to leave their evening camp, they had been attacked by Arab fighters, who had looted the baggage and were at that very moment heading towards Moses Wells. Some hours later, after this harbinger of doom had ridden off, another of the camel drivers walked into the village with a similar tale and warning. Fearing for their lives, the Greek families who owned the local market gardens fled to Suez and informed the British authorities of their visitors. At dawn the next day, they were joined by a number of their employees, who brought news that during the night Moses Wells had been attacked, the houses broken into and the contents stolen and all the crops destroyed. On hearing the reports, Admiral Sir William Hewitt sent a telegram to the British Consul in Jerusalem asking him to contact Sheikh Misleh, one of the chiefs Palmer was to meet at Nakhl, to discover whether the Englishman had arrived. He also sent a group of soldiers to Moses Wells to bring back the second camel driver for questioning. On arrival, they were met by the remaining gardeners, some of whom had been severely beaten. Blaming the British for the attack, they refused to allow the cameleer to leave, and, not wishing to exacerbate the situation, the soldiers returned to Suez empty handed.

By August 14th, Hewitt was convinced that the three Englishmen had come to harm. The telegraph line had not been cut and Misleh had informed the Jerusalem Consul that he had gone to the Nakhl meeting only to find that Palmer and Charrington had not arrived, and, after waiting two days with no news, had returned home. Ordered to send another person to cut the telegraph, Hewitt asked Mr Pickard, who Gill had earlier rejected for the operation, to undertake the assignment and also to investigate the fate of the party. Landed on the Syrian coast by a naval frigate, Pickard made his way to the town of Gaza, where he bribed the local telegraphists to halt all communications on the line. Although ordered to cut the wires himself, for reasons that only emerged a few months later, he instead persuaded the local telegraphy manager and the Arabs employed to service the line to perform the job in return for a large sum of money and British protection if the rebels discovered their actions. Informed that the deed was done, he then turned his attention to his second task. Questioning a number of Arabs who had recently returned from the desert, he learnt that some Bedouin had come to their camp a few days previously with the news that two white men had been murdered at a dried up river bed, known as Wady Sidr, located around forty miles from the Gulf of Suez coastal town of Tor. Another Westerner had escaped, and, after staying at the tents of the Terabin tribe, had left for Suez.

Hewitt calculated that it would take the escapee two days to walk to Suez. When the man failed to appear, a Captain Foote was dispatched to Tor to unearth further information. Once he had arrived, he and the Greek Consul of Suez, who accompanied him, were to interview the monks at the Greek monastery in the town, who had good relations with the local Bedouin, and a Sheikh Moussa, whose Towarah tribe controlled the surrounding desert. To many, Moussa was a thug. He had achieved his great wealth by attacking and murdering a clerk and four soldiers carrying the wages of workmen building a nearby palace, had later robbed a Turkish merchant, ironically to finance a pilgrimage to Mecca, and, in 1869/70, had been imprisoned for refusing to help guard the new Suez Canal. To the British he was a possible ally. His tribe had a close relationship with Europeans, accompanying travellers through the desert and depending on the monastery at Tor for food, and enjoyed an excellent reputation, the explorer Richard Burton writing in 1879 that they were the 'most good-humoured and sociable of men'.[1] Moreover, there were rumours that Moussa supported the British cause. On arrival at Tor, Foote interviewed the monks, all of whom refused to help, fearing reprisals from the rebels if they revealed all they knew. Moussa was at his camp and refused a request to attend a meeting. Interviews with three of his chiefs, however, did yield fresh intelligence: the party had been attacked, but one Englishman had escaped and the other two were held prisoner and would soon be ransomed.

Colonel Charles Warren's involvement with the Palmer party began long before he was asked to organise a search. A well built forty-two-year-old, noted for his long drooping moustache and ever present monocle, he was an instructor at School of Military Engineering at Chatham when the Egyptian emergency flared up and immediately volunteered for active service. His request was denied, but on July 30th, the day before Palmer emerged from the desert from his first mission, he was asked to use his considerable knowledge of the Middle East to write a report on how the Bedouin tribes living alongside the Suez Canal could be persuaded to protect it from attack. Why he was required to produce such a report is something of a mystery; by the time it was completed Palmer, Gill and Charrington had already left for Nakhl. Possible explanations are military incompetence or perhaps the need for a back-up plan if the Palmer mission failed and Bedouin support was still needed.

Warren was asked to lead the search for the unfortunate Englishmen on August 24th. His completion of the report, limited knowledge of Arabic and acquaintance with Palmer (he had first met the Professor in Jerusalem in 1870 and later helped him establish the Society for the Study of Arabic at St John's College, Cambridge), made him the obvious candidate for the job. He also appears to have been given a secret mission 'of what we cannot speak'; presumably to collect intelligence regarding Arabi's military plans. Asked to choose three army personnel to help him achieve his goals, he picked Lieutenants Alfred Haynes and Edmund Merceron Burton and Quartermaster Sergeant James Kennedy. Haynes and Burton, at respectively twenty and twenty-two years of age, were at the start of their careers and were believed to have the stamina and the intelligence that the search would require. Kennedy, by comparison, was about to retire after 21 years service, but had accompanied the Colonel on his South African adventures during which he had proved himself to be both tenacious and loyal.[2]

Warren arrived in Suez just eleven days later and spent his first full day in the town questioning Captain Foote on his recent visit to Tor and the Greek families who had fled Moses Wells prior to it being sacked. The interviews suggested that he should begin the search at Tor. Foote strongly suspected that the monks at the town's Greek monastery knew far more than they had revealed and the Greek families had heard a rumour that a Sheikh Nassar had been involved in the attack on the Englishmen; Warren supposing that they meant Sheikh Moussa, though it later emerged they were actually referring to Sheikh Sofieh. The following day, he visited the local prison to meet two Arab fighters, who had recently been captured during a skirmish with British forces, and offered them their liberty if they agreed to take letters to their sheikhs asking them to join the proposed search party. Both refused, declaring that they would be killed if they embarked on such an errand.[3]

After interviewing Foote and the Greek market gardeners, Warren requested and obtained permission to travel to Tor, where he planned to collect intelligence from the town's monastic order and the inhabitants and arrange a meeting with Sheikh Moussa to discover what he knew about the disappearance and to persuade him to provide camels and men for a search party; entering the desert without an escort being akin to suicide. To encourage the monks to talk, he also proposed taking food, which he intended to use as a bargaining chip. The war had prevented supplies reaching the town with the result that the monks were close to starvation and their relations with the Arab inhabitants, to whom they gave food, were becoming strained. By giving them the provisions, he also increased the chances that the monastery would be attacked by desert Bedouins, who were also hungry, when his party left, which would allow him to use the promise of continued British protection as a further inducement to help.

The party chosen to accompany Warren comprised Haynes and Kennedy; the British Consul, George West, who had been stationed in Suez since 1853 and knew some of the sheikhs of the area; the Greek Consul to act as translator during the interviews with the monks; and Colonel Osman Bey Rafat, who the Khedive had insisted be involved in the search for the Englishmen. The mismatched group boarded HMS Cockatrice early in the morning of September 6th with one ton of biscuits, over five tons of wheat and almost one ton of beans. On arrival, they were greeted like returning heroes. Groups of monks gathered on the beach and carried them triumphantly to land on their shoulders. After the departure of Captain Foote, the town had been approached by one of the sheikhs of the area and his fighters, who had only been deterred from sacking the monastery and slaughtering its inhabitants by local residents, who, dependent on the monks for food, had vowed to defend them if necessary to the death. Since then, rumours of an imminent attack had become a daily occurrence.

Warren's attempts to obtain information were initially unsuccessful. The Governor, 'a man with little mind or enterprise', claimed to know nothing about the missing Englishmen, as did the 'white headed, humble and venerable' Archbishop, though he promised to make enquiries. Discovering that he was a friend of a former Patriarch of the Greek Orthodox Church of Jerusalem to whom he had become close during his stay in the city from 1867-70 and believing further help would be forthcoming, Warren handed over the food. The local inhabitants of the town were equally uncooperative, having heard from messengers sent by the pro-nationalist Governor of El Arish that Arabi had vanquished the British in several battles, and, in revenge, British forces had committed atrocities, including the murder and consumption of Moslem children. The only exceptions to the general apathy were two Bedouin, who Warren later suspected were fraudsters. The men gave contradictory information. One, who claimed that he had acted as Palmer's servant during his journey through the territory in 1870, reported that he had heard that his old friend and his two companions were held prisoner at a camp somewhere between Wady Gharandel and Nakhl and that he was preparing to go and rescue them when he was told that they had been killed. The other Bedouin insisted that all three were alive and held against their will and 'not kindly treated' close to Nakhl. Warren chose to believe the latter and arranged for him, plus Palmer's supposed ex-servant, to take a letter to the prisoners, for which they were paid £10 with the promise of an additional £50 if they brought back a reply and £100 if they returned with the men themselves. The Bedouin left Tor clutching their £10 and were never seen again.[4]

Warren then struck lucky. A Greek priest related that a Bedouin hailing from the Mount Sinai region had come to the monastery for food and whilst eating his meal had given an account of the attack on the party. According to the man, it was Sheikh Sofieh who had persuaded the three Englishmen to ride ahead of the baggage camels. This advance party had been ambushed by Hawetat fighters at Wady Sudr, and not Wady Sidr, as the Gaza Arabs questioned by Pickard had asserted, and during the fire fight that ensued a camel had been killed and Sofieh and his nephew had escaped, but the other members of the group had eventually been made prisoner and taken to the attackers' camp some distance from Nakhl. An attempt by Sofieh to pay a ransom had failed and it was now the intention of the Hawetat kidnappers to hand the prisoners over to Arabi. On hearing the story, Warren asked the Greek Consul to write a letter to the Greek monastery on Mount Sinai asking if this account could be supported by other testimony. A few days later, the monastery Treasurer arrived in Tor and confirmed that other Bedouin had given similar descriptions of the fate of the Englishmen. He also stated that Sheikh Moussa, on hearing of the attack on the party, had sent men to his various tribal leaders to collect further information and asserted that the Sheikh held a neutral stance in the war. He had ignored a letter from the Governor of El Arish urging him to attack the Tor monastery and butcher the Christians he found there, even though it later emerged that he had been threatened with the loss if 'his own head' if he failed to carry out the order.

Convinced that the party was still alive and Moussa could be trusted and held vital details of the attack, Warren contacted the Sheikh. A letter was written requesting an interview and fighters to accompany Warren on the search for the Englishmen, which was dispatched to Moussa's camp by the tribal leader who had attempted to sack Tor after the departure of Captain Foote. Paid £2 and threatened with arrest if he refused to act as courier, he left for Moussa's tents the following day. Whilst he was gone, Warren planned his next move. He decided that he would split his party. Haynes, the British Consul and himself, accompanied by the escort to be provided by Sheikh Moussa would go to Nakhl. On arrival, the party would approach Sheikh Misleh of the Teyahah tribe and pay him a fee to act as a go-between for the ransom of the prisoners, which was expected to involve a sum of between £4,000 and £5,000. If the Hawetat complied, that would be the end of the matter. If they did not, the captives would be rescued by force.

The Greek consul and Colonel Osman Bey Rafat, meanwhile, were to return to Suez on HMS Cockatrice, along with a report of all that occurred and a request for the ransom money. The Consul was of no further use to the mission and it had been discovered that Rafat had been actively sabotaging the investigation, failing to pass on information that he had obtained and threatening Bedouins with injury if they revealed what they knew of the attack to other members of Warren's team. Why he was acting in this way was a mystery. Two possibilities were that he was a secret supporter of the nationalist cause or that the Khedive for some unknown reason did not want the Palmer party to be rescued. Warren reported the Colonel's actions to Admiral Hewitt, and to hide his discovery of his nefarious activities, asked the Colonel to travel to Cairo to investigate the possibility that the prisoners had already been handed over to the rebels.

HMS Cockatrice left Tor on September 24th, returning three days later with the ransom money and Lieutenant Edmund Merceron Burton, who had received the order to decamp to Egypt late and had only arrived in Suez a few days previously. He brought additional stores and news that he had recently been told by a Bedouin that the Englishmen were being held prisoner near Marbrook, a small town just outside Nakhl. To say the least, Warren welcomed the ship's return. During its absence, there had been constant rumours of an attack by pro-Arabi desert Bedouin and the party had been forced to hole up in the monastery, taking turns to keep watch.

Sheikh Moussa's reply to Warren's letter never arrived; its courier disappeared either killed or more likely abandoned his mission. Warren, however, obtained information from the Sheikh in two letters from the Mount Sinai monastery. In the first, the monastery's Archbishop revealed that the Sheikh, through a messenger, had informed him that his tribe refused to allow their chief to have anything to do with the British and that the kidnapped Englishmen were dead. On hearing of their disappearance, Moussa had sent a man to Nakhl, who had been told by the Governor of the town that 'he had killed them with his own hand' on the order of Arabi. In the second letter, the Treasurer of the monastery, reported that the Bedouin sent by Moussa to obtain information about the attack from his tribal leaders had returned with the news that Palmer and his two companions in fact were alive and held prisoner at a location close to Nakhl.

The two communications only increased Warren's determination to raise a rescue party. He therefore again wrote to Moussa requesting an escort plus an additional 100 men to guard Tor whilst he was away. To encourage the Sheikh to comply, he offered to feed the guards and pay a reasonable sum for their work and informed him that the war was finally over; the Turkish Sultan had sent 6,000 troops to support the British and Arabi had fled the country. The latter information was untrue and Warren was later accused of a cynical lie; an allegation that he and the Admiralty strenuously denied. The information was supposedly in a Bombay telegram sent to Admiral Hewitt and had been passed to Lieutenant Edmund Merceron Burton just prior to his departure for Tor. Unfortunately, Hewitt was unable to produce the telegram; the original had been lost and the Director of Telegraph had kept no copies. It was also never explained why an Admiral stationed in Suez and cognizant of all that occurred in the region would believe intelligence emanating from India. Ironically, having falsely informed Moussa that the war was at an end, the day after the letter was dispatched, HMS Dragon steamed into Tor with the news that this was indeed the case and carrying a copy of the proclamation of peace, which Warren read out to the inhabitants of the town before calling for three cheers for the Khedive.

Moussa replied to the second letter by sending a runner to the Mount Sinai Monastery with a message that he and the men requested were about to leave for Tor. Rather than awaiting his arrival, Warren decided to move his party four miles into the desert where they would camp and intercept the Sheikh and his fighters as they approached the town. Although such a move would potentially be dangerous, removing the four men and their interpreter and cook from the protection of HMS Cockatrice and exposing them to attack from Arabi sympathisers unaware of the declaration of peace, it would ultimately encourage Moussa to join the rescue party. Alerted by his spies that Warren was to meet him in the desert, any fears that he harboured of arrest as soon as he entered Tor would be dispelled. Warren thus set about purchasing the equipment and supplies that would be needed for the journey to Nakhl, failing only to obtain camels. Angry that they were again ruled by the British, the Tor townsfolk refused to hire out their animals. Donkeys were thus procured onto which the party loaded themselves and their baggage.

A day after the party had settled into their new camp, they were visited by the Governor of Tor, who had delivered Warren's letter to Moussa and had just returned from the Sheikh's camp. He brought bad news; Moussa would be five days late, as he had to travel to Nakhl to purchase the search party's camels. Believing that he rather wished to confirm that Arabi had been defeated before joining the British cause, Warren proposed that the party head for Moussa's tents and ordered the Governor to force his citizens to provide the requisite camels. Alas, his persuasive powers proved as poor as Warren's and he arrived the next day with fifteen more donkeys and one camel and a warning that anyone entering the desert without safe conduct was unlikely to emerge alive. Aware that the donkeys would only transport them as far as Moussa's encampment and that they would be stranded if they arrived to find the Sheikh gone, Warren reluctantly reverted to his initial plan. After six more days of excessive heat, swarms of mosquitoes and rancid food and still no sign of the elusive Sheikh, Warren sent for the Governor, who assured him that Moussa would show up. Unconvinced, he obtained a runner from Tor and sent the Sheikh a further message – if he did not arrive within the next four days his behaviour would be brought to the attention of the Khedive. When he again failed to appear, the Governor was again consulted and said what he had perhaps always known – that Moussa would probably not come. Exasperated, Warren struck camp and he and the party rode back to Tor on their donkeys, where after paying off their cook and bidding adieu to the Archbishop, they boarded HMS Cockatrice and sailed to Suez 'not at all sorry to leave the miserable town…behind [them]'.[5]

Chapter 7

The Anglo-Egyptian War

British forces began to arrive in Alexandria from August 8th, the day the Palmer party left Suez for the desert. Over the following nine days, 31,000 men were disembarked and marched to Ramleh on the outskirts of the port, where a vast tent city covering over one square mile gradually grew up. The landing was an elaborate hoax. Wolseley wished Arabi to believe that he intended to march from Ramleh to Cairo up the Nile valley and that the great battle of the war would take place at Kafr Dawr, a few miles from Alexandria. In reality, he intended to leave part of his force at Ramleh to protect Alexandria from an attack from Kafr Dawr, but to move the majority of his men and equipment by ship eastward along the Mediterranean coast to Port Said and then 85 kilometres up the Suez Canal to Ismailia, a small town on the west bank of the waterway. From there, he would follow the railway and the Sweetwater Canal west to the Egyptian stronghold of Tel-el-Kebir, and, after its capture, advance on Cairo via the town of Zagazig. The advantages of the route were that progress would not be hindered by irrigation ditches, which littered the Nile valley, the railway and the Sweetwater Canal could be used to transport his army's supplies and the waterway would provide drinking water. Its downsides were that the Suez Canal was supposedly neutral territory and both Port Said and Ismailia contained small numbers of Egyptian troops with another 800 encamped at Nefiche, a railway junction a short distance from Ismailia, and even more at Chalfouf, a town further down the waterway. More significantly, the enemy could prevent his ships reaching their destination by simply blocking the Canal. The mock landing at Alexandria was thus designed both to fool Arabi into continuing to concentrate his best men and arms at Kafr Dawr, leaving Port Said, Ismailia and Tel-el-Kebir lightly defended and easier to take, and to reduce the likelihood that the Canal would be obstructed.[1]

The transhipment of men and artillery to Ismailia occurred on August 18th. To prevent Arabi learning the true purpose of the journey, obstructing the Canal and rushing troops to Port Said and Ismailia, Wolseley informed his officers and the newspaper correspondents who had flocked to Egypt to cover the war that he intended to sail to Abourkir, a small coastal town occupied by Egyptian forces 23 miles east of Alexandria. Here, he would disembark his troops, who would advance on Kafr Dawr, whilst the men left in Ramleh made a frontal attack on the fortifications. In the event, this subterfuge was not wholly necessary. Although there was still a possibility that the rebels would race men to Port Said and Ismailia, the danger that they would block the Canal had passed. The previous evening, Arabi had reluctantly ordered that the entrance of the waterway be blocked with sunken ships, but the message had been sent to Ismailia via Cairo, and, by the time it arrived, the British had passed through the Canal.

On reaching Aboukir Bay, the convoy duly anchored, the war ships positioning themselves nearest the shore. However, as the latter made visible preparations to bombard the town, four of the troop ships surreptitiously weighed anchor and headed east for Port Said, followed after nightfall by the other transporters, and, some hours later, by the battle ships. As this ruse de guerre was taking place, British ships moored off Nefiche began shelling the enemy encampment, and, during the evening, British troops launched attacks on Port Said and Ismailia. At Port Said, marines on the two ships anchored some distance from the town were landed at 3am. So quietly were they disembarked that those onboard a French vessel berthed close by were completely unaware of what was occurring. The men surrounded the Egyptian barracks, successfully ordering the sleeping occupants to surrender, posted a line of sentries across the narrow strip of land that separated the European part of the town from the native quarter and then stormed the headquarters of the Suez Canal Company to prevent information being telegraphed to the firm's other offices on the waterway. Meanwhile at Ismailia marines from the four boats that had been moored off the port since late July easily captured the European district and moved onto the native quarter. Here there was some resistance from Egyptian guardhouses, which was rapidly quelled by five rounds of shells fired from one of the ships berthed on the Canal.

The next morning, troops were dispatched to Nefiche and Chalfouf. The men that marched from Ismailia to Nefiche arrived to find it abandoned. The shells of the previous day had hit a fully loaded train and destroyed the railway station, causing the Egyptian troops camped in the town to flee, leaving behind thirty trucks of provisions and ammunition. Chalfouf was the scene of a minor massacre. The two gun vessels sent from Suez to land soldiers came upon 600 rebel soldiers positioned along the bank of the Canal to halt such an attack. Most were old reservists who had been chained at the ankles to stop them running away. Faced with Gatling guns, they stood little chance, and, at the end of the fire fight, almost 200 lay dead and the rest wounded.

Wolseley's ships sailed into Ismailia on August 21st. Over the following three days, men and supplies were unloaded and plans made for the march on Tel-el-Kebir. In the event, the advance did not go to plan. News reached Wolseley that the Sweetwater Canal had been damned by Arabi close to Magfur, a small village approximately six miles from Ismailia, and that water levels were dropping. Fearing that his troops would be deprived of water and the movement of supplies disrupted, he decided to clear the blockage. Following the waterway, his force of three squadrons of cavalry, 1,000 infantry and two artillery guns arrived at the dam to find it defended by a small number of Egyptians. After charging the position, the cavalry chased the fleeing defenders, but were hampered by some irrigation channels that their horses baulked at jumping. Most of the soldiers therefore escaped. A number, however, were captured, and under questioning divulged that there was a second dam a short distance away where the Canal ran parallel to a series of low sandy hills, behind which ran the railway line to Tel-el-Kebir. Wolseley thus continued to follow the waterway, but as he rode past the hills, their ridges began to fill with Egyptian fighters, later estimated to number 7-8,000, the line of men stretching along the skyline to both his left and right. Moreover, beyond the mounds of sand, black columns of locomotive smoke could be seen, indicating the arrival of yet more troops.

Wolseley had two alternatives: to send messages to Ismailia and Nefiche requesting reinforcements and to hold his position until they arrived or to beat a hasty retreat. He chose the former option, ordering his men to dig trenches. Almost immediately, the enemy's twelve artillery guns opened up, but remarkably did little damage. Many of the shells fell short or long, as the gunners were aiming into the sun, those with percussion fuses sank deep into the soft sand before detonating and those with time fuses exploded in the air. The two Royal Artillery guns returned more accurate fire and the unequal artillery exchange continued for several hours until Rashid Pasha, the Egyptian commander, convinced that his foe had been sufficiently weakened, sent his infantry down the slope to finish them off. His misapprehension regarding the destructive power of his artillery soon became apparent; the advancing soldiers were cruelly cut down by British rifle fire. He then made the decision that lost him the battle. Ordering a retreat, he intensified his artillery barrage, bringing into service six more Krupp guns. Alas, the new cannons had little impact, and, during the afternoon, British reinforcements began to arrive from Nefiche and down the Canal from Ismailia. They brought with them more artillery and Gatling guns that kept the Egyptians at bay and allowed an advance to be made to the foot of the slope. Many later argued that Wolseley should at this point in the engagement have launched a full-scale attack on the ridge. Instead, he maintained his position until early evening when all firing ceased; both his own troops and his reinforcements, many of whom had spent the day marching through hot sun, were exhausted and more divisions were expected to arrive during the night.

At 5.30am the following morning his rested and greatly expanded force gingerly moved up the sand hills, expecting at any moment to be felled by a barrage of rifle and artillery fire. None came. After discovering from a brave officer sent to the brow that there was not an Egyptian to be seen, the troops raced to the ridge from which they had a panoramic view of a long stretch of open desert neatly bisected by the Sweetwater Canal and the railway line along which were moving several trains full of rebel troops. Realising that there was not a moment to be lost, Wolseley immediately ordered the cavalry and the horse artillery to Mahsameh, the next station down the line. Unfortunately, the town proved to be well defended and a frustrating hour was spent bombarding its occupants with artillery and rifle fire as the locomotives sped by and many of the men camped around the station loaded themselves and their equipment onto still more trains. Nonetheless, the settlement was eventually taken and seven Krupp guns, large quantities of rifles and ammunition and two stationary trains loaded with provisions were captured.

After establishing camps at Magfur and Mahsameh, Wolseley sent Major General Gerald Graham and a detachment of the Fourth Dragoons to capture and hold the town of Kassassin, three or four miles down the line from Mahsameh, which contained a lock that he feared the rebels might use to cut off the Sweetwater Canal water supply or disrupt the passage of supplies. The township was found to be deserted and Graham began its fortification, enjoying the next morning an enormous stroke of luck. At approximately 10am a train full of Egyptian troops and camels unexpectedly arrived from Tel-el-Kebir and deposited on the platform Mahmoud Fehmu, Arabi's second-in-command, who intended to scout the area. About to unload the men and animals, the other officers on the train suddenly noticed the presence of British soldiers and frantically ordered the driver to rapidly reverse back to Tel-el-Kebir, unaware that Fehmu had alighted. The second most important nationalist leader in the country thus found himself marooned. Immediately arrested and his identity revealed by captured Egyptian prisoners, he underwent intensive interrogation during which he disclosed details of Tel-el-Kebir's defences, which he had helped to design.

The Battles of Kassassin

It was at Kassassin that two of the major battles of the war were fought. At 9.30am two days after Graham's arrival, Egyptian cavalry appeared on the hills approximately a mile to the north of the town. Graham immediately called his troops to arms and sent a signal to Mahsameh requesting that British cavalry be prepared for action. The Egyptian horsemen then disappeared, only to return at noon with two heavy guns. After a number of shells had been fired, all of which fell short, the Egyptian cavalry began pouring down the hillside. Following textbook military procedure, Graham marched half of the 1,800 men at his disposal into the desert and ordered them to open fire when the horsemen came within 800 yards of their position. Although the first volley was ineffective, a second was more deadly and the rebels rapidly retreated.

Graham assumed that the attack was over and ordered his men back to camp. In fact the strange events of the morning were merely a precursor designed to probe Graham's position and exhaust his troops by keeping them out in the blazing sun. At 4.30pm, the enemy re-appeared; this time in strength. As twelve guns opened fire, a line of approximately 8,000 rebel infantrymen at least a mile in length slowly advanced towards the town, supported by 1,000 cavalry. The fear this sight must have struck in Graham can only be imagined. Outnumbered four to one, his force possessed only four 13 pounder guns for which there was limited ammunition owing to supply difficulties. His only chance of survival was to follow the tactics of Wolseley at Magfur – that is to call for reinforcements and somehow hold out until they arrived. He thus sent a signal to Mahsameh requesting that a battalion of Royal Marines and General Drury Lowe's cavalry, which had been on stand-by since earlier that morning, be dispatched to Kassassin immediately; one hour later sending a messenger to Drury Lowe to ask him to attack the left flank of the advancing nationalist army. He then ordered his own artillery to return fire.

Far more accurate than their Egyptian counterpart, the British guns halted the infantry advance. After their ammunition was exhausted, an Egyptian Krupp gun that had been commandeered at Mahsameh was brought into action; mounted on a railway truck that was pushed by a detachment of marines forwards and backwards along the railway line that ran through the town it proved a difficult target for the enemy artillery, and, during the battle, fired 93 rounds. Its valiant efforts, however, were ultimately inadequate. The enemy infantry remorselessly advanced to within a few hundred yards of the British lines and would have overrun them had it not been for withering rifle fire and the appearance of the Royal Marines and six guns. Their arrival marked the turning point of the engagement. At approximately 6.45pm, expecting Drury Lowe's cavalry to shortly attack the left flank of the Egyptian infantry, Graham ordered his men and the reinforcements to advance in echelon formation. Firing steady volleys by company, they moved forward two to three miles, the enemy, mostly comprising young poorly trained recruits, falling back before them and only once attempting to make a stand. By 8.45pm, with no sign of the cavalry and the light failing, the advance was halted; Graham fearing that his men could mistake detached sections of the enemy for comrades. Ordering them back to Kassassin, he assumed the battle was over.

In fact, the most celebrated part of the engagement was yet to come. At 4pm, having been prepared for action for most of the day, General Drury Lowe had allowed his cavalry to unsaddle their horses and partake of a much needed meal. This had hardly been consumed when Graham's signal arrived and he and his units saddled up and set out for Kassassin, bringing with them four artillery guns. Progress was slow. Men and horses had spent several hours waiting in the hot sun and were exhausted and the terrain over which they galloped comprised soft sand. The journey was further prolonged by the fact that Graham's messenger was unable to locate the cavalry and had his horse collapse under him, forcing another mount to be found and borrowed. Drury Lowe was thus halfway to Kassassin before he was ordered to change course. More time was then lost and further complications ensued from the vagueness of the order. Graham failed to inform Drury Lowe where he could find 'the left flank' of the advancing Egyptian army and the messenger added that Graham 'was only just able to hold his own', which whilst true when he had left Kassassin was no longer the case.[2]

The enemy was finally located by the flash of their guns and musketry in the enveloping darkness. Taking his units in a wide sweep to their rear, Drury Lowe was preparing to advance when he and his men were suddenly fired upon; their presence had been spotted and the guns that had been bombarding Graham had been turned in their direction. Luckily, the gunners' appreciation of range was poor and most of the volleys overshot. Keeping a cool head, Drury Lowe ordered his horsemen to wheel outwards, thus putting them further out of the Egyptian artillery's range and allowing his own four cannon to have an unrestricted target. Several rounds were let off, but whilst they were firing hundreds of enemy infantrymen appeared. In ordinary circumstances, Drury Lowe would have made a tactical retreat. However, believing that Graham's very survival was at stake, he moved his horsemen back to their original position and ordered them to draw their swords. There then followed one of the most glorious episodes in British military annals.

Outnumbered and under intense rifle and artillery fire, the cavalry charged. The Egyptian soldiers maintained their position until the thundering mass of horse flesh was within 100 yards of them, at which point they threw down their weapons and ran. It was too late; they were rode over and hacked down. At the Egyptian artillery, the gunners received similar treatment. The horsemen then wheeled around to finish off as many of the fleeing enemy as possible. When the units had reformed at least 400 rebels were dead and twice or three times that number wounded, as compared to eleven cavalry men killed and 67 injured. Fearful that Graham was besieged, Drury Lowe allowed his men a short rest and then raced to Kassassin, leaving the enemy's abandoned artillery to be collected at a later date. When he returned the following morning, he found that during the night Arabi had not only removed the nine guns, but that local Bedouin had mutilated the corpses of the Egyptian and British fallen – lopping off feet, hands and genitals and ripping open abdomens.

In the aftermath of the battle, whilst Drury Lowe was hailed a hero, Graham was castigated. His failure to post sentries had allowed the camp to be surprised by the Egyptian onslaught and his cryptic second message and the messenger's addendum had prevented a simultaneous cavalry/infantry counter-attack and led to the loss of the enemy's artillery and the atrocities committed on the British dead. He was even blamed for the lack of ammunition, even though he was not responsible for its non-delivery. A close friend of Wolseley, he nonetheless retained his command of Kassassin and thus had to suffer the embarrassment of a second surprise attack on the town twelve days later.

Arabi's final attempt to crush Kassassin was motivated by the need for a great victory against the British, which would rally his men and perhaps slow Wolseley's preparations for the inevitable showdown at Tel-el-Kebir. Although he had been told by Bedouin spies that the town continued to be lightly defended, he did not underestimate the difficulties of his task. The attack was to be two pronged and involve large numbers of troops. While 13,000 infantrymen, plus several squadron of cavalry, thousands of Bedouin tribesmen and 24 artillery pieces, advanced on the town from Tel-el-Kebir in the west, between 1,500 and 8,000 men, the numbers given differ, and more guns would move northwards from Salahieh. Both armies would march during the night, launching a surprise attack the following morning.

The approaching armies were first spotted by Redvers Buller, who was returning from a spying expedition to Tel-el-Kebir and rushed to Kassassin to raise the alarm. At around the same time, a group of fifty Bengal lancers riding out to relieve outpost patrols spied an advancing rebel battalion. The officer in charge sent two men back to town, and, to prevent the Egyptians giving chase, he and the remaining members of the unit dismounted and opened fire, a sandy ridge providing scanty shelter. Rapidly surrounded, they remounted their horses and with lances lowered charged through the Egyptian line and galloped home. They arrived to find Graham's divisions in full battle order.

Arabi's plan to bombard the British position whilst his infantry advanced and a portion of his troops worked their way to its rear, rapidly unravelled. Despite being fewer in number, the British guns had a far more devastating impact than their Egyptian counterparts; firing was more accurate and rapid and the ammunition of a superior quality. Although some Egyptian shells fell within the British camp, causing horses and cattle to stampede through the tents, most again undershot or exploded in the air. The nationalist infantry advance, meanwhile, was slowed by intense rife fire and the attempt to flank Kassassin was halted by Drury Lowe's horsemen charging the troops involved; the

Egyptian cavalry though making an appearance failed to engage. After a mere ninety minutes, Graham was sufficiently confident to order an advance. As the various regiments moved forward, firing rapid volleys, the enemy first fell back and were then in full retreat, heading towards Tel-el-Kebir.

The Battle of Tel-el-Kebir

Wolseley launched his attack on Tel-el-Kebir seventeen days after the capture of Kassassin. The delay was partly due to the need to rest both men and horses, await the arrival of reinforcements and to collect information on Arabi's defences. Intelligence officers made a number of reconnaissance trips to Tel-el-Kebir, on one occasion getting to within a mile of the camp. A more important factor was the difficulty of transporting supplies to the front. Aware that the British depended on the Sweetwater Canal and the Ismailia-Cairo railway to move goods, Arabi had sabotaged both forms of transport. The Canal had been blocked and the railway had been rendered useless by the removal of rails, obstructions and the commandeering of all but one of its locomotives. Until the Canal and railway were again made serviceable, Wolseley thus had to move goods by land, which was equally difficult. The British possessed few mules, many of which were in poor condition, and hardly any camels, and the heavy wagons brought from England sank into the sand when fully loaded and became unmoveable. For a number of days, it appeared that the whole campaign would have to be abandoned; cavalry horses went without forage and soldiers at Kassassin were forced to live on biscuits and whatever they could loot from neighbouring villages. Gradually, however, the situation improved – Canal and rail blockages were cleared, new tracks laid, a locomotive obtained from Suez and additional mules shipped to Egypt from Cyprus, Malta and Italy. Thus, by early September, everything was ready for the final battle of the war.

The Egyptian defences at Tel-el-Kebir were formidable. In

front of and to the rear of the town were a series of trenches. These ran northwards from the Sweetwater Canal and the Ismailia-Cairo railway line, which were to the left of the camp, for over two miles. In front of the trenches was an earthen parapet five to six feet high, and, in front of this, was a dry ditch, eight to twelve feet wide and five to nine feet deep, broken in several places by gun emplacements. Within the encampment were 18,000 troops, three regiments of cavalry, 6,000 Bedouin tribesmen and 60-70 guns. By comparison, the British force comprised 11,000 infantry, 2,000 cavalry and sixty guns.

Taking the town would be difficult. Wolseley had two choices. He could either launch a frontal assault or move his troops around the encampment and attack it from its left or right. He chose the former option. Marching his men to either side of the town would be tiring and difficult. To the left, there was the Sweetwater Canal, which would have to be crossed, and soft cultivated ground, over which it would be impossible to move guns. On the hills to the right, there were nine batteries of artillery that could strafe any advancing troops. Having chosen a frontal assault, he then had to determine the timing of the attack, finally choosing daybreak after an overnight march from Kassassin. There were a number of reasons. Buller had discovered that the Egyptians failed to man the outposts in front of their defences at night, making it possible to approach them under cover of darkness. An early morning attack would also have the advantage of surprise and ensure that the fighting took place in relatively low temperatures and similar raids following night time marches had recently been successful in Basutoland and Afghanistan.

As regards the nature of the battle, Wolseley decided that there would be three separate actions. The main assault on the most heavily defended sections of the entrenchments would be conducted by the Second Division under Lieutenant General Edward Hamley on the left and the First Division commanded by

General David Thomas Willis on the right. Between these two companies would be artillery commanded by Colonel Goodenough. Hamley, Willis and Goodenough and their men would march to Tel-el-Kebir across the desert in the formation of the attack, the Second Division on the left, the First Division on the right and the artillery in the centre and would arrive and attack simultaneously. The more lightly fortified extreme right and left of the encampment, meanwhile, would be dealt with respectively by the cavalry led by Drury Lowe and Indian troops under the command of General David Thomas MacPherson. The cavalry would ride to their position, halt and advance on the sound of gunfire. The Indian brigade would march along the southern bank of the Sweetwater Canal, arriving and attacking after the main assault had begun; the later stages of their journey was through a heavily populated area and it was feared that the inhabitants would alert Arabi of their presence. On victory, MacPherson and his troops would then march on Zagazig, a rebel stronghold just outside Cairo, while Drury Lowe and his horsemen would race to Cairo itself to prevent the nationalists torching the city and massacring its European residents.

The First and Second Divisions and the artillery marched out of Kassassin in the early evening of September 12th, leaving their camp fires burning to fool the enemy. To ensure that they arrived at their positions at the correct time, the Indian brigade and cavalry departed some time later. Willis, Hamley and Goodenough moved their men to 'Nine Hill', a sand dune just outside the town. Here, they were formed into the order of battle, informed that talking and smoking during the march was strictly prohibited and each soldier given 100 rounds of ammunition and a tot of strong rum. Wolseley then rode along the line, which stretched for almost half a mile, and, after a short morale boosting speech, gave the order to advance. To help the units find their way in the dark, posts had earlier been placed in the sand and officers equipped with compasses to enable them to navigate by the light of the stars. Despite these precautions, several halts had to be made to bring the formation back in line. The final halt occurred at 3am and lasted almost an hour, during which the men rested and the formations were tightened. The army then moved forward to within 1,000 yards of the Egyptian defences, where bayonets were fixed; it having been decided that no rifles would be fired until the men were within the enemy's lines in order to maintain surprise.

Suddenly, the air was rent by a single rifle shot, followed seconds later by a barrage of bullets and shells, described by one British officer as 'like wild-fowl in flight'.[3] They had been spotted; some said by an observant sentry, though others laid the blame on Bedouin spies, who had observed them leaving Kassassin and had forewarned Arabi of their approach, or a comet that at that moment had streaked through the sky lighting up the landscape. According to Wolseley's plan, the British artillery should have immediately responded. It remained silent; there was insufficient light for accuracy, and, despite all the efforts to keep a straight line, Hamley's Second Division was forward of the guns and in their line of fire. The two Divisions thus began their assault with no cover. In addition to being ahead of the artillery, Hamley was also forward of Willis. It was therefore his Second Division, led by the Highland Brigade, that attacked the defences first.

On the first shots being fired, bugles were sounded, the bagpipe and drums struck up and the Highlanders stormed forward, fired at by Egyptian troops from behind their earthen parapet. The men in the centre of the attack easily overcame the ditch and climbed the parapet, groups forming to help one another over. Those to their left and right had a more difficult time, facing a higher and almost perpendicular ditch wall and Sudanese fighters who kept up an accurate and deadly rain of fire. After the first wave of men had fallen, Hamley sent in reinforcements, who ascended the ditch side by climbing over the bodies of fallen comrades and overcame the Sudanese defenders by sheer scale of numbers. They were followed by Goodenough's men who manhandled artillery through the ditch and over the parapet, setting up their guns atop the trenches and firing shrapnel into the camp beyond. Catching up with those in the centre of the attack, the reinforcements surged into the enemy trenches, slaughtering all they found, and thence into the camp itself. Firing at the fleeing Egyptians, they captured Arabi's headquarters and the main bridge that crossed the Sweetwater Canal before calling a halt at 6.45am.

Because they were not in the correct position, Willis's First Division had to cross a 900 yard stretch of desert to reach the Egyptian defences. Adopting the regular attack formation, they ran 600 yards, fired a volley and then another after a further 150 yard sprint. Many failed to reach the ditch alive; those who succeeded found its width to be such that it was possible to jump across and that the subsequent parapet was also lower than elsewhere on the line. Joined by reinforcements and artillery, which fired into the camp beyond, they rushed through the trenches, bayoneting the fleeing inhabitants, and into the encampment where they captured twelve guns.

The cavalry were two miles from the encampment when the first shots were heard. Increasing their pace, they charged through the defences on the extreme right of Tel-el-Kebir, silencing two batteries of guns as they went, and then swung to their left racing along the rear of the camp towards the Sweetwater Canal, mowing down Arabi fighters attempting to escape from the advancing First and Second Divisions. As they broke through the fortifications, Macpherson and the Indian brigade, moving along the Canal bank on the extreme left of the encampment, were fired upon by an artillery emplacement protecting approximately 400 Egyptian infantrymen. Returning fire, Macpherson ordered the Seaforth Highlanders to capture the guns. Advancing in rushes, firing volleys when they paused and covered by marines on the opposite bank of the Canal armed with Gatling guns, they stormed the battery, cutting down its gunners. Seeing their cover disappear, the Egyptian infantry threw down their rifles and ran, pursued by the Bengal cavalry.

By 9am, roughly four hours after the start of the battle, the fighting was over. British losses were 57 killed and 380 wounded. Approximately 2,000 Egyptians lay dead and an unknown number wounded. During the rest of the day, the infantry moved through the trenches searching for injured enemy soldiers; those that could be saved were sent to the military hospital and the remainder bayoneted. They were joined by desert Bedouin, who stripped the Egyptian corpses of their clothes and footwear, killing any fighter found to be still alive. The following morning, the trenches were set ablaze, filling the desert air with the stench of 'roast mutton'.[4]

Arabi's defeat can be blamed on two factors. The defences at Tel-el-Kebir were unfinished at the start of the battle and were far too extensive, causing his troops to be spread too thinly along the line. More importantly, he possessed poor quality officers and men. His Second-in-Command, Mahmoud Fehmu, had been captured by the British, his two best Generals had been wounded at the second battle of Kassassin, his Field Commander was widely believed to be incompetent and his officers were poorly trained and cowardly and at least two had been bribed by the Khedive to aid the British attack.[5] The men they led were equally below par. Many of the best soldiers were at Kafr Dawr and other garrisons. Those at Tel-el-Kebir were largely raw recruits with little or no training and low morale, their confidence shattered by the two defeats at Kassassin and the Turkish Sultan's repudiation of Arabi a few days prior to the action.

On realising the battle was lost, Arabi, along with a few of his chief officers, rode to Belbeis, where he caught a train to Cairo. On arrival, he countermanded a revolutionary council order that the city be set alight and awaited the British. He did not have long to wait. Following Wolseley's battle plan, at the conclusion of the fighting Macpherson and the Bengal cavalry galloped to Zagazig, the rebel stronghold just outside Cairo, whilst Drury Lowe and his horsemen raced to the capital itself. Tearing into Zagazig's railway sidings, Macpherson discovered five trains filled with troops about to leave for Tel-el-Kebir. At the sight of the British, four of the engine drivers either surrendered or ran from their locomotives and the fifth, who attempted to move his train, was shot in the head. Horrified and unarmed, the soldiers in the railway carriages gave themselves up and the town was quickly secured. As this was occurring, Drury Lowe reached Cairo's Abbassieh garrison, which contained up to 7,000 troops. Expecting fierce resistance, he was dumbfounded when the commander at once surrendered. Squadrons were then sent to the city's two other fortresses, at the Citadel of Mehemet Ali and Mokattam Hill, housing an additional 4,000 men, which again immediately capitulated. Ordered to a meeting at Abbassieh, Arabi arrived at 1.30pm. Greeted politely, he was asked to formerly surrender. After ensuring that the British would not annex his country, he agreed and ceremoniously presented Drury Lowe with his sword. The war, which from the bombardment of Alexandria had lasted a mere 66 days, was over.

Chapter 8

The Admiralty Search: Cairo and Akabah

Warren returned from Tor to 'an exceedingly hot' Suez on September 25th. His intention was to obtain thirty Egyptian or British soldiers to accompany him into the desert in search of the Professor and his companions and then to travel to Zagazig, a railway town some distance from Cairo. Here, he would meet with Mr Pickard, who lived in Cairo, to discover more of what he had learnt when arranging the cutting of the telegraph lines at Gaza, arrest and question three of Moussa's relatives about the Sheikh's possible involvement in Palmer's disappearance and interview a Bedouin who was rumoured to have taken rebel messages to the Governor of Nakhl. He had also been asked to investigate claims that the Indian battalion that had relieved the town after the battle of Tel-el-Kebir had murdered and destroyed the property of its residents. On completing his work, he would then return to Suez, throw Moussa's relatives in jail, where they would remain until the Sheikh deigned to appear, and, with his party of fighters, enter the desert.

Unfortunately, the first part of the scheme rapidly fell apart. Neither the Governor of Suez nor Admiral Hewitt would provide Warren with the men needed for the search party. The Governor, 'a fine old man of Turkish descent', doubted that there was one soldier in Suez who genuinely supported the Khedive and could be trusted not to cut Warren's throat as soon as the party left the town.[1] The Admiral feared for the lives of Indian cavalrymen entering the desert so soon after the defeat of Arabi at Tel-el-Kebir and pointed out that there were operational difficulties in sending horses on such a long journey. Two hundred and fifty camels would be required to carry the necessary water supplies and the intense heat would cause progress to be painfully slow.

The Admiral put forward an alternate far more ambitious plan proposed by the Khedive himself – that Warren be accompanied in his search for Palmer by Sheikh Salami Shedide, who would persuade the leaders of all the tribes east of Suez to also join the expedition. One of the richest and most powerful men in the country, Shedide was Chief of the Hawetat tribe, which had been closely allied to the ruling power since 1811 when it had assisted the Khedive recapture of Turkish territory in the Arabian Peninsula seized by the House of Saud. During the war, he had initially supported the rebels, pledging that his tribesmen would fight alongside them, but had then switched sides, stealing the 5,000 rifles with which Arabi had armed his men. Warren initially rejected the proposal; Shedide was the ultimate head of the tribe that had been accused of capturing Palmer's party, and, at the time of the ambush, had been a supporter of Arabi. After some consideration, however, he relented and agreed to travel to Cairo to formally request the appointment of the great sheikh, before proceeding to Zagazig, as originally intended.[2]

The journey to Cairo was neither swift nor comfortable. Warren, accompanied by Haynes and an Arab who could identify Sheikh Moussa's relatives, caught a freight train to the city. The train departed almost six hours late and then abruptly halted eight miles outside Cairo station, which had been bombed by pro-Arabi terrorists. After a night without food, water or information, and wishing to waste no more time, the party alighted and walked with their baggage the remaining distance. Arriving in a 'famished and miserable state', Warren met the Minister of the Interior, who regretfully informed him that Salami Shedide was needed in Cairo to calm the growing discontent, and that Salami's younger brother, Sard, would be joining the search party. There then occurred the first of a series of farcical incidents, which should have warned Warren that all was not what it appeared. In the early afternoon, Salami Shedide called at Warren's hotel, informed him that he had required all the sheikhs of the region to travel to Suez to join the search party and introduced him to a man he claimed to be his younger brother. Even to Warren, who had little experience of Bedouins, the claim was preposterous. The man was many decades older than Salami, had difficulty walking and was poorly dressed. On being challenged as to the true identity of his companion, Salami continued to insist that he was his brother and only accepted that this was not the case when Warren threatened to inform his superiors of his suspicions. 'Not in the least abashed, but highly amused at being found out in a lie', Salami faithfully promised to send his real brother and his baggage over to the hotel within the hour.[3] Warren waited until late afternoon, and, when no one appeared, set off for Zagazig, leaving word that Sard Shedide should go direct to Suez.

The two days Warren spent in Zagazig, a railway junction of around 40,000 inhabitants, were less than fruitful. Sheikh Moussa's relatives were arrested, but professed to know nothing about the attack on the Englishmen, the rebels' supposed messenger claimed that he had never left the town during the whole of the war and Mr Pickard had little to add regarding his trip to Gaza apart from a rumour that a message had been sent from nationalists in Cairo to those who had attacked the party via the Governor of El Arish. On the plus side, it was discovered that the Indian battalion when relieving the settlement after the battle of Tel-el-Kebir had harmed none of the residents nor stolen or destroyed their property and that the false claims had been made in the hope of obtaining compensation from the British government.

On his return to Suez, Warren placed Moussa's relations in the local gaol and busied himself with administrative work while awaiting the arrival of Sard Shedide, who rode into town with his uncle, other family members and a large retinue of Bedouin fighters the following day. Sard, 'a morose young man', proved extremely helpful.[4] He confirmed Warren's suspicions that Sheikh Moussa and his tribe had been involved in the attack on Palmer, and, when Moussa failed to respond to a message informing him of the fate of his relatives and demanding that he present himself in Suez, wrote a letter to the Sheikh ordering him to join the search party. He also agreed to collect information about Palmer's disappearance from the various sheikhs as they arrived in Suez, and, on the morning of October 6th, led a raid on Moses Wells to capture four rebel spies.

The presence of these Bedouin in Moses Wells had first been reported whilst Warren was in Zagazig by a messenger sent to Nakhl to request the Governor's surrender. Captured by Hawetat and Terabin fighters before he had reached his destination, beaten up, stripped of all his clothes apart from a cloth around his loins and kept prisoner for three days, the runner had returned to Suez, stopping off at Moses Wells. Here, he had spotted four men who he learnt had recently travelled to Suez to gain information on the progress of Warren's investigations. One had been heard boasting that he had killed an Englishman and another was identified as a son of the sheikh who had accompanied Palmer's party. Attempts by Lieutenant Burton, who had remained in Suez during Warren's trip to Cairo, to arrange a raid on Moses Wells to capture the men had ended in failure. The Governor of Suez refused point blank to provide him with Egyptian soldiers and the local British commander, after offering to assist, had changed his mind, deeming the mission too dangerous. Shedide's willingness to complete the task was thus much welcomed by Warren, though the results were less than satisfactory. Of the nine men captured, none were the spies, who it appeared had ridden off on being warned of the approaching fighters. The Bedouin arrested nonetheless were questioned and then thrown in jail, where they remained for over a month.

Although impressed by Sard Shedide, Warren was dissatisfied with the sheikhs who were to form his search party. Sard reported that all denied any knowledge of Palmer's disappearance, and, when on October 6th, Warren called them together to plan the route of the expedition, he was astonished when they unanimously refused to leave Suez unless they were accompanied by at least 150 of their own men. Despite Warren's entreaties, they refused to budge from their decision and the trip was postponed until the fighters and camels arrived. In the event, their intransigence led to a discovery that completely altered Warren's perspective of the case. With little to detain him in Suez, he decided to sail to Dhahab, a fishing village on the coast of the Gulf of Akabah, and then onto the nearby fort town of Akabah, to find out whether any news of Palmer's disappearance had been received there.

The trip to Akabah had to be delayed a day. The water level of the Sweetwater Canal, which provided Suez with its water supply, was found to have fallen and Warren was asked to investigate. Travelling down the Canal with an escort of native cavalry, he discovered that more water than usual was being absorbed by the mud banks, which had become excessively dry during the period in which it had been blocked by Arabi, and its contents had ceased to flow. The following morning, accompanied by the ever loyal Haynes, three sheikhs and the Egyptian official who was to become the new Governor of Nakhl, he boarded the HMS Eclipse, whose sailors immediately 'made pets [of the sheikhs] as though they had been a superior race of monkeys', and sailed out of a harbour packed with the ships of the East India Squadron preparing to transport home the Indian heroes of Tel-el-Kebir.

The journey to Dhahab was slow and tortuous. After sailing down the Gulf of Suez, HMS Eclipse entered the adjoining Gulf of Akabah, along which no English steamer had previously sailed. Aware that the Gulf possessed treacherous sunken reefs and rocks, the Captain proceeded gingerly, constantly halting to take depth soundings. Dhahab comprised a few mud huts housing around a dozen families. Anchoring in the bay, the party went ashore escorted by six marines only to find the village deserted, the inhabitants having fled on their approach. A camel was thus commandeered and one of the sheikhs sent into the surrounding hills to make contact with the fleeing villagers whilst the rest of the party lay under bushes talking and admiring the 'beautiful effects of the sun setting behind the granite mountains'.[5] Several hours later, the sheikh returned to report that he had come across two men who had confirmed that Palmer had been kidnapped by Moussa's Towarah tribe.

Re-boarding HMS Eclipse, the party sailed to Akabah, a series of mud huts scattered along the seashore that housed around 1,000 Arabs and behind which stood a magnificent tenth century fort. Their arrival caused much consternation. Viewing the shoreline through binoculars, Warren noticed a green Arabi flag being rapidly lowered from atop the fort and heavily armed men taking up position behind the stone walls that protected the town and fort from the sea. Realising that he had stumbled across an Arabi stronghold, his first reaction was to shell the fort. Such a response, however, could destroy any chance of obtaining information about Palmer's whereabouts and there was the possibility that the Professor and his companions were held prisoner in some deep dungeon. He therefore determined to resolve the situation by peaceful means. Two boats were lowered; into one of which clambered Warren, Haynes, one of the sheikhs and the Egyptian official and twelve soldiers and into the other twenty marines. These were rowed to a break in the sea walls below which on the beach stood a uniformed man identified as the Governor of the town. Anchoring just offshore, Warren used a megaphone to inform the Governor that the war was over and Arabi defeated. Obviously suspicious or hard of hearing, the Governor ordered one of his soldiers to swim to Warren's boat to obtain more details of the defeat, and, on the soldier's return, boarded a skiff and rowed to within a few feet of the boat. More assurances of the defeat of Arabi were then communicated and the Governor finally allowed Warren and his non-military companions to land.

On setting foot on the beach, the group was immediately surrounded by an armed mob, who demanded that they be shot or carried to the fort and held prisoner. Warren's response was to order the Governor to read to the crowd the Khedive's proclamation of peace. The response was utter disbelief, and, as the horde surged forward, one of the sheikhs fell to his knees and began to pray, believing his life on earth was about to end. With the insouciance for which the English were renowned, Warren cracked a joke, loudly informing him that he was facing in the wrong direction, a comment that 'raised a laugh'. He then required his interpreter to read the proclamation a second time, ordered the governor to send the people away and politely asked him and his officers to take coffee with him on the beach. Cushions and drinks were brought from the fort, and, when both sides were seated, he produced a letter from the Governor of Suez and Arabic newspaper cuttings that proved that Arabi was defeated, and, to demonstrate his good faith and that life had returned to normal, purchased some sheep – for which he paid an exorbitant price. By this time, the sun had begun to set and the mob, which had dispersed, had begun to drift back and the women begun to wail. Fearful of further disorder, Warren and Haynes returned to HMS Eclipse, leaving the sheikhs and the Egyptian official on shore to discover whether the Palmer party were indeed held prisoner in the town.

On landing the following morning, Warren found that the town's hatred of the British had not abated. Accompanied by Haynes and four soldiers, he was again surrounded by an armed mob from which he was rescued by the Governor, who led the party to the fort closely followed by the baying crowd. During the ascent, he was joined by the sheikhs and the Egyptian official, who had spent the night on shore. The sheikhs claimed they had discovered nothing, except that party had been taken by the

Towarah. The Egyptian official, however, had ascertained that the Governor was in possession of an important letter that related to the Palmer case.

Once inside the fort, coffee was again called for and the Governor informed that the fort and town would be shelled out of existence if Akabah continued to support Arabi and that he would be arrested and tried for treason if he failed to hand over the mysterious correspondence. Surprisingly, the Governor at first denied the existence of the letter and then refused to allow Warren to read it, and, it was only after more threats, that the missive was finally produced. From the Governor of Nakhl, whose seal it bore, it claimed that Arabi had won an important victory against the British and urged the Governor of Akabah to defend his town from attack. More significantly, it stated that the Palmer party had been murdered by Sheikh ibu Murshed of the Hawetat tribe close to Wady Sudr, and, on hearing of their deaths, Salami Shedide, who a mere two weeks previously had assured Warren that he knew nothing of Palmer's disappearance, had instructed the tribe's other chiefs to send any other Christians captured in the desert to Cairo. For Warren, the letter was devastating, not only did it finally prove that Palmer, Gill and Charrington were dead, but it exonerated his chief suspects, Sheikh Moussa and the Towarah tribe, and implicated the Shedide family in the crime. Salami Shedide was the ultimate head the Hawetat tribe and the fact that he had sent instructions to subordinates after the murder suggested that he may also have ordered them to carry out the killings.

Taking the letter, Warren immediately reboarded HMS Eclipse and sailed to Suez, where he demanded an immediate interview with Sard Shedide. Presented with the letter, the young man declared it a crude forgery and reiterated that neither he nor his brother had known anything of Palmer's disappearance prior to meeting Warren. He similarly denied that he had deliberately let the spies at Moses Wells escape and was outraged that Warren had the temerity to question his honour by accusing him of failing to question the sheikhs who had joined the search party and encouraging them to implicate the Towarah. The Shedide family, he insisted, had no influence over Bedouin sheikhdom, a claim Warren dismissed as 'palpably ridiculous'.[6]

One would have thought that Warren, having discovered the Shedide's involvement in the affair, would have immediately dismissed Sard from the search for Palmer and his companions. In fact, he continued to employ him. There was the possibility that if Sard was sent packing his brother would instruct the tribal sheikhs gathered in Suez to return home, allowing the murderers to escape justice. There was also no direct evidence that Shedide had ordered the murder, or, if this was the case, that Sard had known of or countenanced the instruction. Warren thus merely gave Sard a furious dressing down, accused him of being an 'old woman', a remark that 'stirred him up a good deal', and warned him that any suspicions that he was acting against the interests of the British government would be immediately reported to the Khedive.[7]

On his return to Suez, Warren discovered that the 150 fighters the sheikhs had insisted were essential for the protection of the search party had still not arrived. Initially angry, he later accepted that the delay was again fortuitous, allowing him to interview a number of witnesses plus Sheikh Moussa. A few days after his meeting with Shedide, Sulieman Zahr, the Bedouin who had rented Palmer his camels at Moses Wells appeared in Suez and gave his story, and, soon afterwards, one of the monks at the Mount Sinai monastery arrived, bringing with him a Bedouin from Wady Sudr who named three of the attackers and three of the murderers, information that he claimed he had obtained from Hawetat and Terabin friends. One of the attackers he identified was Sheikh Sualem Abu Farag, an important Hawetat chief, who was known to have commanded the Bedouin called upon by Arabi to defend Cairo. Coincidentally, a few days later Salami

Shedide, presumably unaware that Warren had connected Farag to the murder, sent the Sheikh to Suez to help in the search for Palmer's killers. Farag, 'a little wiry fellow with small black eyes and a determined look on his browned sedate face', arrived several days later covered in bruises and with a broken arm. On his journey to Suez, he had been captured by Indian troops, who disbelieving his story had beaten him up and sent him back to Cairo, where Shedide had given him a letter explaining his mission. Unfortunately, on his second attempt to reach Suez he was again arrested, received another battering and was only allowed to proceed after Shedide's letter had been translated. His reception in Suez was far less warm than he must have expected. Warren had him taken to the interrogation room, where, after several hours of discussion, a deal was apparently struck – he would escape prosecution if he genuinely helped the British locate Palmer's murderers and told them all he knew. Farag, perhaps weakened by his beatings, accepted the offer. He denied that he was involved in the ambush, but admitted that Salami Shedide had ordered him to co-ordinate the attack and that he had twice sent him to the town of El Arish to 'discourage' Hawetat tribesmen from talking to the authorities. Warren immediately confronted Sard Shedide with the accusations, but was informed that they were despicable lies and that Farag held a grudge against the Shedide family.

Sheikh Moussa finally appeared in Suez on October 19th bringing with him a number of Towarah fighters and two of the camel drivers on Palmer's ill-fated expedition, one of whom had heard that the order to attack the party had come from the Shedides. A tall and dignified middle-aged man, free of the weapons that usually bedecked chiefs, Moussa profusely apologised for his behaviour during the previous few weeks.[8] He had intended to meet with both Foote and Warren, but had been prevented from doing so by the rebels. On his way to the meeting with Lieutenant Foote, he had been approached by a supporter of Arabi, who had informed him that on entering Tor he would be arrested for the murder of the Englishmen and 'would lose his head'. Believing what he had been told was true, he had turned back. As regards the appointment with Warren, he had arrived four days after the British had left, as the Governor of Nakhl, who had been asked to supply some of the requested camels, had deliberately delayed sending them until the deadline had elapsed. His reluctance to come to Suez, meanwhile, was related to the murder four years earlier of an Algerian, who like Palmer had been travelling through the desert. Rather than arresting the Hawetat tribesmen responsible, Fasil Shedide, Salami Shedide's father, had falsified evidence and placed the blame on the Towarah, imprisoning Moussa and a fellow chief, who were only released when the Egyptian authorities discovered the true culprit. Aware that the Shedides were involved in the search for Palmer, Moussa, not unnaturally, had been initially unwilling to respond to the entreaties to come to Suez.

His apologies were gladly accepted by Warren. Recent army reports had shown that the Towarah had rejected Arabi's entreaties to join the rebellion and confirmed that Moussa had refused to support a Hawetat plan to attack Tor. Moreover, the Governor of Tor had discovered that when Warren had bivouacked outside the town to await Moussa's arrival the Sheikh had secretly posted sentries around the camp to protect it from attack. Assuring his new ally that his tribe were no longer implicated in Palmer's murder, Warren invited him to join the great search party.

Chapter 9

The Camel Drivers' Story

The account of Palmer's and his companions' journey from Moses Wells to the point at which they parted from the baggage, as related to Warren by the residents of the town and the camel drivers who accompanied them, contained a number of puzzles. The party left the beach below Moses Wells just after sunrise bound for Wady Kahalin, where they intended to camp for the night. After approximately an hour, Sheikh Sofieh rode back to the town to engage another camel driver and returned with the man at approximately 11am. At noon, the party halted at a small oasis for lunch, and, whilst they were eating, were joined by Salim ibu Subdeh, the Arab who on the beach at Moses Wells had warned Sheikh Sofieh against entering the desert, and his companion, Mosellam ibu Aiyeneh. After the meal, Aiyeneh had a short conversation with Sofieh, at the end of which the old guide was seen to give the Arab two sovereigns; one of the camel drivers claimed that the Sheikh had told him that he had asked the Bedouin to make some purchases on his behalf in Syria. Aiyeneh then rode off, whilst Subdeh stayed, as he was travelling in the same direction as the party.

Wady Kahalin was reached just as the sun was about to set. Tents were pitched, food prepared and eaten, and, just as the Englishmen were retiring for the night, two tired and dusty middle-aged Arabs accompanied by a young boy walked into the camp. Asking to stay the night, they were allowed to pitch their tent next to those of the party. The next morning, they were gone, along with two of the baggage camels. It was assumed that the animals had been stolen and it was decided that the party would remain at Wady Kahalin until they had been retrieved; a decision that made little sense. The lost camels had been lightly loaded and were not needed to carry the party's baggage to Sofieh's camp, the monetary loss was relatively small and regaining the camels would not only be dangerous, but would also delay the party and perhaps prevent it reaching Nakhl at the appointed hour. Any reasonable person would either have accepted the loss of the camels or despatched two of the cameleers to bring them back whilst the rest of the company continued on its journey.

Three men were chosen to hunt the thieves, one of whom was Sofieh's teenage nephew. Some distance from the camp, the tracks of the robbers parted company; one had ridden off and the other two had carried on with the stolen animals. The three Bedouin followed the thieves with the camels and spied them, one of the middle-aged men and the young boy, in the distance. Asking his colleagues to wait, Sofieh's nephew rode up to them. They talked and shared water and the nephew then returned to his companions with the stolen camels, having allowed the thieves to go on their way. The treatment of the third robber, whose tracks the search party then followed, was somewhat different. Sofieh's nephew and another of the cameleers savagely beat him with cudgels.

Warren later apprehended only the thieves who had been allowed to escape. The young boy was uncommunicative, but let slip that he and his two companions had left Moses Wells at approximately the same time as Palmer's party and shortly afterwards had met Salim ibu Subdeh. His master, at first, denied that such a meeting had ever occurred, but later admitted that Subdeh had indeed passed the group. His friend had run after the departing Bedouin to beg for a spare coin and had a short conversation with him. He had then returned and informed them that Subdeh was trying to find the three Englishmen who had left Moses Wells a few hours previously, as their guide owed him money, and had asked him whether he knew of their whereabouts.

As regards the theft and retrieval of the camels, the thief gave contradictory and muddled answers. He first claimed that the camels were taken because they had been browsing some distance from the camp and were thought to be strays. When it was pointed out that the animals were marked, he changed his story; the brand had been discovered some distance from the camp, but they had lacked the time to return them. When told that there was evidence that the animals had been grazing just twenty yards from the tents, he admitted to their theft, but claimed that the idea to steal them had come from his friend and that he was a mere accomplice. As to why Sofieh's nephew had allowed him to escape, the only reason he gave was that they both belonged to the same tribe.

On their return to camp, the three Bedouins who had retrieved the camels found that Salim ibu Subdeh had gone on alone and that it had been decided that the party was to be split. Whilst the recaptured camels were loaded, the three Englishmen, Sheikh Sofieh and his nephew and Gill's attendant would ride onto Sofieh's camp. The baggage camels and the cameleers would then follow, bivouacking in the desert at sunset and then setting out for Sofieh's tents the following morning. The reason put forward for the decision was that the theft had so alarmed Sofieh that he wished to get his charges to the safety of his camp before nightfall. Travelling with the baggage camels would slow progress, particularly as the stolen animals and those involved in the pursuit of the thieves were exhausted. An explanation that again made little sense to Warren. If Sofieh believed the theft presaged an attack, why did he halt the party at Wady Kahalin while the camels were retrieved? Also, dividing the company actually increased the chances of attack, Bedouin being reluctant to take on large groups, and reduced its ability to defend itself if it was set upon.

The cameleers left the camp at 4pm, around an hour after Sofieh and the Englishmen had departed. Following their employers' tracks, they rode until 9pm when at a spring at the entrance of Wady Sudr they bivouacked for the night. At approximately 3am, a rider had passed close by their tents, and, in the morning they had noted his tracks, but thought nothing more of the incident. As dawn broke, the camels were reloaded and they started for Sofieh's tents, but had scarcely gone 300 yards when around fifty Hawetat and Terabin tribesmen charged down the valley towards them shouting and firing rifles and revolvers. The cameleers fled to nearby rocks. Ordered to emerge, all complied apart from Palmer's cook and one of the camel drivers, who made a dash for freedom down the valley but were shot at. Dragged back to their companions, both were searched and the cook found to possess £21, which was stolen along with his shoes. The cook was then bound and informed that he was to be taken back to the raiders' camp, most probably because he was a Jew.

Brought together, the cameleers were told that their masters had been captured, but that Sofieh and his nephew had escaped and were asked if they knew of their whereabouts; to encourage them to talk the attackers added that they had been ordered by Arabi not only to kill all Christians travelling through the desert, but also any Towarah accompanying them. On discovering that the Sheikh and his nephew had been last seen the previous afternoon, the raiders then strode over to the baggage camels, threw the luggage onto the ground and rifled through the contents, smashing open the boxes with stones. Loading the plunder onto their own camels to which the leads of the party's beasts were attached, they began to leave, but found their way barred by the cameleers. Two claimed that the camels they were stealing belonged to themselves and should not be taken and another demanded that the attackers give up the camel on which Charrington had been riding, which he insisted he owned.

Asked later why these false claims had been made, the cameleers insisted that they were a cunning rouse to stop the attackers stealing Zahr's and Sofieh's camels. Warren believed otherwise, suspecting that they intended to keep the animals for themselves, a suspicion supported by their failure to return them until ordered to do so some months later. Whatever, after some discussion, the attackers agreed to leave the party's camels with the cameleers and to allow the 'owner' of Charrington's camel to accompany them to their camp, where he would be reunited with his property.

According to the 'owner' of Charrington's camel, he and the raiders proceeded up the valley for three miles. The leader than dismounted and asked his men to place on a carpet all the goods that had been looted so that they could be fairly distributed. The suggestion was met with anger by some and it was eventually decided that each man should keep what he had taken. It was during this argument that another party of four or five Bedouin arrived, one of whom rode the camel that the cameleer claimed as his own. After more discussion, the camel was returned and the cameleer told to leave; his assertion that he pleaded with the attackers for the lives of his employers and asked to be taken to them being regarded by Warren as 'pure tosh'. On departing, the cameleer rode to Moses Wells to inform its residents of the attack and that he had heard some of the assailants discussing plundering the town. On the way, he passed close by, but failed to notice one of his companions, who was walking to the oasis with the same purpose in mind.

Chapter 10

William Gill

William Gill was the polar opposite of Professor Edward Palmer. Whereas the man who led him to his death was a gregarious egotistical extrovert who loved life, Gill was shy, modest and 'morbid'. He preferred his own company, rarely mentioned his many achievements and often disclosed to close friends that he did 'not wish to live long' and fervently hoped that he 'would die before old age'. At social gatherings he appeared morose and melancholy, saying little and leaving early. He never married; indeed appears never to have had any form of relationship with a woman. While the great Cambridge professor privately mocked the conventions of his time, Gill embraced them. He was deeply religious, praying for twenty minutes each morning, intensely patriotic with a 'burning desire…to make some sacrifice for the Country which he loved' and had an intense sense of duty. As a schoolboy, he voluntarily rose several hours before the rest of his family to study, and, on reaching adulthood, spent every evening writing vast journals in which he recorded in immense detail the minutia of his life. Unlike the excitable Palmer, he remained calm even in the most trying of situations, and rarely displayed the 'ardent' 'soul of fire' that some insisted existed beneath his impassive facade. Both men, however, shared one personality trait – restlessness. Palmer pursued innumerable careers and interests. Gill was 'a man to whom action — action — action — was everything'. He spent the final nine years of his life constantly on the move. Asked why, his only reply was that 'life is worthless without activity'.[1]

He was born three years after Palmer in Bangalore, India, to Major Robert Gill of the Madras Native Infantry and his much younger wife, the former Frances Rickerby. The marriage was an unhappy one. Gill's father spent much of his time pursuing his army career, hunting tigers, slaughtering over 150 during his lifetime, and dallying with his Indian mistress. The relationship broke down in 1852 when he was discharged from the army on medical grounds and decided to remain in India. His wife, along with their five children, returned to England, took a house in Hove, and, thereafter, appears to have had little further contact with her husband, who after his Indian paramour was murdered, supposedly for consorting with a white man, found himself a new Anglo-Indian 'wife' with whom he had two daughters. Filling his days sketching the frescos of the Ajanta caves and photographing other ancient monuments, he died in 1875 while travelling from Ajanta to Bhusawal and was buried in the Catholic Cemetery at Bhusawain.

Gill became a day pupil at Brighton College, winning prizes for divinity, mathematics and drawing, and, after six months of private tutoring, entered the Royal Military Academy, Woolwich. Commissioned in 1869, he served in England and for eighteen months in India and appeared to be destined to live out his days as a career soldier. A life changing event then occurred. The legend, which Gill did nothing to contradict, was that he was left a fortune by an old gentleman, whose hat he had retrieved whilst walking down Fleet Street on a windy day. In reality, the money came from a distant relative. His mother's sister had inherited from her cousin, the merchant John Rutherford, half of his estate. When she died, the money passed to her husband Frederick Heusch, another merchant and one of the wealthiest Jews in Britain, who, on his death, left his considerable fortune to Gill, his closest male relative. Overnight, the non-descript Indian army officer became one of the richest young men in England; worth in today's values approximately twelve million pounds. Needless to say, he told only his closest friends of his good fortune, omitting to inform them of the sheer size of his inheritance.[2]

Regarding his newfound wealth as a 'trust committed to him by God to be used for his glory and for the benefit of his fellow man', he gave large sums to various charities, paid for the education at an English convent of his Anglo-Indian step-sisters, and, taking extended leave from the army, began to travel the globe, gathering military intelligence along the way.[3] His first journey was to Persia with Colonel Valentine Baker, the leader of the expedition, and Captain Clayton of the Nineteenth Lancers. Baker was a seasoned cavalry officer, who had served with distinction in the African Kaffir and Crimean wars. The journey was supposedly a private trip, undertaken whilst both he and Clayton were on leave from the army. In reality, it was a military and diplomatic enterprise. Since 1870, there had been much concern about the threat posed to India, the jewel in Britain's Imperial crown, by Russia. Baker's mission was to survey the region between Tehran and the Artek river through which the Tsar could launch an attack on the sub-continent and to note any valuable political, geographical or strategic information that could prove useful to the British. Gill was recruited to map the area and sketch important sites, whilst his two companions collected intelligence. The three men were also to attempt to settle the disputed boundary between Persia and Russia. The Persian Shah claimed that the territory to the north of the Artek contained towns and villages predominantly inhabited by his citizens and was thus part of Persia. A claim disputed by Russia, which insisted that Persians only inhabited the area to the south of the river and the district belonged to the Tsar.[4]

The party left Charring Cross Station in April 1873, accompanied by over a ton of luggage, including such essentials as Harvey and Worcester sauce and tins of Pea and Mulligatawny soup. At Vienna, they switched from railway to water transport, taking steamers down the Danube and across the Black Sea, before boarding a further train bound for the Georgia city of Teflis. Here, they awaited the return of the Grand Duke Michael, whose permission was required to visit Russian territory. Unaware of the true intentions of their polite English visitors and gratified by their interest in the town, the local Russian commanders took them on tours of the various military facilities. After visiting the topographical division and carefully examining the most up-to-date maps of the region, they proceeded to the arsenal, the army hospital and the local military school, where they noted the training methods adopted. In the evenings, they attended various social gatherings at which further useful intelligence was gathered.

Finally, after a delay of two weeks, the Grand Duke returned, gave Baker the requested permissions, and the party set forth for Tehran, the Persian capital, from where their expedition would officially begin. The trip by carriage, schooner across the Caspian Sea, steamer, horse and pony was extremely pleasant. The men passed the time talking, reading, shooting pelicans and hares and hunting with hawks, and, on arriving at the town of Ashourado, again, threw themselves into the local social scene, discovering the views of ordinary Russians on their country's southern expansion. On reaching Tehran, they explored the bazaars, buying carpets and knives, and arranged transportation for the journey ahead – hiring nineteen mules and five horses and employing nineteen locals as servants, cooks and muleteers.

The expedition hit its first difficulties on the journey from Tehran to Mashhad, a large town bordering Afghanistan and Turkmenistan. During their stay in Tehran, both Baker and Clayton had been taken ill with fever. Both recovered, but a few miles outside the city, Clayton experienced violent cholera-like convulsions and it was decided that he would return to England. Baker and Gill rode on, through the Elburz mountains and the forests of Mazanderan, but were the victims of further misfortunes. A servant who had returned to a village alone to replace a sick mule was savagely beaten. It later emerged that he had revealed to his assailants the route of the party, and, several days later, the muleteers who left camp early whilst Gill and Baker breakfasted were ambushed. Luckily, one man escaped and raised the alarm. Accompanied by their faithful servants, Baker and Gill immediately rode to the place of the attack where they found their men, the remains of the baggage and two groups of robbers. Not thinking of the consequences, they charged, guns ablaze, the smaller group of twenty raiders, who fled. Turning their horses, they then launched a frontal attack on the second larger band; 'about half a dozen timid spirits turned and ran; then a tremor seemed to go through the ranks of the remainder, and, in another moment, the whole body was scattered and flying over the fields in all directions'.[5] Baker and Gill took off in pursuit, capturing three prisoners, who they later allowed to escape, fearing that their companions would attempt a bloody rescue.

Some days later, the party had an even more dangerous encounter. Its path was blocked by a dozen men armed with guns, spears and sticks. The leader approached the Englishmen with a 'menacing air' and attempted to seize the bridle of Baker's pony.[6] Baker grabbed the man's hair and placed the muzzle of his revolver on his temple; at which point men who had been hiding in the rocks at either side of the road made their presence known by rising and levelling their rifles at the Englishmen. Baker kept the leader covered; warning that he would be the first to die if the gang did not retreat. In the event, at this moment a number of the roadside attackers opened fire and began to throw stones, and Baker, Gill and their men raced to a nearby fallen tree, behind which they returned fire. Oddly, the stones did more damage than the bullets; Baker was twice hit on the head, his skull saved only by his doughty pith helmet, and Gill suffered a broken arm. A stalemate then set in; eventually broken by the arrival of two servants of the Governor of the district, who acted as peace-makers. Baker took the gang leader prisoner, but later released him on being assured by the Governor's servants that their employer would punish him for his behaviour.

There were yet more problems on the long trek from Mashhad to the river Artek. Disputes with the members of the expedition became common. At a village outside Mashhad, a number of the muleteers refused to continue the journey and proceeded to steal and sell the party's supplies. Baker demanded that the local headman arrest them and that the four ringleaders be whipped, though he personally blamed himself for their actions having 'been too lenient and…spared the rod overmuch'.[7] Bodyguards recruited to escort the party through a particularly dangerous region then abandoned them, claiming that the journey was too perilous, and, at Boojnood, the cook and one of the servants were discovered to be deliberately over-purchasing supplies in order to sell the excess and pocket the proceeds. Baker reported the two men to the town's Governor, who threw them in jail, though it was subsequently discovered that they were released on the departure of the party.

Both Gill and Baker also again came close to death. While scrambling down a hillside, Gill rested for a moment and leaned his loaded half-cocked rife against a rock. The gun slipped and went off, firing a bullet into his right leg. Luckily, he was wearing high leather riding boots and suffered only flesh wounds. Baker was less fortunate. He fell ill with dysentery, and, by October, rarely slept and was 'reduced to a shadow…dying by inches'.[8] Gill nursed him for five weeks and he recovered sufficiently to continue their journey, but was then struck down by malaria. The river Artek was reached in mid-November and the two men celebrated with a bottle of champagne. As Baker's condition had deteriorated further, it was decided to end the expedition there and to return to Tehran and thence to the Caspian Sea. The journey was a 'nightmare'. Baker rode clinging to his pony's mane, too ill and exhausted to sit up in his saddle. Five miles from the Caspian, he fell to the ground and was carried to the steamer on a stretcher.

The two men spent over a month at Baku, a small town on the southern edge of the Caspian Sea, where Baker received medical attention and recuperated. On his recovery, they decided to return to England through Russia, which would avoid the tedium of retracing their steps and give them an opportunity to collect more intelligence on that country's military intensions. Buying warm clothes, they crossed the Russian steppes by carriage, and, when the snow made further progress impossible, by sledge, using the long lines of telegraph poles as their guide. On arriving at Moscow and St Petersburg, they again threw themselves into the local social scene, dining at the British embassies and befriending Russian military officers with whom they exchanged views on the likelihood of war between their respective countries. Finally, on December 4th, 1873, they boarded a train for England, arriving at Charring Cross Station four days later and eight months after starting out on their hazardous adventure.

The expedition had not been a complete success. The Russians had denied them access to the area to the south of the Artek river, despite their possession of the permit issued by the Grand Duke, supposedly because of military engagements in the territory, and the King barred them from entering Afghanistan on the flimsy grounds that the party had no official standing. Nonetheless, it had achieved a great deal. Much military intelligence was collected and Gill's map of the territory greatly added to the knowledge of the geography of the region, forming the basis of the new map of Persia that was being compiled by the India Office. The pair also settled the debate over the location of the Persian/Russian boundary, proving beyond doubt that there were Persian towns and villages in the area north of the Artek river.

Both Gill and Baker wrote accounts of their epic journey. Gill's article appeared in the October 1874 edition of the *Geographical* magazine and Baker's book, *Clouds to the East*, was published in 1876, but sold barely a copy. It appeared whilst Baker was serving a one year sentence with hard labour for a rape committed on a train travelling from Portsmouth to Waterloo. At 5.15pm on 17th June 1876, as the train passed through Walton Station at forty miles per hour, a railway company bricklayer saw a young woman hanging from the door of a first class compartment. Believing she was attempting to jump, he informed the station-master, who sent a signal that the locomotive was to be brought to a halt using the emergency breaking system. The scene that met the railway employees when they reached the halted train was one of confusion. The woman claimed that soon after the start of the journey, Baker had tried to make small talk with her, asking her whether she believed in mesmerism. She had politely replied, but 'he would not leave her alone' and had then 'insulted' her, an euphemism for sexual assault. At the subsequent trial, Baker denied the charge, but was found guilty, partly because he declined to testify in his own defence, refusing to impugn the honour of the young woman further by calling her a liar, but largely due to the weight of evidence against him. Two passengers in the adjacent compartment testified that when the train was halted and Baker stepped from his carriage, his flies were undone, and a police constable claimed that on his arrest at Waterloo Station the suspect had said 'I am sorry I did it'.[9]

The trial destroyed Baker's life. He was cashiered from the army, an offer to resign was rejected as it would have allowed him to escape the disgrace of being dismissed, and relatives and friends deserted him. On his release from prison, he immediately left the country never to return. Taking a commission in the Turkish army, he commanded an infantry regiment in the 1877-8 Russo-Turkish war, leading what many believe to be one of the greatest cavalry charges of the century. Of the few friends who remained loyal was Gill, who was convinced of his innocence. He visited him during his trial, giving him moral support, in 1878 met him in Constantinople and the two men regularly corresponded. The continued contact was partly the result of the comradeship that had developed during the eight months they had spent in Persia, but also had a baser foundation. As an officer in the Turkish army, Baker obtained much information of interest to the British military and it seems likely that Gill acted as the conduit of that intelligence.[10]

A few months after returning from Persia, Gill stood for the Conservative party in a by-election in Hackney against the Liberal Charles Reed, a seasoned politician and the owner of a successful London type founding business and the largest private collection of house keys in the Empire. Given that the constituency was 'a hotbed of radicalism' and he possessed none of the characteristics found in a successful politician, Gill stood little chance of victory and duly came bottom of the poll, though he increased the Conservative vote. Claims that the proper procedures had not been followed, however, caused the result to be invalidated and the election was re-held in August. Reed stood down as the main Liberal opponent to be replaced by Henry Fawcett, Cambridge University's Professor of Political Economy, who had been blinded in a shooting accident at the age of twenty-five, and, coincidentally, was a friend of Edward Palmer. Owing to Fawcett's inexperience and strong support from the *Independent* newspaper, the result was far closer; Gill lost by only 1,500 votes, his opponent declaring that he had 'fought a manly, straightforward and upright fight'.[11]

Disillusioned with politics, Gill set forth on his second great journey – a trek through China, Tibet and Burma, which was to take him two years. His professed motive for making the trip was his lust for adventure and a sentimental wish to view the place where one of his friends at Brighton College, Augustus Margary, had died. A diplomat and explorer, Margary and his personal staff had been murdered in Upper Burma the previous year whilst searching for rare orchids. In reality, the expedition had a military goal, again connected to the Russian threat to the Empire. An alternative route by which Russia could attack India was through Tibet, the only Himalayan Kingdom free from

British influence. Gill was to map the area, collect intelligence on Chinese troop deployments and attempt to discover routes that would be taken by an advancing Russian army and could also be used by British traders.[12]

He left London on 30th July 1876, having obtained advice on the journey ahead from Colonel Henry Yule, the eminent Scottish geographer then at the India Office, and Thomas Thornville Cooper, a diplomat and the first European to penetrate the mountains west of the province of Sichuan. After stopping off at Berlin to meet Baron von Richthofen, 'the most illustrious and accomplished of modern travellers in China' and the uncle of the World War One flying ace, the 'Red Baron', he travelled by sea to Singapore. From there, he sailed onto to Saigon, capital of the French colony of Cochin China; Hong Kong; Shanghai, where he discussed his forthcoming expedition with the Consul, Thomas Wade; and finally Peking. Here, he shopped, dined at the finest restaurants, finding the food 'tedious in the extreme', and visited the Temple of Heaven, chipping away some of the Temple's bricks, tiles and glass as souvenirs, and the ruins of the Summer Palace, becoming overcome by 'the sadness of [the building's] desolation'. He then set out on a five week journey to the Great Wall of China and the coast with an employee of the British legation, passing through 'interminable plains...[and] filthy though picturesque villages inhabited by a good humoured population'.[13]

On his return to Peking, Gill slightly altered his itinerary. Unsettled diplomatic relations between Russia and Britain raised the thrilling spectre of war between the two countries in which he could play a significant part. He thus reduced the length of his proposed journey, which he split into two parts: a 1,500 mile trip up the Yangtze river to Chonqing and a trek across Eastern Tibet to Bhamo in Burma. He was accompanied on the journey to Chonqing by two servants, a brown retriever dog he had recently purchased and named 'Tib' and the British representative of the town, Edward Colborne Baber, who was returning to his post after an expedition to the Burmese border to investigate the death of Margary. A confident extrovert, Baber was the same age as Gill, and, since graduating from Cambridge University, had spent his entire career in the Far East.[14]

The party travelled to Hankou by a commercial steamer, 'similar to a Mississippi river boat', and then hired a eighty foot by eleven foot junk, which was rowed by 'ten lusty coolies, shouting to encourage themselves' in the upper reaches of the Yangtze, and, later, hauled through rapids by over 100 hired men. Gill made voluminous notes whilst passing the mouth of the Grand Canal of China, which rather than the magnificent highway imagined by the British was 'in many parts little more than a stinking ditch', and, at Hackou, visited a Russian factory producing brick tea, whose black colouring he discovered was produced by the addition of large amounts of soot. The journey was generally uneventful, disturbed by only three incidents. Baber tried, but failed to catch and flog a Chinese sailor, who had dared to call the two Englishmen 'Devils'. Gill, having decided to leave the junk for a stroll one morning returned to find it had left, forcing him to commandeer a second vessel and give chase. And at Yichang, the local British Consul and his party were attacked by a Chinese mob whilst attempting to mediate between local Chinese and European residents; Gill and Baber being too distant to come to his assistance.

On reaching Chonqing, Gill found that William Mesny, with whom he was to travel to Burma, had not yet arrived. After spending a few days exploring the town and meeting the French Roman Catholic Missionaries working in the area, who he was horrified to find wore artificial plaits and Chinese clothes, he became concerned that he was wasting time. He thus sent a message to Mesny, arranging to meet him at Chengdu, 170 miles to the north, and bid adieu to Baber, who, like himself, was to die at a comparatively young age. Unfortunately, the only person waiting for him when he arrived at Chengdu was a messenger with a note from Mesny that announced that he would be several weeks late. Rather than waiting for him in his 'exceedingly dirty' hotel, Gill decided to take a 400 mile side trip to the mountains of Northern Sichuan, an area no European had previously travelled. Accompanied by an interpreter, sixteen coolies and his faithful dog, he climbed to the highest peak, staying each night at the nearest village, where he was invariably a curiosity followed about 'by a gaping crowd', who when he returned to his room at the local inn made holes in the plaster walls in order to watch him eat and sleep. After admiring the views, hunting deer, hares, pheasants 'and a variety of bird life', and visiting the lamas (Buddhist monks) at a local monastery, who 'though exceedingly polite were excessively dirty and smelt horribly', he and his party boarded a boat and sailed down the river that flowed through the range to within a few days march of Chengdu.[15]

Gill returned to the town on 20th June, a day before the arrival of Mesny, who, dressed in traditional garb and married to a Chinese woman, he concluded had 'turned Chinaman'.[16] The son of a Jersey cobbler, Mesny had become an apprentice brickmaker at the age of eight, and, at twelve, had run away to sea, sailing to Australia, Africa and the Americas, before settling in Hong Kong, where he became a jailer at the local gaol. Becoming bored with a settled life, he took up the profession of gunrunner, selling weapons to both the Chinese government and the rebels they were fighting. Various mishaps, including being caught by the rebels who were somewhat miffed that he was also arming their enemies, convinced him that this was an unhealthy career choice and he entered the Chinese Customs Service, which gave him plenty of opportunities for earning additional sums from individuals loath to pay the full duties. The money he earned, he invested in a ship broking enterprise and a hotel. Unfortunately, he proved as poor a businessman as a gunrunner, and, in 1868, obtained a job as a drill instructor, and, later, as a mercenary for the Chinese Imperial army. Finally, he had found a profession at which he excelled. Leading forces in military campaigns to suppress the Miao, he was rapidly promoted to Colonel and then Major General at the early age of thirty. With no more wars to fight, he became Superintendent of the Kueichou Armouries and returned to business, operating a company for the extraction of mercury and hiring himself out as a guide to Western travellers.[17]

The two mismatched Englishmen set off for Tibet and Burma three weeks later. The departure of the party was a magnificent sight; twenty men carried Gill, Mesny and their servants in sedan chairs and were followed by a long train of forty coolies and over 100 baggage donkeys. Finding his sedan chair uncomfortable, Gill exchanged it for a donkey on leaving the town, only returning when entering and leaving large conurbations, as to do otherwise would have been against the inexorable law of custom and entailed a loss of status that might have had inconvenient consequences. Over the following weeks, the party climbed roads that were sometimes so steep 'that it seemed as if neither ponies nor coolies could possibly mount them' and so slippery that Gill had to exchange his leather boots for straw sandals. As they trudged on, they were passed by streams of mules loaded with opium and brass, a man with a cargo of parrots, and hundreds upon hundreds of coolies carrying tea and logs of wood on their backs, who 'seemed more like beasts of burden than human beings; they never smiled and scarcely ever said a word'.[18]

At Tachienlu, 130 miles from their starting point at Chengdu, they halted for a few days in order to spend time with Bishop Chauveau of the French mission and to purchase souvenirs and a few dozen scarves, 'a horse–load' of tea and 350 turquoise stones, which they hoped to use as currency on the next stage of their journey. An aged frail man dressed in Chinese costume with a long snow white beard, the Bishop had lived in China 32 years and had only months to live. Nonetheless, he showed a keen interest in European affairs and Gill was much impressed by his courtly manners that were of a 'nobleman of the old French regime'. After their meeting, he helped the party exchange its silver bullion for lighter gold ingots and agreed to adopt Gill's dog, Tib, who had become so exhausted that 'much to the discontent of the coolies' he had been carried for the previous few weeks in a sedan chair. The two Englishmen also visited the local monastery, which allowed the ways of the lamas to be observed. Noting that their lands were free from taxation, they never performed manual work and lent money to the local populace at rates of interest exceeded only by the 'Jews of London', Gill concluded that they were 'a curse to the country and the people'.[19]

Refreshed, they continued to climb, occasionally becoming giddy at the lack of oxygen. Gradually, the number of passersby waned and the coolies and mules were replaced by great droves of yaks and half bred oxen. At Batang, on the border between China and Tibet, they paid off and gave gifts to their coolies, who were unwilling to leave their homeland, and replaced them with Tibetans. Soon afterwards they were approached by the head of the town and warned that if they entered Tibet they would 'be obliged to fight [their] way out'.[20] The functionary had heard that the lamas had ordered 6,000 men to guard the frontier and to kill them on sight, and, if they escaped, had forbidden the local population from giving or selling them food, forage or shelter. To avoid any trouble, Gill persuaded the local native chief to send soldiers into the mountains to investigate the truth of the rumours. On discovering they had little basis, he and Mesny, set off on the final lap of the journey, accompanied by the chief and 200 fighters. A few miles outside Batang, their path was blocked by 300 Tibetans, who fired warning shots as they approached. The native chief went forward, and, after some negotiation, they were allowed to peacefully go on their way. No other attempt was made to molest them, and, on leaving Tibetan territory, their armed guard departed.

The trip to Burma was a mournful affair. The country had been torn apart by civil war and plague, both of which had carried off a large proportion of the population. The party passed through scenes of utter devastation; abandoned paddy fields and ruined villages 'where rank weeds and prickly pears usurped the place of smiling vegetable gardens [and] bore pitiful witness to the havoc of the dogs of war'. The sombre mood was intensified when they reached the place of Margery's murder, where Gill paid homage to his deceased schoolmate, whose memory would 'ever be dear to the hearts...of those who value the noble qualities of uprightness, courage and determination'. To avoid his own party suffering the same fate as his childhood friend, before entering the region he had employed twenty native fighters and purchased large quantities of opium, which as custom dictated he gave to the heads of the villages through which they passed. The precautions were a success and there were only two minor confrontations. Soon after leaving the scene of Margery's death, a group of twenty or thirty robbers fired a shot, but ran way when Gill 'sprang down and clapped a couple of cartridges' into his rifle. Further along the track, an elderly Chinese man with a gun demanded that they walked rather than rode past his house, but abandoned his stance on Mesny calling out 'if you shoot, you are a dead man'.[21]

Finally, on 1st November 1877 they reached Bhamo, where they were greeted by none other than Thomas Thornville Cooper, whose advice Gill had sought prior to leaving England and who had been appointed the region's political agent. As he shook Cooper's hand ('Oh, the pleasure of a hearty British shake of the hand!'), a feeling of 'peace, ease and contentment quite indescribable' came over Gill – he had achieved his goal.[22] The three Englishmen spent a week in the town celebrating the end of the expedition before parting for a final time. Five months later, Cooper was dead at the age of just forty; murdered in his own home by one of his guards angry at a punishment the political agent had inflicted upon him. Mesny returned to life as a businessman, variously managing the Shanghai office of the New York Life Assurance Co, representing the Lartigue railway construction company and Messrs Reiss & Co. and becoming the owner of Shanghai's Olympia skating ring and a local newspaper. All the ventures failed and he died in Hankow in poverty and obscurity in 1919.[23]

The success of the expedition was reflected in the decision of the Royal Geographical Society to award Gill its Founders medal and the Paris Geographical Society to bestow a further gold medallion. Gill had created a detailed two miles to the inch scale map of Western China and Tibet that extended over 42 sheets. Furthermore, he had collected much information on the various tribes encountered and the strength and capabilities of the Chinese army and had brought back a previously unknown species of oak tree, later named in his honour, Quercus Gilliana, and a manuscript written in an unknown ancient ideographic script, which he donated to the British Museum. His two volume account of the journey, *The River of Golden Sand,* was published in 1880 and achieved respectful, though not high sales.

By the time the book appeared, Gill was in the border town of Giurgiu waiting for a pass that would allow himself and a friend to enter Bulgaria. Their professed reason for the trip was to visit the battlefields of the Russo-Turkish war, which had just come to an end. The real motive was to determine whether the Russians had begun to occupy the provinces about to be detached from Turkey during the peace negotiations. The Russians were onto them almost immediately. In Giurgiu, the hotel staff took an inordinate interest in their movements; they were followed – there appeared 'around every corner…someone who was trying to look as if he did not see us'; and it later emerged that their correspondence to England had been opened and read. When the pass failed to materialize, Gill and his companion attempted to cross the border illegally, but were arrested by two Russian soldiers, who took them back to Giurgiu, where they were placed on a train to Bucharest.[24]

Disillusioned by the failure of the Balkans escapade, on his return to London Gill appears to have attempted to move away from his quasi-intelligence work; reactivating his commission and making a second attempt to become an MP. Both initiatives failed. The army sent him to Constantinople to help map the new border between Turkey and Russia that had been laid down in the post-war peace negotiations. However, disagreements between the British and the Russians prevented any work being undertaken, and, after six months hunting, exploring Constantinople, socialising and collecting intelligence from the Russians involved in the project, he was recalled home. His nascent political career was similarly unsuccessful. Campaigning for Home Rule in Ireland as the Conservative candidate for the seat of Nottingham in the 1880 election, he was roundly defeated by his Liberal opponents, largely because of his 'lack of energy at the commencement of the battle'.[25]

He thus reluctantly returned to the world he knew best. In August 1880, he travelled at his own expense and in a private capacity to Afghanistan, where the British had just suffered a major defeat at Maiwand. Setting out from Qandahar in the southern part of the country to support 6,000 supposedly pro-British tribesmen in suppressing a rebellion against the Amir, two brigades comprising 2,700 British and Indian troops and led by Brigadier George Burrows had been ambushed by 25,000 Afghans. Although they fought with considerable bravery, the British were routed, 969 men were killed and 177 wounded. Gill's brief was to travel to the region and collect information on the location and strength of the Afghan forces. Unfortunately, by the time he arrived the rebels had been defeated and he therefore joined Major General Charles Macgregor in an expedition against the Maris, another rebel group. Although his role was to survey the country through which the company passed, 'he was always ready to lend a hand where he could be useful' and was mentioned in dispatches.[26]

On the surrender of the Maris, Gill sailed from Karachi to Southern Persia and his next mission. Over the following four months, he travelled across Persia to Tehran and then to Mashad, which he had last visited with Baker in 1873, creating a detailed map of the area. From Mashad, he had hoped to travel to Marv in Turkmenistan, one of the Turkish states that Russia had hopes of acquiring. Alas, the Russians had become aware of his presence at the border and made an official complaint to the British government, who, claiming complete ignorance of Gill's activities, nonetheless, suggested that he return to England.[27]

His final expedition before his fatal meeting with Palmer was a nine month private journey through the provinces of Tripolitania and Cyrenaica, which together form modern Libya and lie between Tunis and Egypt. The British government feared that France, which had earlier that summer invaded Tunisia, would advance into the region and Gill was asked to map the area, report on its inhabitants and discover any evidence of French reconnoitres. After a brief sojourn in Sicily, where he climbed Mount Etna, he sailed to Malta to meet his guide, Khalil Attick, to whom he became unusually close and with whom he was later to die. The son of an employee of the British Mission School at Beirut, Attick proved to be 'as sharp as a needle', arranging hotels and itineraries, and, on one occasion, saving his master a great deal of time and trouble by forging his signature. The two men went by steamer to Tripoli, where they waited for three months for the authorities in Constantinople to issue a travel permit; Gill making use of the delay by travelling to the coast and the hill country south west of the city, where he collected a mass of useful information.[28]

The permit never arrived, and, as in the Balkans, Gill set off on his expedition without permission. He arrived at Benghazi by steamer on April 6th, and, to avoid any suspicion that he was to enter the desert, sent his luggage in small consignments to a farmhouse two miles away, where he would pick it up when he rode out of the town on a supposedly day long excursion. All went well until the final consignment, which was spotted and followed by a suspicious Turkish policeman, who immediately arrested Gill, Attrek and the camel drivers transporting the equipment. Gill was mortified; 'Spilt milk, spilt milk, in huge cans full! It's no use crying over it, but it's uncommonly hard to help it'. Enormous bribes succeeded in saving himself and Attrek from imprisonment, but failed to release the camel drivers, who served long sentences for their crimes. After paying the bribes, he and Attrek were escorted to a steamer bound for Malta, from where Gill was summoned to Constantinople for a meeting with the British Ambassador for Turkey, who informed him in no uncertain terms of his view of his behaviour. After this well deserved 'wigging', he returned to his apartment in London and was planning a trip to Asia Minor or Syria when he received the fateful call from Lord Northbrook.[29]

Chapter 11

The Admiralty Search: Nakhl and Gattieh

Colonel Charles Warren's search expedition finally left Moses Wells on October 19th and comprised fifteen sheikhs, 370 Bedouin fighters and 200 pack camels, 75 of which carried grain to be delivered to the town of Nakhl, which had received no food supplies for six months and was close to starvation. As Sard Shedide had refused to be the ultimate commander of the Bedouins, claiming that he was too young to give orders to chiefs older than himself, Warren split the Arabs into three geographical groups, each led by a single sheikh. He himself was accompanied by Lieutenants Haynes and Burton, the new Governor of Nakhl, two Syrian interpreters, a Turkish cook of doubtful culinary ability and Sheikh Sualem Abu Farag, who had implicated the Shedides in Palmer's disappearance and had been given immunity from prosecution. To further ensure Farag's co-operation, Warren had taken his son hostage and had placed him in the custody of Sard Shedide's uncle; a distinctly odd decision, as it gave the Shedides a hold over Farag, making him less likely to make further accusations.

The expedition had public and concealed goals. Warren informed Sard Shedide that they would first travel to Nakhl, following the usual direct route. On arrival, the new Governor would be installed, the grain unloaded and the expedition split into two parts. The Hawetat and Terabin sheikhs and their followers, whose tribes were implicated in the attack, would investigate Palmers' disappearance amongst their own people, whilst Warren and the other sheikhs would travel to Gattieh, where it was rumoured that Sheikh Sofieh, the Englishmen's guide, was in hiding. In reality, Warren intended to follow Palmer's route to Nakhl – in order to collect evidence of the attacks and murder and to search for Palmer's, Gill's and Charrington's journals, which could contain clues as to the identity of the murderers, and, more importantly, politically embarrassing details of the true purpose of their missions. The false route prevented Sard arranging for the destruction of evidence or the collection of the journals and Warren suspected that he may have arranged for the party to be attacked on the Nakhl road. On arrival at Nakhl, the grain would only be handed over to the townsfolk if they provided information regarding Palmer's disappearance and murder, and, before the expedition split, Warren intended to arrest and question the old Governor and collect any evidence that implicated him in the murder.

Although numerically impressive, the success of the expedition was far from assured. The sheikhs of tribes not implicated in the Palmer attack had little interest in the mission, having only joined on the orders of Salami Shedide. Most of the sheikhs distrusted their fellow chiefs and were reluctant to use force against any of the culprits or capture them in case they died or were executed and a blood feud was generated – Bedouin custom dictating that the family of a murdered man had the duty and right to kill the murderer, or, if this was not possible, the murderer's close relatives. There was also the danger that the expedition would be set upon by Bedouin still loyal to Arabi or by the men involved in Palmer's murder or that the Governor of Nakhl would defend his town with force. For Warren, Haynes and Burton, an even greater threat was violence from the search party itself. Many of the Bedouin had a few weeks previously been fighting the British and had seen their comrades slaughtered at the battles of Kassassin and Tel-el-Kebir. Hostages were therefore taken for the safe return of the English members of the expedition and a messenger was to be sent to Suez each day with a signed note from Warren assuring the Governor that all was well. For additional safety, Warren, Haynes and Burton rode during the day with Sheikh Moussa and his Towarah fighters and at night camped separately from the rest of the search party, built a barricade of trunks and stores around their tents and slept with loaded rifles and revolvers. When dealing with the Bedouin on a day-to-day basis, Warren acted as though 'he had a guard of 5,000 British soldiers just around the corner', liberally abusing and swearing at even the most prominent sheikhs in the belief that such behaviour instilled fear and awe.[1]

The expedition hit difficulties before it even started. The rations, provided by the Governor of Suez, comprised mouldy biscuits infested with maggots. Approached by the sheikhs who threatened to mutiny if they were not replaced, Warren took one of the biscuits, munched it with self-evident gratification and declared it the finest morsel that had ever touched his lips. He also arranged for the delivery of fresh supplies. A few hours later, the expedition having got underway, Sard Shedide rode up to Warren to point out that they were heading in the wrong direction. On being told of the new route, he halted the caravan and refused to allow it to proceed unless the direct road to Nakhl was taken, claiming that they possessed insufficient water to travel via Wady Sudr and that the roughness of the terrain would injure their camels. Warren simply rode on – sending Burton back to the caravan to inform the sheikhs that if any of his party did not return the British government would ensure that every last one of them would hang. Sualem Abu Farag, the only man in the expedition who rode a horse, galloped after Warren, and, soon afterwards, the whole caravan was docilely following in his wake.

The expedition reached Palmer's first encampment in ten hours. Bivouacking there for the night, it then proceeded to his final camping ground, and, from there, headed for Wady Sudr. On arriving around a mile from the small oasis where the baggage was plundered, Warren ordered the Bedouins to dismount, form themselves into a human line and walk forward combing the desert for any traces of baggage. After a few hundred yards, a small piece of tin was discovered, followed by planks of wood, straw and a sponge. At the oasis, Warren went forward alone and searched for, found and made plaster casts of the tracks of the attackers, who appeared to have charged from the south, plus those of a camel coming from the opposite direction, which had passed within a few yards of the spring. The area on the other side of the oasis was then scoured and more debris found, including old newspapers, parts of maps, letters written to Charrington by his brother and a mutilated copy of Byron's *Don Juan* on the first page of which was the inscription 'John Charrington, 1823'.

Ordering the Bedouin to remount, Warren led the expedition towards the location of the ambush, noting that they covered the distance far more rapidly than the Palmer party, which must have moved at a relatively slow pace. At the entrance to Wady Sudr, the Bedouin again dismounted, formed an arc and walked up the valley in search of the whitened bones of a camel Warren had been informed had been killed in the attack. Unfortunately, after four hot and irksome hours no skeleton was found and Warren decided to bivouac for the night; his frustration at the situation finding expression the following morning when the late arrival of his porridge prompted him to kick the cook into the fire on which his breakfast was cooking.

Accepting that they were unlikely to find the place of the ambush, Warren decided to make for Nakhl, but soon after leaving camp spotted in the near distance three Bedouin riding camels. On noticing the expedition, the Arabs began to gallop away and Warren ordered his entire force to charge in pursuit. At the same time, two more Bedouin were spied making for undergrowth in a nearby oasis. Confident that the expedition would capture the fleeing fugitives, Warren and Haynes sped to the palm trees, where they arrested a crippled old man, a well dressed woman and four children and awaited the reappearance of the search party. Amazingly, the sheikhs returned empty handed, claiming that the Bedouin had fired at them and had escaped. Not believing a word of their excuses, Warren was incandescent with rage, even more so when informed by Sualem Abu Farag that one of the escaped Bedouin was Sheikh ibu Murshed, who in the letter discovered at Akabah had been identified by the Governor of Nakhl as Palmer's murderer. His only consolation was that the captured woman was identified as Murshed's wife and the elderly man one of his workers. Moreover, the old man was found to be carrying a tobacco pouch marked 'H. Charrington'.

Gathering his search party together, Warren moved them plus a flock of sheep and goats that the old man had been guarding to a further oasis a few miles distance, which was more easily defended if Murshed returned with his tribe and attempted to rescue his wife, which Bedouin lore dictated was his duty. Here, he bivouacked and interrogated his prisoners. Whereas Murshed's wife refused to speak, the old man was eventually persuaded to talk by Sheikh Moussa to whose tribe he belonged. He recounted that on the evening of the murder a rider had appeared at Murshed's camp bringing information that Palmer was travelling towards Wady Sudr. After speaking with the Bedouin, the Sheikh and some of his fighters had ridden off. On their return, Murshed had given him the tobacco pouch and he had heard from others that the three Englishmen and their two servants had been killed and their bodies dumped in a ravine, the location of which he described in detail. He believed that four of the bodies had been eaten by vultures, but that one was still intact, having fallen into a pool of water. Life had then returned to normal until a few days previously when the tribe had been informed that the British had discovered that the Palmer party had been murdered and were about to mount an expedition to round up the culprits. On hearing the news, all the attackers had fled except Murshed, who had been assured that the hunt for the murderers would not commence until after the expedition had travelled to Nakhl. As for the current location of his employer, the old man guessed that he had returned to his camp ten miles distant.

On hearing the old man's tale, Warren determined the next morning to go to the ravine to recover the bodies, fearing that otherwise vultures, rainfall or Murshed would remove all remaining traces of them. In order to increase his chances of success, he decided to divide the expedition into three. That night and before informing the sheikhs of his plan, he sent seventy Hawetat fighters, plus Sualem Abu Farag, his 'eyes and ears', and one of the children captured the previous day to act as a guide, to Murshed's camp with instructions to take everyone they found there prisoner, women and children included. The attack on the encampment would hopefully prevent Murshed attempting to remove the bodies or prevent Warren reaching the ravine and many of those captured were certain to be relatives of the murderers/attackers and could be held as hostages. The following morning the expedition was again split. The majority of the Bedouins were told that they would remain in camp under the command of the Governor of Nakhl, who to prevent any of his charges sneaking out to inform Murshed of the attempt to recover the bodies or the attack on his tents was instructed to post pickets and to shoot anyone attempting to leave. The remainder, approximately sixty fighters, were directed to accompany Warren to the murder site; an order that was vehemently opposed by their sheikhs, who deemed the mission suicidal. After much argument, they relented, though their men remained apprehensive, and, shortly after Warren had left the camp, half suddenly turned around their camels and rode back. Informed by Haynes, who was sent after them, that if they did not reconsider their decision they would be tried for desertion, all reluctantly returned.

As a concession, Warren directed Sard Shedide and four of his men to act as scouts, riding some distance in front of the main party, though within sight of them, to warn of any approaching attack. On re-entering Wady Sudr and rounding a corner, all five disappeared. After a wasted hour searching for them, during which he came upon and arrested an elderly woman, who he suspected was a spy, Warren gave up and proceeded to the mountainous area at the end of the Wady. Here, his party dismounted and climbed to the ravine, which proved to be a gully approximately fifty feet deep and twenty feet wide that stretched for several miles; above and alongside of each side of which ran two ledges that variously narrowed and broadened.

The presumed murder site was reached at midday. Rather than immediately descend into the gully, Warren decided to break for lunch, fearful that the sights that his men were about to encounter would put them off food for a considerable period. It was after he had finished his first boiled egg that voices were heard at the bottom of the ravine some distance away. Warren went to investigate and found Sard Shedide and the other four scouts who had disappeared on the journey to the place of the murder apparently searching for bones. After making his presence known, Warren sent for the rest of his party and using ropes descended to the floor of the ravine, where he confronted Shedide. Not at all nonplussed, Sard claimed that he and his fellow scouts had become lost and having accidentally stumbled on a gully that matched the description given by Murshed's employee they had descended – eager to obtain the evidence needed to bring Palmer's wicked murderers to justice. Speechless at the audacity of the man, who had obviously intended to remove the remains before the search party arrived, Warren stalked off and ordered his men to commence their own search.

After an hour of combing through the reeds and rock pools, a bone was found, followed by a skull, a jawbone, numerous ribs, a pair of socks monogrammed 'W.G' with the feet still in them, a small hernia truss and a pair of long johns encrusted with blood and human excrement. All were carefully placed in a blanket, apart from the trousers, which Warren burnt not wishing others to discover that an Englishman had not faced death with calm equanimity. Continuing the search until early evening, the party then ascended and began to examine the ledge, finding traces of dried blood, which suggested that at least one of those murdered had been killed or wounded before entering the gully. On the other side of the ravine more blood stains were seen, which Warren presumed belonged to the cook, who he conjectured had been killed on the opposite ledge some time after the murder of the rest of the party and had been brought to the place of execution by a different route. After ordering Haynes to sketch the site and storing the human remains in a tin-lined cartridge box, Warren, with a heavy heart, finally ordered his party back to camp.

The following day began badly. Shedide refused to start for Nakhl until the return of the Hawetats sent to attack Murshed's camp, arguing that these fierce fighters would be crucial to victory if the Governor of Nakhl resisted their entry into his town. Suspecting that Sard was attempting to delay the party in order to give Murshed time to organise an attack or an ambush, Warren insisted that they leave immediately, but to no avail. Coffee was thus called for, and, five long hours later, the expedition set off on the understanding that no attempt would be made to enter Nakhl until the Hawetats returned. They reappeared some time later. Not one prisoner had been captured. Indeed, they had not even reached Murshed's encampment. Ambushed by Murshed soon after leaving Warren, they claimed they had been forced to retreat under a hail of bullets. Later, questioning Sualem Abu Farag, Warren discovered that the ambushers had been hostile Bedouin unconnected to Murshed, the Hawetats had not returned fire, the only injury suffered was a slight arm wound, and, after the non-battle, no attempt had been made to complete the journey to Murshed's tents.

Nakhl was the chief stopping point on the Hajj pilgrimage

route from Cairo to Mecca. Consisting of a 'wretched' square stone built fort surrounded by mud huts and water tanks, it stood on slightly raised ground in the midst of a flint strewn desert plain.[2] Approximately a mile from the town, Warren's party was approached by a contingent of armed Egyptian soldiers, who warned him that if any attempt was made to enter he and his men would be shelled. Warren replied that he had merely come to replace the Governor now that the war was over and to deliver provisions, and, eventually, the soldiers allowed one of the sheikhs to take a message to this effect to the fort. Soon afterwards, four army officers arrived and requested that the new Governor accompany them. Aware that he would not come out of Nakhl alive, Warren asked the officers to take back a polite note from the new Governor requesting a meeting with his predecessor and his officials and his own less polite threat that if they did not appear he would pile the grain he had carried from Suez into a heap and set it ablaze. The officials eventually duly appeared, and, having read the new Governor's letter of appointment, rapturously embraced him and triumphantly led their new-found friends into Nakhl.

Once in the fort, Warren interviewed all the officials, discovering from the Chief Clerk that the old Governor had been away from Nakhl at the time of Palmer's murder and had returned on a camel belonging to Sheikh Sofieh, the party's guide. He then questioned the Governor himself. Variously described as 'shabby', 'a battered hulk' and 'seedy looking', Ali Effendi was a former Egyptian soldier who it was discovered eked out his scanty salary by charging travellers exorbitant fees for the drawing up of safe conduct contracts with local sheikhs.[3] Warren began by informing him that he was aware that he had told one of Sheikh Moussa's men that he had killed the Palmer party 'with his own hand' and had written a letter to his Akabah counterpart, which suggested that he was a supporter of Arabi and that the Shedides were also involved in the murder. Effendi categorically denied both making the confession and writing the note, and, when Warren produced the letter, claimed that he had forgotten its existence, and, in any case, could not possibly comment on the contents as it was a private correspondence.

Warren then turned to the Governor's movements during the week of the murder. Effendi declared that he had nothing to hide and admitted that he had left Nakhl on August 7th, the day before Palmer and his companions had started for the desert. He had obtained leave to be away from the fort from his superiors and had intended to travel to Suez, where he hoped to purchase provisions for Ramadan and deliver some of his town's letters. Aware of the worsening political situation, he had first ridden to the encampment of Sheikh Sofieh, Palmer's guide. He had hoped that the Sheikh would escort him to Suez and wanted to discover whether he had any information on the progress of the war and the Syrian officer who had supposedly ridden from Sheikh Misleh's tents to Suez a few weeks previously. On arrival, Sofieh's sons had told him that their father had gone to Moses Wells, but would soon return. He thus remained at the camp for two days, but, when Sofieh failed to appear, travelled to the tents of the Sheikh's blind brother, believing Sofieh may have called in to see his sibling on his trip home. Again, finding no sign of the elusive Sheikh, he decided to cross the desert alone and the next day rode to Marbrook, a town on the route to Suez. Here, he discovered the desert to be in turmoil and that Sofieh had gone to Moses Wells to escort three English gentlemen to Nakhl, calling first at his camp to change camels. The Governor thus abandoned his Suez trip and returned to Sofieh's tents intending to accompany the party to Nakhl.

He found Sofia in a state of almost nervous collapse. The Sheikh told him that his party had been ambushed and named the five leaders of the attack, but refused to hand over for safe keeping the money the Englishmen had been carrying or to go Nakhl to sign a statement recording what had occurred. The next morning, the Governor therefore returned home alone, riding on one of Sofieh's camels, as his own beast had become lame. He had made no attempt to rescue Palmer's party, as he was fearful that the miscreants who had captured them would harm or kill him and he had no powers of arrest, the incident having occurred outside his area of jurisdiction. Although he had dearly wanted to immediately report the incident to the British authorities, he was unable to do so owing to his inability to travel to Suez and Sofieh's refusal to provide a statement.

Wishing to check the Governor's story, Warren made no attempt to question him on its details. Nonetheless, he was already convinced that the Governor had left Nakhl in order to personally supervise or monitor the attack on Palmer and his companions. It was highly unusual for a governor to personally undertake minor tasks such as the purchase of provisions and the delivery of letters, and, in any case, Ramadan was over when he had left Nakhl. Moreover, he had travelled to Sofieh's brother's tents on the morning of August 10th, the day of the ambush, and the camp was just five miles from the location of the attack. The Governor, along with his wife and children, was thus arrested, and, after their apartments had been searched for any property belonging to Palmer, Gill or Charrington, they were sent back to Suez under an armed guard, where they were thrown in jail.

Having interviewed the Governor, Warren carried out the second part of his search agenda. The expedition was divided into two. The Hawetat and Terabin Bedouins, led by Sard Shedide, were sent to their tribal territories with orders to hunt down and arrest Palmer's attackers and murderers. Warren, Haynes, Burton, Sheikh Moussa and the remaining 100 Bedouins, meanwhile, prepared to ride to Gattieh, where they hoped to arrest Sheikh Sofieh. In the event, the party was lucky to survive the journey with their lives. To reach Gattieh, they had to cross 110 miles of waterless desert. By only the second day, water had become scarce, and, by the third day, camels had begun to collapse and were left behind, in some cases with their owners, who were loath to abandon them.

There were three reasons for the near disaster. First, as Warren should have been aware, the route was passable only in the spring when there were regular rainfalls and water holding desert grasses and bushes flourished. Second, the party comprised mostly Bedouin from regions around the Nile and town-dwelling sheikhs whose camels were unused to travelling long distances and who had little knowledge of the desert. They watered their camels, the day before leaving Nakhl, with the result that the animals would not drink on the day of departure, and carried insufficient water for their own use, much of which they drank during the first two days of the journey, and, when their own water ran out, surreptitiously emptied the barrels that carried the emergency supplies. Water also ran low because the journey took far longer than expected. Progress was slowed by the Bedouins' reluctance to make early starts, very soft sand, a guide who appeared to be unsure of their exact route, and an incident that occurred on the first day of the trip that had not only wasted a whole afternoon, but exhausted and increased the thirst of both men and beasts. Four Arabs riding two camels were spotted on the far horizon and Warren ordered his men to capture them. Most of his 100 fighters duly raced off in pursuit, whilst he took a plaster cast of the camel tracks and sent a man to retrace the riders' route. The pursuers returned several hours later, needless to say, empty handed, declaring that they had been fired at and outrun. They also alleged that one of the fugitives was none other than Sheikh Sofieh, the very man they were travelling to Gattieh to arrest; a claim disbelieved by Warren who suspected it was a ploy designed to persuade him to return to the safety of Nakhl and to disguise the true identity of the four Arabs – the Bedouin sent to retrace the riders' route having discovered that they had most probably come from Sard Shedide's expedition and were spies.

By the fourth day, the situation had become desperate. As vultures flitted among the sand dunes waiting for prey, more camels collapsed and the Bedouins, their mouths cracked and voices hoarse, took up a continuous cry of 'mowyah, mowyah' ('water, water'). Some rode up to the Englishmen and, 'pointing to their mouths in the most piteous way', unsuccessfully begged a drink from their private supplies. More disturbingly for Warren, Haynes had begun to act 'queerly'. The previous morning he had attempted to thrash a Bedouin he claimed had insulted him, and later had become convinced that the Arabs were planning to take him prisoner and had asked his companions for poison. Relief came at dawn the following day, when the guide returned from a foray to report that he had found water a short distance away. The column raced to the well, where men and beasts drank their fill, several camels expiring from over-drinking. After arranging for men to be dispatched with water to the Bedouin and camels left behind, the party moved to a second well, where the water was less rank. It was here that Hayne's condition worsened; he was now delirious and was 'spitting up a great deal of phlegm'. Fearful that he was close to death, Warren abandoned the trip to Gattieh and set out for Ismailia, eighty miles distant, strapping his faithful lieutenant on a stretcher constructed of spears and robes and carried by four Bedouins. Luckily, the party came upon a Hawetat tribesman, who agreed to guide them to the town, but had difficulty crossing the Suez Canal; officials only agreeing to flag down a passing ship on receiving a bribe of £10 and the full force of Warren's considerable wrath. On arrival at Ismailia, Haynes received medical attention and was personally nursed for the following five days by his commanding officer, who regarded the young man as a surrogate son.[4]

Chapter 12

Charles Warren: Pre-Search Life

Charles Warren had an extraordinary life. He was variously an engineer, a fighting soldier, an administrator, an archaeologist, an aspirant politician and a policeman. Twice he was hailed a national hero, yet his career ended in disgrace with his reputation in tatters. In his prime, he was admired by all. Later, he was regarded as an arrogant monster renowned for his vindictiveness, foul temper, tactlessness, lack of humour and bigoted religious views. A contemporary writer concluded that he was 'a difficult man to get along with' and was 'apt to conduct himself in a controversy which is not only resented by his opponents, but is not always pleasing to impartial observers'. Others were more blunt, describing him as 'cranky', 'crotchety' and possessed of a 'disagreeable temper [that] unfits him for holding any important position'.[1]

He was born in Bangor, North Wales in 1840, the third child of Colonel Charles Warren, who had served under the Duke of Wellington in the post-Waterloo march to Paris and seen active service in India and Africa. Four months after his birth, his father embarked for service in China, and, on his return, the family joined him in Colchester and then Winchester where he was quartered. Like Edward Palmer, Warren lost his mother at an early age. Suffering from tuberculosis, she and her children were sent to Paris, where it was hoped that the milder climate would ease her condition. It did not. She became seriously ill and on 10th January 1846 died, followed four months later by her daughter Charlotte, who no doubt had contracted her own tuberculosis from her mother. Rather than depositing his remaining three sons with relatives, the Colonel decided to bring them up himself with the help of governesses and the English school system. The children thus followed their father to Ireland, his next posting, where they lived in army accommodation in Limerick. Various parts of Ireland at that time were in a state of rebellion and Warren's main memory of the barracks was watching Irish prisoners marched from their cells to a central square where they were executed by firing squad.

On attaining school age, he was sent to join his elder brother, John, at a Grammar School at Bridgenorth, Shropshire, run by a Dr Thomas Rowley, who adopted the educational practices of Dr Arnold at the far superior Rugby School. The brothers occupied their own room, and, when John attained the age of eighteen and left, Charles was joined by his younger brother Billy. On Rowley's retirement, he and Billy were transferred to the Grammar School in the nearby town of Wem. Deciding that he would make a fine soldier, his father then moved him to Cheltenham College, which specialised in preparing boys for an army career, followed by the Royal Military College at Sandhurst, where he revealed an unusual ability for science and numbers, winning at the end of his first year the prize for mathematics. Believing he was more suited to the Corps of the Royal Engineers than one of the line regiments, his father thus enrolled him in the Royal Military Academy, Woolwich. His time there was unhappy. He was the victim of severe bullying, thrashed daily with belts and tennis bats, which only halted when the college authorities discovered the harassment and dismissed the perpetrators. He also experienced further family bereavement. His elder brother, John, had joined his father's regiment and father and son had been sent to the Crimea and fought in the Battle of Inkerman, where both were wounded. Colonel Charles Warren survived.[2] His son, whose leg had been accidently run though with a bayonet belonging to a fellow British officer, died of gangrene at Scutari hospital several days later.

Warren joined the Royal Engineers just before his eighteenth birthday, and, after the usual two years training at the School of

Military Engineering at Chatham, was sent to Gibraltar, where he spent the five happiest years of his life. His duties were less than onerous. In addition to managing his unit, he maintained and constructed barracks and fortifications, completed a trigonometrical survey of the island, and, for several months, made the eastern face of its cliffs inaccessible to possible invaders by blowing up any crags and filling in any crevices that could serve as footholds. It was whilst he was engaged on the latter task that he believed his life was saved by God. One night he dreamt that he was working on a ledge when his men hurled boulders down the cliff face unaware of his presence. Warren stepped back and was struck by a rock and killed. The following day, he found himself on that exact ledge, and, when a number of boulders hurtled towards him, leapt forwards rather than back, escaping death by inches. Away from his duties, he became a keen rock climber; invented a battery slide lever, which allowed guns to be moved by one rather than four men and eventually became a standard piece of equipment; joined the Freemasons, becoming in 1862 the Master of the local lodge; and spent most of his vacations travelling through Spain with his fellow officers. He also maintained an almost daily correspondence with his sweetheart, Fanny Haydon, a childhood friend, who in August 1864 he married. After a brief honeymoon in Scotland, he and his new wife returned to Gibraltar, where she learnt the ways of an army wife and joined her husband on his explorations of the Spanish countryside.

Warren returned to Chatham in 1865 as Assistant Instructor of Surveying at the School of Military Engineering. His commanders had been more than impressed by his 50 feet to one inch survey of Gibraltar and the two models of the Island that he had constructed on the same scale, one of which was proudly on display at the School. It was his surveying skills that also helped him win his next posting, which gave him his lifelong nickname of 'the Mole'. The Palestine Exploration Fund required an officer to map the districts to the north east and south west of Jerusalem and to undertake excavations on Temple Mount, the walled-in area in the south-eastern corner of the Old City, in order to answer important questions of biblical archaeology, including the true sites of the temples constructed by King Solomon and Zerubbabel, the Holy Sepulchre and the churches built by the Emperor Constantine. Three candidates were in contention for the post, which was eventually offered to Warren, partly because of his surveying expertise, but largely his climbing and diplomatic skills. Despite his recent marriage, he enthusiastically accepted; a committed Christian and staunch freemason, he savoured the opportunity to obtain both evidence of his faith and proof that masons had been involved in the construction of the temples, thus enabling the antiquity of freemasonry to be traced back to biblical times.[3]

He, his team of five and eight mule-loads of equipment arrived in Jerusalem in February 1867 only to find that the firmin or letter from the Moslem Turkish authorities that controlled Palestine giving them permission to excavate on Temple Mount, which is also a Moslem shrine, had not yet arrived. Attempts to persuade the Turkish Governor to allow digging to begin failed, and, when the firmin finally appeared, Warren was astounded to discover that it not only forbade excavations within forty feet of the Mount, but also in and around other Moslem and Christian holy places. Unable to comprehend the Turks objections to his proposed excavations, which a contemporary commentator compared to the Dean of Westminster opposing Moslem plans to dig up the Chancel of Westminster Abbey, he at first simply ignored the letter's contents.[4] Arriving at a site, he would inform its guardian that he had permission to excavate, waving the firmin around, but never letting the individual read it. When his deception was discovered, he would simply move to the next site and repeat the procedure. Eventually, he ran out of sites and was forced to adopt other strategies. Shafts of up to 125 feet were sunk forty feet from Temple Mount and tunnels of up to 600 feet dug horizontally from the bottom of the shafts to the walls he wished to examine. To excavate within prohibited buildings, he bribed officials or he and his team dressed as Moslems and rapidly completed their work whilst accomplices distracted the guards and prevented other worshippers entering.

Lack of permission to excavate was not the only problem faced. The work was dangerous. The local labourers employed were notoriously careless – stones that had been hauled to the top of shafts were often allowed to fall back down. Tunnellers were at constant risk from collapsing walls and roofs, suffocation and drowning; Warren almost died when a tunnel suddenly began to fill with water leaving him just four inches of breathing space. When they emerged from their excavations, they risked attack from Moslem worshippers, who would have 'torn [them] in pieces' had they discovered them desecrating their holy sites, and, having often crawled through freezing water and raw sewage, were prone to fever and disease.[5] Warren also lacked money. Although the Palestine Exploration Fund paid him his £300 preliminary expenses, it provided only half of the additional payments promised over the following ten months; the extra subscriptions that it had hoped the project would attract failing to materialise. For a number of months, Warren thus had to finance the £1,000 cost of the expedition himself, selling his investments to do so and bringing his family close to penury. Eventually, the Fund paid the sum owed, obtaining some of the funds from freemason lodges eager to discover the historical linage of their organisation, but continued to make payments in arrears, forcing the leader of its expedition to make up the difference.

Warren brought the project to an end in January 1870. A new firmin had arrived from Constantinople that forbade all excavation and he was 'knocked up with fever and fatigue', though the former had been alleviated by staring at a mark in the ceiling and hypnotising himself back to health.[6] He was also utterly disillusioned with the Palestine Exploration Fund, which had not only failed to fully finance the expedition, but in its lust for publicity and funds had damaged his reputation by claiming in a letter to the *Times* that he had been the true discoverer of the 'Moabite stone', a piece of stonework found at Dibhan, Moab, which contained inscriptions in an ancient unknown language. Alarmed that friends would believe he was attempting to steal others' glory, he had been forced to write his own letter to the newspaper putting forward the true facts; an act that led to yet another bust-up with the Fund. No doubt angered at Warren's rebuke, Captain Charles Wilson, a prominent member of the Fund's board, publicly disparaged the accuracy of the architectural plans drawn up in Jerusalem; comments that were published by James Ferguson, an amateur archaeologist who had made a fortune producing indigo in India and disputed Warren's findings. Fearing again for his reputation, Warren demanded that the Fund hold a special committee to determine the quality of his work, and, after its vindication, published a pamphlet savagely attacking Ferguson's accusation and raft of theories.[7]

He spent the rest of that year writing the official report of the expedition, which detailed his many achievements for which he was elected a Fellow of the Royal Geographical Society. He had created a detailed topological map of Jerusalem and the surrounding area; found a water shaft, which he humbly named after himself, and a series of tunnels that he identified as a major water system; and, most significantly, discovered evidence that the first settlement existed outside the mediaeval walls of the old city. Moreover, there was some proof that masons had indeed been involved in the construction of Solomon's Temple. Having delivered the report and begun writing a book about his many trials and tribulations, eventually finished and published in 1876, he returned to his military duties. For the following three years, still intermittently troubled by fever, he was the Engineer to the School of Gunnery at Shroeburyness, where he worked on improving the efficiency of heavy guns and invented and patented a smokeless kitchen range in his spare time. He then spent a year as Engineer in charge of the gunpowder and small arms factories at Waltham Abbey and Enfield. He found both roles interesting and relished the time they allowed him to spend with his wife and growing family, which now comprised two sons and two daughters. Nonetheless, they failed to fulfil his desire for action and achievement, and, he was seriously considering leaving the army to take up an engineering post in Australia, when in 1876 he was offered the post of Special Commissioner of the Griqualand West Survey.

The survey was necessitated by the discovery in 1870 of diamonds at the junction of the Vaal and Orange rivers in central South Africa, which led to a dispute over the ownership of the region. The Orange Free State, an independent Boer republic, declared that the area was part of its territory; whilst Chief Nicholas Waterboer, leader of the Griqua, pointed out that his tribe had been granted the land by the British in an 1834 treaty. As tension grew, the British Governor of the Cape was asked to mediate, and, after forming a committee to consider the evidence, ruled in favour of the Griqua people, who asked the British to take over the land, fearful of attack from their powerful neighbour. In 1873, therefore, the territory became the British colony of Griqualand West. To the Orange Free State, the British annexation was a cynical land grab and its government continued to pursue its claims until 1876 when it agreed after long negotiations to accept the annexation in return for a one-off payment of £90,000 and the creation of a mutually acceptable boundary.[8]

Warren's task was to survey the colony's outer reaches with the Free State's surveyor, Joseph E. de Villiers, to draw up a three miles-to-the inch scale map and to mark the boundary via the construction at intervals of one to three miles of 8 to 16 foot boulder cairns. The work was far from easy. Owing to the high demand for labour from the local mining industry, it was difficult to recruit sufficient staff and those employed had to be paid high wages and were the 'scum of Kimberley'; 'a sullen, scowling, discontented lot', who were often drunk, prone to fights and were 'incapable of doing a good day's work'. Prevented by law from whipping them into submission, Warren resorted to bribes, giving them coffee if they started work on time and cheap red wine when they performed their tasks satisfactorily. Other problems arose from the climate and the animal life of the region. Mirages made it difficult to take theodolite readings, high temperatures shortened the working day to a few hours in the early morning and evening and the torrential downpours of the rainy season washed away tents and caused wagons to become marooned in seas of mud. Cairns meanwhile were regularly dismantled by baboons and the party attacked by swarms of 'flies and winged monsters', and, on one memorable occasion, by an irate ostrich. The local human population was hardly less intimidating. The London and South African Exploration Company pressured him to divert the boundary line to ensure that their farms were in British territory and local Boers were reluctant to sell him food, preferring to 'let their milk spoil or their sheep die' than allow them to be eaten by a British officer. When this was not the case, they charged extortionate prices, a cabbage costing 18s 6d. Each morning at sunrise, Warren was thus obliged to troop off into the surrounding countryside to shoot snipe and teal for the camp's evening meal.[9]

The expedition was completed after five long months, and, as a sign of the government's appreciation, Warren was made a companion of St Michael and St George, an award presented to individuals who had rendered important non-military service in a foreign country. Intending to return home after a short tour of South Africa, he was instead ordered to Cape Town to meet the High Commissioner of Southern Africa, Sir Bartle Frere, who offered him the post of Griqualand West's Land Claims

Commissioner. The Orange River State's jibe that Britain's annexation of Griqualand West was a cynical land grab was nothing less than the truth. One of the first acts of the new British Governor had been to set up a special court to determine who owned each piece of land. Since the Griqua possessed no paper titles, could not afford legal representation and were unlikely to farm commercially, few of their claims were successful and the majority of the land was awarded to white settlers.[10] Many of the land court's decisions, however, were subsequently challenged by other white claimants and the Commissioner was to prevent these cases reaching the High Court of Appeal.

Initially, Warren was reluctant to take the post; he longed to return to his family and believed the chances of the Commissioner successfully persuading petitioners to give up their claims were low. Flattery and self-interest persuaded him to change his mind. The Governor insisted he was 'the only person competent' to take on the role, predicted that the agricultural economy of Griqualand West would collapse if he refused it and promised that 'the Home Government would mark their appreciation'. The work was a 'weary business'. Rather than determining legal ownership of a plot of land, he invited all the claimants to a meeting at which he mediated an agreement, which generally involved the eventual victor financially compensating the other plaintiffs for dropping their claims. He then met each of the four members of the colony's Executive Council to obtain their approval of the agreement and finally sought the consent of the Governor himself. Over five tortuous months, he dealt with 200 cases, only seven of which proceeded to the High Court. Although sympathetic to the Griqua cause, arguing that the provision of land would help to 'civilise' them, he acquiesced to the establishment view and ensured that few of their claims were successful.[11]

As a relief from the monotony of his Commissioner role, he also assisted the Executive Council and arbitrated in a dispute over the ownership of the Kimberley mine, for which he was paid £200. The arbitration meetings were fraught with tension, one owner regularly arriving with a pickaxe that he significantly laid on the table, but a compromise was eventually achieved. So impressed was the Mine's new Board of Directors at his abilities that it offered him the post of Mine Engineer at a salary of £2,000 pa, later raised to £3,000 pa, and the London and South African Exploration Co. asked him to report on the best methods of working their African mines. Other job offers followed – the leadership of an archaeological project to excavate the ancient Ceylon cities of Anaradharpona and Pollinarniva, the completion of a survey of Natal and the post of Land Claims Commissioner of Transvaal. He was tempted only by the latter two roles, which would advance his public career, finally plumping for the Commissioner job as he 'would much rather do work which deals with individuals than with things' and he had no wish to repeat the experiences of the Griqualand West survey.[12]

In the event, he never took up the appointment. As he was preparing to journey to Pretoria, he was ordered to fight in the Gcaleka-Fengu war that was then raging in the Southern Cape. To say the least, he was delighted. After 22 years in the army, he had yet to see action and be 'blooded'. The conflict had begun with inter-tribal strife between the Gcaleka and Fengu tribes, whose ancient rivalry had deepened as the prosperity of the two peoples had diverged. As the Fengu became involved in urban trade and flourished, the Gcaleka descended into poverty; their harvests destroyed by drought and their cattle killed by disease. A bar fight between a Fengu and a Gcaleka at a wedding party rapidly escalated into inter-tribal violence and thence into war. Although the conflict had nothing to do with them, the British government decided to become involved on the side of the Fengu. The reason was again land. The Gcaleka occupied their own independent state and it was believed that their defeat would allow the territory to be annexed. The first stage of the war was over in three weeks. Cape paramilitaries swiftly defeated an army of 8,000 Gcaleka gunmen and occupied Gcalekaland. The surviving Gcaleka, however, regrouped and counterattacked, marching into the Cape where they joined forces with their close kin, the Ngqika, at King William's Town.[13]

Warren's orders were to proceed to Kimberley, take command of the Diamond Fields Horse, a volunteer cavalry unit, and then travel with the volunteers the 600 miles to King William's Town to take on the combined Gcaleka and Ngqika armies.[14] The task was far from easy. His men were untrained, few having previously handled rifles, and many did not own a horse. Lacking time, Warren decided to march them to their destination, purchasing mounts and drilling them on the way. Twenty-five days after setting off from Kimberley, they arrived in the environs of King William's Town, where they joined with the Frontier Light Horse under the command of Redvers Buller, who twenty years later was to destroy Warren's career and reputation. Their first meeting was a foretaste of things to come. Asked by Warren why he was carrying a large stick, Buller replied that it was for beating his men. To which Warren remarked 'take care you don't strike my men by accident or you may get shot', a comment to which Buller took strong exception.[15]

Warren's involvement in the Gcaleka-Fengu war embraced a catastrophe and a great victory. The fiasco occurred at Petrie Bush. Owing to communications problems, he had not been informed that a sweep of dense jungle involving 4,000 men had been abandoned. The Diamond Horse thus advanced on foot through the bush alone. On eventually realising they had no support, Warren decided they should retrace their steps, but by this time the Gcaleka had been alerted to their presence. As they retreated, his Captain and Lieutenant were shot dead and he himself was felled by a partly cut tree that the enemy toppled onto him on hearing his approach. Although he was seriously injured with several broken ribs, he retained command and eventually returned his men to safety. His great victory was at Debe Nek. Discovering that a large number of Gcaleka were marching through the countryside to join their compatriots, he and his unit of 75 took up position ahead of the advancing army in a roadside ditch. As 1,600 warriors approached to within 600 yards, his men opened fire. The first wave of fighters fell and the rest retreated, but rapidly regrouped and launched assault after assault on the ditch and attempted, but failed to surround it. Ordered to aim for the Chiefs, the battle finally ended when one of Warren's men shot the overall commander through the head at which point his warriors fled, pursued by the Diamond Horse who hacked 'the cowards' down with their bayonets. Several hundred Gcaleka warriors were killed and an equivalent number wounded; British losses were one trooper and two horses.

After Debe Nek, the Diamond Horse took part in several further engagements, distinguishing themselves at the battle of Makabili Kili Heights, where they captured 450 of the enemy's women and children and large herds of cattle. By May, the conflict was over and Warren returned to King William's Town, where he received the personal thanks of General Frederic Thesiger, the Commander of British troops in Africa. This, however, was not the end of his war. Although the Gcaleka were defeated, their rebellion had encouraged other tribes to rise up against the British, including the Griqua and the Balaros and Batlapin. Having effectively had their land stolen by the British, the Griqua rebelled against their colonial masters in 1878.[16] Familiar with the colony and with a growing reputation as a soldier, Warren was appointed Chief of Staff of the Griqualand West Field Force, under Colonel William Lanyon, and given the task of putting down the uprising.[17] The first Griqua fighters were encountered in the Northern Cape and were dispatched with ease. Major battles then took place at Paardefloof and Witsand Heights, fortified mountain strongholds that Warren stormed with a total loss of just three killed and one wounded.

Having staunched the Griqua rebellion, he next turned to the Balaros and Batlapin of Bechuanaland, who had seen precious firewood carted away by white settlers to whom they had lost their land. Hearing rumours that both the Gcaleka and the Griqua had overcome the British, the two tribes began to indiscriminately kill settlers and threaten the lives of traders and missionaries. Warren, now in command of the Field Force, was ordered to the Kuruman mission station, which had been besieged by the Balaros for five days. Joining with two other units, his men relieved the town and the combined force then attacked the enemy at Gomaperi, slaughtering many warriors and capturing their wagons and cattle. The survivors fled to the Batalapin fortress on the side of Takoon Mountain, closely pursued by Warren, who on arrival requested their surrender, promising that only those who had killed settlers would be punished. On their refusal, he brought up heavy guns and shelled the fortifications for several hours. Confident that any resistance would be minimal, he and his men then charged to the foot of the fortress, where they dismounted and fought their way inside. At the end of the action, 200 Batalapin and Balaros lay dead; the British having lost just five men.

Warren's final battle occurred in the Lange Berg range of mountains. The Gcaleka, Griqua, Balaros and Batlapin fighters who had survived the British onslaught made common cause and established a camp in the valley of the Gamgagiana river. Warren's plan of attack involved a pincer movement – units were to attack the rebels from the top and the bottom of the valley, while Warren and two companies of light infantry and two units of Zulus climbed over the top of Mokolukue's Mountain and stormed them from the side. The plan was only partially successful. Although many warriors were killed, many escaped fleeing to the neighbouring Gobatsie Mountain, where they holed up in a fortification that could easily repulse a direct attack. Warren thus had a seven pound field gun dragged to the top of the mountain from where it shelled the rebel fortress below. Having 'softened up' the rebels, he then led a frontal attack that wiped out large numbers of the enemy.

Warren emerged from the rebel wars a hero. On his return to Kimberley, he was chaired around the market square amidst the cheers of thousands of spectators. A town in the Northern Cape was renamed Warrenton in his honour and he was successively promoted to Major and then Brevet Lieutenant-Colonel.[18] As a further sign of the British government's appreciation, he was appointed acting Administrator of Griqualand West, and over the following few months disarmed the African inhabitants, strengthened the protection of the colony's borders and rounded up a number of rebel leaders. He stayed in the post for a mere eight months. Missing his family and still suffering from the injury that he had sustained at Petrie Bush, he returned home in October 1879. After several months recuperating and writing reports for the Colonial Office on his African adventures, he was appointed Chief Instructor of Surveying at the School of Military Engineering at Chatham, a role he performed until he embarked on his great search for the Palmer party.

Chapter 13

The Admiralty Search: Suez, Nakhl and Mount Sinai

Warren returned to Suez to discover that the abandoned journey to Gattieh had been unnecessary. Whilst he and his men had been facing death in the desert, Sheikh Sofieh had ridden into Suez and surrendered himself to the authorities. To say the least, Warren was keen to interview him. Over the previous two months, he had made assiduous enquires about the murdered party's guide and had discovered a number of disturbing facts. Sofieh had told Palmer that he was Sheikh of the Lehewat, a tribe controlling the desert between Suez and Nakhl. In reality, he was not a sheikh, but a wealthy hirer of camels to pilgrims and travellers, and had not been a member of the Lehewat tribe for several years, having been expelled for some unknown offence. The Lehewat, moreover, lived many miles from Suez to the south of Palestine and had no power over the desert to the east of the town. By agreeing to guide Palmer through territory over which he had no control, Sofieh had thus placed the party in grave danger.

Sofieh's interrogation was a fraught affair. The old man appeared confused, constantly contradicted himself and 'habitually worked himself up into such an excited state that it was difficult to clear his facts from the mass of verbiage in which they were wound'.[1] Warren began by inquiring why he had hidden his true identity from his employer. After initially insisting that he was the Lehewat's Chief, Sofieh eventually admitted that this was not the case, but could give no reason for his subterfuge. He was then asked to describe his journeys with the Professor from the time they first met to when the party bound for Nakhl decided to ride ahead of the baggage train. Little new information was forthcoming, though much was omitted – Salim ibu Subdeh's warning not to enter the desert, Sofieh's return to Moses Wells to recruit another camel driver after the party had left the town and the hunt for the camel thieves. There were also downright lies – he claimed that he had taken the letter Palmer had written after meeting Sheikh Misleh asking for instructions into Suez, spending a day in the town; that during the journey to Moses Wells, he and his employer had travelled during the day; that the meeting at Nakhl was with Sheikh Suileman rather than with his brother, Sheikh Misleh; and that he had carried the naval sword presented to him by Admiral Hewitt into the desert.

His narrative of subsequent events was more detailed and left no doubt as to who had acted in the most heroic fashion. On entering Wady Sudr, at approximately 11pm, the party was fired upon by approximately 25-30 Bedouin hidden among rocks at either side of the trail. His nephew's camel was hit in the jaw and collapsed in a heap, and, as bullets ripped the air around them, the rest of the party kneeled their own camels, behind which they crouched. Palmer threw Sofieh a pistol and ordered the nephew to escape on his own camel, on which was secured a case, the moment he and the guide began to return fire. Both let off a barrage of bullets and the nephew made his getaway. There was then another intense exchange of shots, during which Sofieh's camel rose and galloped off down the Wady. Exposed and aware that the battle was lost and help urgently needed, Sofieh bounded after the animal, which he eventually captured, remounted and rode to his camp.

Here, he collected his two sons and four or five other Bedouin and returned to the place of the attack, where he found his five former companions, stripped to their underwear, sitting in a line and guarded by four of the assailants. Unfortunately, as he and his fellow rescuers rode up, the rest of the attack party arrived from plundering the baggage, preventing them from setting the Englishmen and their attendants free. After both sides dismounted, Sofieh draped his own cloak around Palmer, thus signifying to the attackers that he regarded him as one of his own family, and proffered £150 of his own money for their release. When this overture was rejected, he additionally offered fifty camels and promised on Allah that there would be no retribution for the dastardly deed that had occurred. The attackers' response was that they had been instructed by Arabi to capture and hand over to the nationalists in Cairo all Christians and intended to follow these orders. Asked by Warren whether Palmer had spoken during these exchanges Sofieh stated that the Professor had told him to offer the £150 and camels, but later that he had merely croaked the words 'Metter! Metter!' and later still that he had said nothing. Beating Sofieh till he spat blood, the assailants had then threatened to kill him if he and his rescue party did not leave.[2]

Utterly heartbroken at abandoning his British friends, Sofieh had returned to his camp, where the next day he was visited by the Governor of Nakhl to whom he related the story of the ambush and gave the names of 22 of the Bedouin who had attacked the party, the four men who had guarded the prisoners and four of the chiefs with whom he had negotiated; information that he passed onto Warren. On asked to return to Nakhl to provide a statement, he had refused as he suspected that the Governor had some involvement in the outrage and wished him harm. During his first stay at his camp, the Governor had informed his sons that he intended to report their father to Arabi for fraternisation with the enemy and he had then gone to a local Sheikh's camp (and not to Sofia's blind brother's tents as the Governor claimed), where it was possible he had met the attackers or their representatives. Questioned about the Shedides' involvement in the attack, Sofia claimed that he had heard that an Arab, named Ali Soweyer, had brought a message to Sheikh ibu Murshed prior to the attack informing him of the party's location, but stated that he did not know from whom the message originated, and, later, that the Egyptian government would not allow him to divulge this information. Pressed on whether the source of the message was the Shedides, he would only say that they 'know about it'.[3] After the departure of the Governor, he had been visited by Sheikh Suileman, whose brother Palmer was to meet at Nakhl, and gave him an account of what had occurred. Two days later, he had left his camp, and, with his nephew, had ridden to Wady el Hadj, where the latter had concealed the case strapped to the camel on which he had escaped to make sure that it was safely hidden. From there, he had travelled to various towns on business, including Gattieh, immediately returning to Suez on discovering that the British wished to interview him.

On the morning after the interview, Warren travelled with Sofieh and a number of Bedouin to Wady el Hadj to recover the £3,000 in gold sovereigns Palmer had carried into the desert. Fearful that the cash would be stolen on the return journey, he told the sheikhs present in Suez that he was returning to Nakhl. On arriving at the head of the Wady, Sofieh dismounted by a terrfa tree and then solemnly paced a certain number of steps up the rock strewn slope of the valley side, halted and began to clear away some loose stones to expose a crevice, which contained a small leather case. The case was handed to Warren, who discovered that it held a black leather bag and a small locked despatch box. Sofieh took the bag and 'and went through a pantomime in trying to open it, playing with [it] as though he were a monkey'.[4] Recovering the bag, Warren pressed its spring catch and found that it contained various small articles, such as scissors and brushes, and one cotton sack in which was found £999 in English gold sovereigns. Expecting the remainder of the money to be in the despatch box, this was forced open, but proved to contain only notepaper, some letters written by Palmer, £235 in English sovereigns, notes and Turkish lire and Mr Hammond's IOU for £100.[5]

Realising that the £2,000 was missing, Warren rounded upon Sofieh, accusing him and his nephew of stealing the money. Agitated and in tears, the old man denied the allegation, claiming that he had been unaware that Palmer had been carrying such a large sum and that neither he nor his relative had opened the black bag. Warren was unconvinced. It was unlikely that Palmer had divided the money between two camels, and, even if this was the case and it had been stolen by the attackers, the theft and the expenditure of such a large sum would have soon become public knowledge. The only possible explanation was that Sofieh had taken the money and had been in cahoots with those who had organised the attack; on the day of the murder deliberately splitting the party to weaken its ability to defend itself and slowing the progress of the three Europeans and their attendants in order to allow the preparation of a night ambush. As planned, during the attack his nephew had escaped with the camel carrying the gold, which no doubt was shared with the Governor of Nakhl, Sheikh ibu Murshed and possibly the Shedides.[6]

By the time the party had arrived back in Suez, Sofieh appears to have descended into madness; constantly repeating the names of the men involved in the attack. Warren placed him on HMS Carysfort, where he would be safe from the Shedides, and sent Bedouin into the desert to arrest the Sheikh of the Lehewat and to find Sard Shedide and request his return. He also began to question the witnesses that Shedide and the other sheikhs were beginning to send into Suez, all of whom were immediately imprisoned to prevent them absconding. Initially, most claimed to possess no information or gave details that they believed were already known. Gradually, however, through continual cross-examination, they became more loquacious, though some of the information appeared to have been obtained from fellow prisoners or fabricated in an attempt to escape Suez gaol. After two long weeks of interrogation and using the information obtained from Sofieh and others, a voluminous list of all the

Bedouin who had attacked the party, baggage train and Moses Wells had been compiled and this was dispatched to the Governor of Gaza and sheikhs in outlying areas with a note asking them to arrest any of the fugitives found to be living in their territories.

The Lehewat Sheikh arrived several days after being summoned. Claiming that he lacked the necessary power to order Sofieh's nephew and sons to give themselves up, he was thrown in jail and only released when he agreed to do what was asked of him. Soon after he had departed, Sofieh's sons were brought in by Lehewat tribesmen. 'Neither nice looking fellows', they professed to know nothing of their father's activities. They were followed by Sofieh's nephew, who insisted that he would have come earlier had he not had to search for some stray camels. His account of the attack added two incidents to that of his uncle's narrative. Around 1,000 yards before the ambush, the party had ridden past two sleeping Bedouin, who the young man had been dissuaded from shooting by Palmer, and these men were still asleep, despite the noise of the gunfire, when he passed them on his escape from the ambush. He also claimed that after the attack had begun, he had cried out to the assailants, begging them to stop shooting. As regards his movements after his escape, he had retraced the route of the party and proceeded to Wady el Hadj, where he had hidden the case that had been strapped to Palmer's camel. Asked whether he had passed the cameleers and the baggage, and, if so, why he had not alerted them to the attack, he agreed that he must have ridden by, but was too far away to notice them, a claim disproved by the casts of his camel tracks and a cameleer's recollection of having heard him ride past. After concealing the case, he had then returned to his uncle's camp and both of them had gone back to the hiding place to ensure that all was well. He confirmed that neither he nor Sofieh had opened the case, though he later let slip that the money was with the brushes, which suggested that he had not only opened the case, but also the leather bag it contained.[7]

Two days after the nephew's interrogation, Sard Shedide arrived in Suez, bringing with him one of the suspected murderers, Salim Sheyk, who declared that he was innocent of all crimes. Warren's interview with Sard descended into a tirade of accusations. In addition to his criticism of the Sheikh's actions during the search for the bodies of the murdered Englishmen, Warren had fresh allegations. Sard's tribesmen had allowed two hostages to escape whilst supposedly guarding them, one of whom was the son of Sualem Abu Farag, who had implicated the Shedides in the murders and had been promised immunity from prosecution. The following day, Farag himself had disappeared; Warren suspecting that Shedide had made a deal with the fugitive, who had agreed to abscond and thus not testify against the family in return for his son's freedom. Moreover, Sard had apprehended just one of the named murderers and there was evidence that he had advised Salim Sheyk not to speak during his interrogation and told other witnesses what they could and could not reveal.

Sard denied everything. He was not to blame for the escape of the hostages, who had cunningly outwitted their guards, and he had failed to apprehend the accused because of a series of unfortunate incidents. After leaving Nakhl, his guide's camel had fallen ill, forcing his party to return to the town, and, when they had next ventured out, they had become hopelessly lost, ran out of food and water and feared they were about to die until rescued by Salim Sheyk, who by an amazing coincidence happened to ride by. So traumatic were these experiences that he refused to re-enter the desert, proposing that a circular letter requesting help be sent to all the minor sheikhs of the district and that he be allowed to go to Cairo to arrest and hold as hostages relatives of the main culprits. Warren, needless to say, refused both requests and instead placed Sard under arrest and threw him in jail. When the next day, his uncle suggested that other hostages could escape if Sard was not released, he too was imprisoned.

Warren's next decision is difficult to understand. Having rid himself of one member of the Shedide family, he requested the assistance of another, Sard's elder brother Salami, even though he strongly suspected that it was Salami who had ordered the attack on Palmer's party and the Sheikh two months previously in Cairo had tried to fob him off with a bogus brother. One explanation may be that the appointment was demanded by the Egyptian government. A more likely reason is that Warren believed that Salami, as head of the Hawetat tribe and one of the most powerful men in the country, would have greater success than his younger brother in forcing the Bedouin of the desert to give up the culprits. Initially, Salami proved uncooperative. He professed complete ignorance of the details of Palmer's murder and only acknowledged that he was the chief of his tribe when a number of Hawetat prisoners were paraded before him, all of whom genuflected and declared him their great and only ruler.

Threatened that he and his entire family would be charged for their part in the murder, Salami became more accommodating. After a great deal of prevarication, he agreed to interview Salim Sheyk, the suspected murderer captured by his brother, who had denied any involvement in the affair.[8] Sheyk was duly brought in, and, when ordered by his chief to give a full and honest account of what had occurred, not only described the attack and murder, but named the five assassins and admitted that he had helped to arrange the murders. Salami was then ordered to sign a contract in which he agreed to bring in all the identified attackers and murderers plus other witnesses who had not yet been questioned, including all those present at Moses Wells at the time of the arrival of the Palmer party and the Bedouin who accompanied Meter ibu Sofieh on his ransom mission – a total of sixty people. These were to be handed over to the authorities at Nakhl within 21 days; 26 during the first ten days of his mission, a further 26 in the following ten days and the remainder by

December 26th. Salami again baulked, claiming that he would be killed if he undertook such a venture, which would in any case take at least two months to complete. Assured that if he did not sign, he would be immediately arrested, he acquiesced, but demanded that during the 21 days no other search party and especially no Europeans should enter the desert; a condition to which Warren agreed.

A few days after leaving Suez, Salami returned bringing with him a number of witnesses and was again dispatched into the desert. Two days earlier, a resident of Moses Wells, acting on behalf of Sheikh ibu Murshed, the alleged organiser of the ambush who had narrowly escaped capture during Warren's trip to the murder site, had offered the British a deal – Murshed claimed that he had captured Ali Schwair, one of the named murderers, and would hand him over if his wife and children who had been taken hostage and were presently languishing in jail were released. During interrogation, the intermediary revealed that Murshed was staying at a camp near Nakhl and Warren ordered Salami to travel there and arrest the two men. Salami appeared reluctant. Claiming that he had urgent business in Cairo, he finally entered the desert a week later and then simply vanished. After thirteen days, Warren sent out a spy, who on his return reported that Salami had failed to capture either Murshed or Schwair, but was presently scouring the desert for the other miscreants.

Convinced that Salami would have as much success as his brother, Warren asked the four principal Sheikhs of the Terabin tribe to take over. Initially refusing to become involved, they finally agreed after spending seven 'hellish' days in gaol. He also decided to break his agreement with Salami not to enter the desert during the Sheikh's hunt for the culprits and to make a new trip to the murder site. Here, he would go over the ground again for clues, the fear of attack from Murshed causing the original investigation to be rushed; investigate the geological features of the region and identify sites described in Exodus for a paper he hoped to write for the Palestine Exploration Fund; and take Spencer Calmeyer Charrington, the landowning elder brother of Lieutenant Charrington, and his sister, Katherine Charrington, to the place of their sibling's death. A funeral service for the dead men would then be conducted and a memorial cairn built.[9]

The Charringtons had arrived in Egypt several weeks earlier with Gill's brother, the lawyer Robert Thomas Gill, and his friend Edward Houndle, a Chief Clerk in the Office of the Adjutant General. Both families were unhappy at the Admiralty's failure to inform them of the progress of the search for their relatives, expressing their concern in a letter to the *Times* written by Gill's friend Colonel Henry Yule. When the Admiralty still failed to provide updates, they decided that their relative's siblings should go to Egypt to discover the reasons for the presumed lack of progress and to 'help' the inquiry. Relations between the Charringtons and the search party almost immediately descended into acrimony. Lieutenant Burton believed Spencer Charrington to be a 'babbling fool' and that he and his sister cared 'not two straws about their brother's death' and were indulging in a 'pleasure trip'. The true cause for his and Warren's dislike of the pair, however, was Spencer Charrington's determination to become involved in the investigation. On arrival, he demanded that he, Gill and Houndle be allowed to be present during the questioning of witnesses and suspects. Warren refused the request, arguing that their presence would force him to avoid questions that could result in answers that would 'hurt their feelings'. Charrington insisted, stating his 'nerves were steeled to anything', and, after an almighty row in which personal insults were exchanged, Warren relented; a decision he was later to bitterly regret. The three men would be allowed to hear the evidence, but were to remain silent, take no notes and to leave when requested to do so.[10]

Two days later, Charrington asked to read the written records of previous interrogations. Warren agreed, but when told that he was taking notes of the Governor of Nakhl's evidence stormed into the room and ordered him to stop writing on the grounds that nothing had been proved against the Governor and that he suspected that the evidence was to be leaked to the press. Yet another argument ensued, Warren only allowing Charrington to leave the room after he had surrendered his notes. A further quarrel then erupted over whether the Charringtons should be allowed to visit the place of their brother's death and observe the collection of evidence. Warren at first refused, believing that they merely wished to satisfy 'a morbid curiosity' and the trip would waste valuable time and be dangerous. After a barrage of complaints, he acquiesced; fearing, as it turned out prophetically, that 'otherwise they will go back to England and tell all kinds of tales against us'.[11]

Before Warren and the Charringtons could start their journey to Wady Sudr, a messenger arrived from Salami Shedide. He had captured three of the five murderers, one of the five headmen that had incited the killings and five of the 22 ambushers, one of whom was a twelve-year-old boy, who had been present at the murder scene. All had been placed in the dungeons of Nakhl's Fort and he was about to return to the desert to start the search for the remaining suspects. Warren immediately abandoned the trip to the murder site and headed for Nakhl, where he also intended to interview Sheikh Misleh about the bargain he had made with Palmer back in mid-July. On arrival, he, Haynes and Burton commenced their interrogation of the prisoners, and, after a mere four days, two of the three murder suspects and the headman accused of inciting the killings had confessed and the third murderer had been implicated by the others. Moreover, the young boy confirmed the identities of both the murderers and headmen. After celebrating their success with a magnificent Christmas dinner, which comprised lamb from Murshed's captured flock and a plum pudding specially made by the Suez Hotel's cook under Burton's close supervision, the three men questioned the alleged attackers, who also confessed. All the prisoners, except one, were then sent to Suez with instructions that those facing the death penalty should be kept separate from the others to ensure that 'they could not be put up to saying that they had been forced to confess by torture or deny their confessions'. The exception was the young boy. Given his age and the 'straightforward and unhesitating manner' in which he had given his evidence, Warren decided that he would not be prosecuted and eventually released him, an odd decision given the crucial nature of his eyewitness evidence.

On their journey to Suez, the prisoners passed Sheikh Suileman, who was heading to Nakhl in place of his brother, Sheikh Misleh, who had a more pressing engagement, and brought with him another suspected attacker. On arrival, Suileman, 'a slightly built, dark complexioned Arab' 'with a tinge of foppishness', described the details of Palmer's deal with his brother, stated that Palmer was travelling to Nakhl to seal this deal and confirmed that after the murder he had visited Meter ibu Sofieh, who had related to him the grisly details of the party's demise. When asked why he had not informed the authorities of the attacks, he swore on Allah that he would have done so had he not had to pursue raiders who had stolen three of his sheep.[12]

On completing all his business at Nakhl, Warren reverted to his previous plan to revisit Wady Sudr and hold a funeral service there. However, rather than heading straight to the murder scene, he decided to go to a nearby Bedouin camp, where a recent message from Shedide stated another purported murderer was hiding out, and then to the Mount Sinai Monastery to interview its Archbishop, the writer of the letter that two months previously had informed Warren that Sheikh Moussa on first learning of the Palmer party's disappearance had sent a man to

Nakhl, who had been told by the Governor that he had killed the Englishmen 'with his own hand'. Moussa had denied the story, perhaps fearful of a blood feud if the Governor was executed, and Warren wished to discover the identity of and then question the tribesman who had made the trip.

Both journeys proved an utter waste of time. The murder suspect had left the Bedouin encampment weeks earlier for Syria, where he owned land, and the Archbishop was away and none of the monks had any further information to impart. Preparing to leave the Monastery, Warren received unsettling news from Suez. A few days previously, Sheikh Sofieh had complained that he had felt unwell and had been transferred from Suez prison to the local French hospital, where, two days later, he had passed away. Fearing foul play, the British Consul had organised a post-mortem, which had concluded that he had died of unspecified natural causes. Warren was not convinced by the finding; suspecting that the Shedides had silenced one of his main witnesses of their involvement in the murder.

From the Monastery, Warren and Haynes travelled to the spot where Palmer's camels were stolen, whilst Burton returned to Suez to ensure that the Nakhl prisoners had arrived safety, to buy more supplies, to further investigate Sofieh's death and to accompany the Charringtons to the murder site. On the journey to the location of Palmer's camp, Warren visited various tribes to inform them that only those guilty of the attack on the Englishmen would be punished and to obtain assurances that they would not approach the party after the arrival of Charrington's sister, who he feared would be alarmed by their appearance. He also called at the tents of Sheikh Moussa, where a sumptuous banquet was held in his honour. Arriving at Palmer's former encampment, he began to retrace the Professor's final journey. Riding to and from the place the camel thief was caught, he found that it must have taken at least five hours to recover the camels. He then moved onto to the oasis where the attack on the baggage occurred, and, from there, to the spot where the looted spoils were divided. Here, he found part of Gill's and Charrington's journals and a number of letters. At the location of the attack on the party, blood stains from the shot camel were discovered, and, after much searching, some pages from Palmer's pocket book. Disappointingly, there were no messages scratched onto the rocks where the men had been held prisoner, though there was a camel track leading from there to the murder site, suggesting that it had recently been visited. At the murder scene, heavy rains had recently swept down the gully and an inch-by-inch search for body parts produced only two pieces of bone, which were buried.

Having exhausted their investigations, the party led by a local Bedouin proceeded to the tents of Sheikh ibu Murshed, who Warren had almost caught on his previous visit. The camp was deserted, but amongst its debris were found pages from newspapers, a part of a portmanteau and army cartridges, which had been broken up and emptied of their gunpowder. The party then rode back to the head of Wady Sudr, where they met up with Burton and the Charringtons. Miss Charrington was visibly upset, not only on account of the death of her brother, but also that of her 52 year old mother, who had died a few days previously supposedly from a 'broken heart'. Palmer's final journal was again retraced, and, at the murder scene, Warren read the funeral service at the end of which, Burton and Haynes fired three volleys of ball cartridges into the cliff opposite; much to the consternation of the Bedouins present, who scattered believing they were under attack.

The site chosen for the memorial to the dead men was a flat-topped peak overlooking the gully into which the bodies had been thrown. During the collection of the building materials, a further exciting discovery was made. Within a cave, the mouth of which was sealed by a large stone, were found two of the naval swords that Palmer had intended to present to Sheikh Misleh when he arrived at Nakhl and some fragments of Western clothing. All the articles were removed and sent back to England. The completed cairn was an impressive 13 foot high and topped with a 10 foot oak cross, brought by Miss Charrington from Suez, on which was cut an inscription informing the world of the dastardly deed that had been committed below. After its construction, a consecration service was held and Sheikh Moussa sent on a tour of the surrounding Bedouin camps to warn the inhabitants that anyone who damaged the memorial in any way would be severely punished.

There then occurred yet another argument with the Charringtons. Warren's dislike of the couple had been further heightened by Spencer Charrington's refusal to help in the construction of the cairn, the insertion by Miss Charrington in a crevice in the rocks of a soda bottle containing a note that gave an account of her and her brother's journey to Egypt and suggested they had played a part in the capture of the murderers, and the inscription on the donated cross. Not only were the names of the party's two servants missing, but Lieutenant Charrington's name was in huge capitals, while those of Palmer and Gill were in much smaller letters and in small case. The inscription also stated in large script that the cross had been donated by the Charrington family and that the party had been 'killed by Bedouin', words that Warren had insisted be removed, as they were both incorrect and inflammatory. When at the end of the service, Spencer Charrington insisted that he and his sister be immediately accompanied back to Suez, as he could not bear to spend the night close to the place where his dear brother died, Warren exploded, informing the couple in the bluntest of terms exactly what he thought of them. Eventually, it was agreed that Burton would take them to Suez the following morning. During the journey another row ensued. At 1pm, Spencer Charrington informed Burton that he intended to split the party; in order to ensure that he and his sister reached civilisation before nightfall, they and an escort would take the horses and fast camels and head for Suez, while the Lieutenant and the majority of the camel drivers would proceed at a more leisurely place. Miffed that Charrington was usurping his own role as leader of the party, Burton vetoed the plan, which would make them all more vulnerable to attack. Charrington, however, was adamant and the two siblings rode off leaving a fuming Burton, who became even more angry on discovering that Spencer Charrington had left instructions with the camel drivers as to the route they should take.

On his own journey to Suez, Warren took time out to investigate the geology and monuments of the region, visiting a number of stone monoliths, an ancient temple, some long abandoned mines and inscriptions said to be the work of the Israelites. He reached Suez in mid-February, by which time the December 26th deadline imposed on Salami Shedide for the capture of the named attackers and murderers had long passed. Unfortunately, no further murderers or assailants had been captured, though a number of witnesses had been brought in and the wives and children of some of the fugitives had been seized as hostages to be freed only when their husbands/fathers gave themselves up. There were also rumours that Salami had refused to arrest one of the murderers when his relatives had offered to hand him over and had actually apprehended Sheikh ibu Murshed, but had subsequently released him – after first providing detailed instructions as to how to avoid recapture. More worryingly, he was accused by the relations of those he had deigned to arrest of stealing their property and had been spotted driving vast herds of camels, sheep and goats to Hawetat camps.

Suspecting that he was deliberately failing to detain suspects who possessed evidence of his own involvement in the affair, Warren ordered Shedide back to Suez and asked for an explanation. Unabashed by his failures, the Sheikh blamed his poor arrest record on the recent heavy rains, which had reduced the need for suspects to travel to water holes where his men waited to catch them, and the refusal of the Terabin to give up those members of their tribe implicated in the crime; an attempt to seize culprits at one camp had supposedly been resisted by an armed force of over 600 fighters. As regards, the escape of some of those arrested and the accusations of theft, the former were unfortunate and the confiscation of the effects of the guilty parties had been ordered by the Khedive to whom the possessions had been handed.[13] Asked by Warren to fulfil his agreement to bring in all sixty suspects and witnesses, Salami equivocated, claiming that he had urgent business to conduct in Cairo and suggesting that he take a month off; the break would allow him to recruit more men, and the suspects would assume that the search was at an end and would leave their hiding places, and, with the arrival of the dry season, would be forced to the desert wells and oasis.

Having nothing to lose, Warren accepted the offer, but insisted that spies be left in the desert to alert Shedide of any new developments. He also set in motion three further initiatives. Towarah Bedouin were sent out to take more hostages and discover the hideouts of the fugitives; four hostages were released on the understanding that other members of their families would be freed if they brought in suspects; and Lieutenant Burton was sent to the former camp of Salim Sheyk, who had admitted helping to arrange the murders, to search for any articles that may have belonged to Palmer, Charrington or Gill. Burton found the encampment deserted and discovered only some straw bales, which may or may not have been looted from Moses Wells.

Chapter 14

The Foreign Office Search

At the same the Admiralty was conducting its search for Palmer and his companions, the Foreign Office was undertaking its own completely separate investigation, which involved Noel Temple Moore, the British Consul of Jerusalem, Moses Shapira, an antiquities dealer, and Richard Burton, the explorer and Consul of Trieste. The son of a Consul General of Beirut, Moore on entering the Foreign Office had followed his father to the Syrian capital, where he was an official in the Consulate and later Vice Consul. His appointment in 1863 as Consul of Jerusalem was partly the result of the good impression he had made on Lord Dufferin, the Foreign Secretary, for whom he had acted as an interpreter during a visit to Syria in 1860, and the Prince of Wales, who he had accompanied on his 1862 tour of Palestine. Both men were impressed by the polite young diplomat and had recommended his appointment as Consul. He was also a superb linguist, fluent in Arabic, Turkish and Persian, and was regarded as a much needed safe pair of hands. His predecessor, James Finn, had prompted outrage among the Palestinian and British Jewish communities when he had imprisoned two Jews, one Dutch and the other Russian, who had obtained certificates that guaranteed them British protection to which they were not entitled.

Moore remained Consul for a remarkable 27 years, during which time he never returned to England, largely because of his miniscule salary and expenses. An indolent individual – apart from the dates, his annual reports are almost identical – and well aware of the reasons for the departure of his predecessor, he kept a low profile, avoiding confrontation and forming amicable relations with everyone he came into contact, particularly the local Jewish community. During his time at Jerusalem, he fiercely opposed the various Turkish restrictions that sought to restrict Jewish immigration and land purchases, granted British protection to Russian Jews and removed many the hindrances faced by Jewish travellers.[1]

He was asked to conduct his own investigation into the disappearance in early October and immediately travelled to Gaza. Here, he hoped to spread the news of a reward he had been permitted to offer for the recovery of the Englishmen and to question Sheikh Jabr, a Teyahah chief who had helped him contact Sheikh Misleh in early September when the Admiralty had asked him to discover whether the Professor had kept his Nakhl appointment, and Reverend Alexander Schapira, who had assisted Palmer during his first mission. Although neither Jabr nor Schapira possessed any useful clues, Moore made two breakthroughs. He discovered that a Turkish officer on the Syrian frontier had recently bought a British rifle from a passing Bedouin, which he had presented to his commanding officer. Obtaining the rifle through the Governor of Gaza, Moore took it to Schapira, who identified it as belonging to Palmer. The Turkish officer was summoned and questioned, but the identity and location of the seller, almost certainly one of the attackers, remained a mystery.

A few days later, he was approached by Sheikh Hussain Effendi El-Husseini, a leading notable, who introduced him to other influential chiefs. Questioning these men, he discovered that Palmer's party had been attacked and murdered at Wady Sudr and that the crime had been committed with the connivance of their guide, Sheikh Sofieh, who had recently used gold coins to make large purchases of goods and animals at El Arish. More significantly, he was given the names of the four Bedouin who had killed the Englishmen, though only after first swearing not to reveal to anyone the source of the information, the sheikhs fearing retribution from the culprits' tribes. Elated with this great success, he telegraphed the information to Suez. Warren, who had a low opinion of Moore derived from the Consul's lethargy during the Colonel's 1867/70 expedition to Jerusalem, delayed replying. He then curtly informed him that he believed that at least some members of the group were still alive and enquiries had revealed that the four Bedouin named as murderers lived in Palestine and had no connection whatsoever with the case.

Undeterred, Moore sought to organise a search party for Palmer and his companions, only to meet with opposition from the Turkish authorities. The Governor of Gaza put pressure on Sheikh El-Husseini, who was to lead and provide the personnel for the expedition, to pull out, and, when Moore decided to command the party himself, refused to provide an escort, pronouncing the mission to be overly dangerous. The Governor's subsequent promise to help Moore form an expedition made up of other sheikhs and their fighters, proved disingenuous. Although his offer of the future goodwill of the Turkish government encouraged chieftains to volunteer for the mission, Moore suspected that he was also behind their subsequent decision to pull out of the deal.

Perhaps concerned at Moore's lack of progress, the Foreign Office in early November 1882 ordered him to return to normal duties, replacing him with Moses Shapira and Richard Burton.[2] Shapira was a strange choice. A Polish Jew who had converted to Christianity, he had arrived at Jerusalem from his native Kiev at the age of 26 to open a shop selling antiquities. He began to supply the major museums of Europe, including the British Museum, and became well known in 1873 when he offered for sale a large quantity of vases and figurines, inscribed with ancient letters almost identical to those found on the 'Moabite stone', the piece of stonework discovered at Dibhan, Moab in 1868. The find created a sensation and Shapira was expected to make his fortune from the sale of the items. Alas, investigations by Charles Trywhitt Drake, with whom Palmer had travelled to the Desert of Tih, and the French archaeologist M. Clermont

Ganneau subsequently proved the pots to be crude forgeries manufactured by a local Arab, who had sold them onto a credulous or perhaps not-so-credulous Shapira.[3]

Shapira was appointed on the recommendation of Palmer's friend Walter Besant on the basis that he had good relations with the Bedouin of the region, from whom he bought his antiquities, and was 'a man who will do anything for money'.[4] He also claimed the Professor was his 'very special friend', though he had met him only once when Palmer had passed through Jerusalem in 1870, and expressed a great desire to rescue him. Moore was asked to approach the dealer, who agreed to become involved in a search for a fee of £200 to £300. Unable to enter the desert himself, he sent his servant on what he claimed was a quasi-business trip, but was probably a normal journey to purchase antiquities, with instructions to 'have an open ear to all he may happen to hear in the Bedouin's tents'. The news with which the servant returned was as astounding as Shapira's discovery of the Moabite pottery. One of the party was alive! Although wounded in the arm and suffering from injuries to his feet and legs, he was in good health and the prisoner of a Sheikh Gad, whose attempts to force him to convert to Islam had been rejected with a cry of 'I will die in my belief'.[5] The servant had obtained the information from two sheikhs who had offered to guide him to Gad's tents for a fee of £50; a proposal he had reluctantly turned down, as he had not the authority nor the funds to pay Gad a ransom for the Christian and he suspected that the prisoner may have been moved to another chief's camp.

The Foreign Office was initially sceptical, but its doubts evaporated when the story appeared to be confirmed by Andrew Graves, the Vice Consul of Jerusalem, who had been left in charge of the Consulate during Moore's absence in Cairo. Graves reported that he had recently received two pieces of information. There was a rumour that several weeks earlier some Bedouins had been approached in the desert by a white man, looking 'sick and sorry', who had announced 'I am under thy protection'.[6] Also, a few days after the return of Shapira's servant, he had been approached by a Sheikh Abdullah Racheed, who had recently arrived in the city and had divulged that he had heard that Palmer had been left for dead at the time of the massacre, but had then come to life, only to be captured by a Sheikh Arar Ben Gazi.

Convinced that Palmer was still alive, the Foreign Office instructed Graves to send Charles Warren news of the exciting developments and to determine whether Sheikh Rasheed was prepared to travel to the tents of Sheikhs Gazi and Gad and pay a ransom for the prisoner. Warren's reply to Graves' telegraph was discouraging. He too had heard the rumours of a white man wondering the desert and had arranged for the individual to be brought to Suez. The man had been found to be a Syrian and to have been driven half-mad by his Bedouin rescuers, who had beaten him every day and 'ill-used him', presumably sexually.[7] He also disclosed in a telegram to Lord Northbrook, that he strongly suspected that the rumours of the lost European had been started by Richard Burton in an attempt to strengthen his contention that one of the party was still alive; Burton having been in Suez when the man was questioned. As for Shapira's claims, the dealer was a proven fraudster and was no doubt attempting to extort money from the government.

Graves, nonetheless, decided to go ahead with the ransom mission, even when he discovered, on contacting Sheikh Rasheed, that Shapira had already asked him to obtain the prisoner's release, an arrangement that suggested the two were in cahoots. He strongly believed that every attempt should be made to find the gallant Englishman if he was still alive and suspected that Warren was deliberately attempting to sabotage the Foreign Office's efforts in order to grab any glory for himself. Needless to say, after paying Sheikh Rasheed £15, he never saw him again, though the Sheikh's servant later brought a letter from Sheikh Gad categorically denying that he was holding a Christian prisoner. As for Shapira, he was quietly dropped by the Foreign Office, but was soon ensconced in yet another scandal. The following year, he attempted to sell sheepskin scrolls supposedly containing the book of Deuteronomy written in characters closely resembling those found on the 'Moabite stone'. The objects were eventually declared forgeries, though many now believe they were genuine, and the antiquarian, bereft of reputation and livelihood and holed up in a decrepit Rotterdam hotel room, took the gentleman's way out with a bullet in the head.[8]

Richard Burton's only contribution to the search for the Englishmen was to infuriate Charles Warren. During the 1870 expedition to the Libanus mountains with Palmer and Drake, he had come to greatly admire the eccentric academic, who shared his interest in occultism, crystal gazing and the Romany language and had supported him during the controversy over the causes of the 1860 Damascus riots. Over the years, they had kept in touch, and, in 1880, he had sent the Professor seventy pages of notes on his journeys through the Middle East. By 1882, he was sixty-one years of age and had been removed as Consul of Damascus, having managed to upset not only his superior, the British Consul General at Beirut, but also the Turkish Governor of Syria and the local Jewish community, who were perturbed when he refused to take action against those who defaulted on loans. After a year in the wilderness, during which he travelled to Iceland, he had been appointed the British Consul at Trieste, a sleepy backwater, where it was hoped he could do little harm. On hearing of the disappearance of his old friend, he announced to his wife that 'if there is any chance of saving dear old Palmer, I will go anywhere and do anything' and immediately began to campaign to be included in a search party. Support came from Gill's brother, the Consul of Jerusalem and the Admiralty, and on October 27th, the Foreign Office permitted him to travel to Gaza to help Noel Temple Moore with his enquiries.[9]

Unfortunately, he was unable to leave Trieste until November 3rd, by which time the Admiralty had withdrawn its support. Palmer and his companions were now known to be dead, the search mission had become a murder investigation and Admiral Hewitt, aware of Burton's reputation, feared friction if he became involved. Burton, nonetheless, demanded that he be allowed to make his own enquiries, pointing out that he had already paid for his passage and arguing that that there was still a possibility that Palmer was alive; none of his clothing having been found at the murder scene.[10] The Foreign Office reluctantly relented and on November 8th Burton arrived at Alexandria, where he questioned Charles Clarke, the editor of the *Egyptian Gazette*. Clarke was on friendly terms with the local Bedouin chiefs and had been asked by Warren to help in the search for the party, but had declined; his house had been looted by English soldiers during the invasion of Alexandria in the belief that he was an employee of Ferdinand de Lesseps and he was convinced 'the game was not worth a candle'. Clarke told Burton that he had heard that Palmer and his companions had been killed, and, in return for this information, received an interview in which the great explorer insisted that the Englishmen were still alive and implicitly criticised the investigation into their disappearance.

Warren first became aware of Burton's involvement in the case on receiving a telegram from him asking whether they could meet in Suez. Before he could decline the request, Burton arrived and at a number of meetings informed him of the many mistakes that had been made in the search for the Englishmen, insisted that they were still alive and proposed that he be allowed to take 500 men to Nakhl to rescue them. Warren declined the kind offer, and, instead, suggested that he continue to Gaza as planned to search for the missing gentlemen and to help in the hunt for the suspects, some of whom were reported to have fled to the city, giving him a list of the 21 miscreants to be arrested. He also began a campaign to ensure that Burton had no further involvement in the affair.

Warren had first met Burton in the 1860s in Jerusalem and regarded him an unscrupulous cad, an opinion that was heightened by the explorer's tale at dinner of how he had placed pottery at an excavation site to fool an archaeologist into believing that he had made a great find. He also feared that Burton's criticisms of Palmer's actions during his two missions would discredit the Professor's good name and that he sought to grab the glory of capturing the Englishman's murderers. Displaying the paranoia that was to blight his later career, he became convinced that the great explorer would ride out with the Gaza sheikhs and arrest each and every culprit, and, if this was not possible, would persuade the British government to allow him to take over the investigation.

To prevent either outcome, Warren sent a telegram to Lord Northbrook and letters to Sir Charles Wilson, head of army intelligence, and Admiral Hewett suggesting that Burton, who had recently expressed an interest in establishing an Egyptian gold mining company, was using his search for Palmer as a cover for exploring the mineral potential of the region and that his involvement would damage the effectiveness of his own efforts. The following day, on reading Charles Clarke's interview, which had been reproduced in the *Pall Mall Gazette*, he dispatched Lieutenant Alfred Haynes to Cairo with instructions to personally plead his case to Wilson and to deliver a letter and speak to Sir Edward Malet, the English Consul General. Neither was helpful. Wilson merely suggested that Burton be telegraphed and politely asked to do nothing until further notice. Malet pretended not to be 'at home', and, when Haynes on his third visit demanded entrance, sympathised, but insisted that he had no authority to act and suggested a meeting with Lord Dufferin, the Ambassador to Istanbul, who had recently been sent to Egypt by the British government to plan the post-war future of the country. Dufferin perfectly understood how Warren must feel 'loosing the fish he had hooked and was just bringing in' to a 'blustering fellow...with a landing net', but insisted he was powerless, suggesting a telegram to Lord Northbrook.[11]

Burton, meanwhile, rather than heading for Gaza as promised, had instead proceeded to Zagazig to ask the Director of Telegraphs to collect information from the local Bedouin sheikhs and had then travelled to Cairo, where he met with Noel Temple Moore to urge him to continue the line of investigation opened up by the discovery of Palmer's rifle and updated Malet and Dufferin on his theory that at least some of the party were alive. Discovering his movements, Warren telegraphed Malet to insist that he be ordered to go to Gaza. Burton complied. His time in the town, however, was short. After questioning the Reverend Alexander Schapira on his impressions of Palmer when he had stayed with him during his first mission and the rumours that a Christian had been seen wandering in the desert, he and the missionary sailed to Jaffa. Here, he interviewed the Turkish Governor and then called on the British Consul, who presented him with a Foreign Office telegram ordering him back to Trieste. Northbrook, fearing that the army would lose the kudos of capturing Palmer's murderers had successfully pressured the Foreign Office to recall Burton, arguing that his presence in Gaza would breach Warren's agreement with Salami Shedide that the British would halt their own hunt for the murderers during the 21 days he was in the desert rounding up suspects. Burton was furious, later writing 'this is simply making a fool of me. They wanted my name while the House of Commons was sitting and then nada [Spanish for nothing]'.[12] Nonetheless, he returned home, where he wrote a severely critical article about the search, which he failed to get published.

Chapter 15

The Ambush

The evidence obtained from the men brought in by Salami Shedide and others revealed the murder of Palmer and his companions to have been a highly organised affair. Rumours in London suggested that Arabi was aware of Palmer's first mission even before he had left England. The source of the intelligence was probably Wilfrid Blunt, a fervent nationalist supporter, who had been alerted that the British government was planning some intrigue by Palmer himself and was a close friend of Walter Besant to whom Palmer had revealed every aspect of his mission prior to his departure for Egypt. Likewise, Arabi commanders knew all about the Professor's second journey into the desert. Details may have come from the camel buyer employed by Palmer on August 2nd to purchase some of the camels required by the Indian army to whom the Professor may have accidentally divulged details of his first mission. The man was a known Arabi spy and an employee of Salami Shedide; it later emerged the he was the 'bogus' brother who Shedide attempted to fob off onto Warren when they first met in Cairo. However, it seems likely that he delivered his intelligence after the Palmer party had begun its mission. On his journey to Cairo, he was captured by rebel forces, who refused to believe that he was carrying important information and beat him, stole the money he had received to purchase the camels and threw him into jail, where he was tortured. Other possible sources are a second nationalist spy based in Suez; Blunt, who would have received the information from Besant with whom Palmer corresponded up to his departure for Nakhl; and Sheikh Misleh. It is possible that the Sheikh passed the nature of the agreement he believed he had made with the British either to his great friend the Governor of

Nakhl, an ardent supporter of Arabi, or his brother, Sheikh Suileman, who had failed to keep his appointment with Palmer because had had been called to Cairo by Sard and Salami Shedide's father.[1]

On being informed that Palmer was to enter the desert a second time, an Arabi official in Cairo, probably Salami Shedide, sent instructions to the Dukilallah tribe and Sheikh ibu Murshed's Hawetat tribe. On August 8th, a messenger was dispatched to the Dukilallah with a letter that ordered them to stop the Christians reaching Nakhl and warned that a decision not to comply with the directive would comprise 'a risk to their throats'.[2] The messenger, however, only reached the tribe's camp after the Englishmen had been murdered. The second instruction requested the Hawetat to capture the party and send them to Cairo, where apparently they would have been held as hostages and Arabi would have revealed to the world the despicable plot to bribe the Bedouin. The message was sent to the fanatical Governor of El Arish. What he then did with the communiqué is the subject of some dispute. Warren implies that he passed it unaltered to his Nakhl counterpart, who in turn relayed to the Hawetat during his first day in the desert. Alternatively, Mr Pickard, the man sent to Gaza to cut the telegraph and investigate the disappearance of the party, and at least one newspaper correspondent believed that he told the Nakhl Governor that the Christians were to be brought in dead or alive and a Hawetat sheikh informed Professor Edward Hull during his 1883 journey through the region that his instruction was 'any Christians running about his country, like rats with no holes' were to be 'finish[ed]…off at once'.[3]

The task of co-ordinating the attack was allocated to Sualem Abu Farag, who informed Warren that he had been given the assignment by Salami Shedide. Farag sent two Bedouin, Salim ibu Subdeh and Ali Schwair, to Moses Wells. Their instructions were to wait for the arrival of the Englishmen, discover their route to Nakhl, communicate this information to the Dukilallah and Hawetat tribes and to slow the party's progress in order to give the tribes' sheikhs sufficient time to prepare an ambush. On arrival at Moses Wells, Subdeh hired three local residents to steal half of the party's camels, which would delay the expedition by forcing the remaining beasts to carry heavier loads, and a further Bedouin, Mosellam ibu Aiyeneh, who lived close to the village. He and Schwair then hunkered down to await the appearance of their foes.

On the afternoon of August 7th, they heard that Sulieman Zahr, the camel trader, had received instructions to send camels down to the beach the following morning. As dawn broke, Subdeh took a constitutional walk around Zahr's enclosure, and, when the animals were led out, called on the Bedouin who he had paid to steal some of the party's camels and told them to start walking to Nakhl. He then rode to the beach. Here, he struck up a conversation with Meter ibu Sofieh, using a warning not to enter the desert as a means of discovering the proposed route of the party. Having obtained this intelligence, he returned to Moses Wells and passed it onto Ali Schwair, who immediately left the oasis for the Dukilallah and Hawetat camps. On arrival at the former, Schwair was appalled to discover that they knew nothing of the proposed attack and had no intention of becoming involved, believing the affair would come to no good. He, nonetheless, continued to the Hawetat tents, informed the tribe's chief, Sheikh ibu Murshed, of the route and progress of the intended prey, and, according to one of the suspects, ordered the Englishmen's murder, adding that if the Hawetat failed to 'kill them, their country would be ruined'.[4] He then rode to the camp of a local sheikh, where he spent the night.

Subdeh, meanwhile, sent word to Mosellam ibu Aiyeneh to join him two miles from Moses Wells, and rode after the Bedouin who were to steal the camels to tell them to proceed to Wady Kahlin, where he had discovered from Sofieh the party would be bivouacking for the night. He then met up with Aiyeneh and they set off after the Englishmen, finding them having a sumptuous lunch at a nearby oasis. After eating with them, Aiyeneh left and rode to Wady Sudr to inform Ali Schwair of the progress of the party and to assure him that they were taking the route Sofieh had indicated. Subdeh stayed – again to monitor the party's progress and to ensure that their camels were indeed stolen. In the event, the theft of the camels did not go to plan; rather than stealing half the animals, the thieves took only two and it seemed likely that the extra loads the remaining beasts would have to carry would have little impact on the speed at which the party travelled. All appeared lost until, much to the amazement of Subdeh, it was decided that the Englishmen and baggage would remain at Wady Kahalin while the stolen camels were retrieved, thus ensuring that the attackers had more than enough time to prepare their ambush. He then had another stroke of luck, it was decided that the group would be split on the return of Bedouin sent to recover the camels, the Englishmen and their attendants riding ahead of the baggage. The party's ability to defend itself was thus greatly reduced. On told that this was to occur, Subdeh made his excuses to Palmer, wished him a pleasant journey and left the camp, riding to Wady Sudr to join Ali Schwair.

Distressed to find that the attacking force would be much smaller than anticipated, Subdeh believed that the operation could still be a success and dispatched Schwair to the Hawetat tents whilst he and another Bedouin made their own way to Wady Sudr. Schwair arrived at Sheikh ibu Murshed's camp at sunset to find its inhabitants celebrating the Feast of the Dead with some visiting Terabin tribesmen. Told that the Englishmen were probably at that moment passing through Wady Sudr, Murshed sent a fighter to Sofieh's camp, either to determine whether the party had already arrived or to inform the Governor of Nakhl, who he may have believed had returned there, that the attack was about to begin. He then mobilised his and the visiting Terabin fighters and rode to the middle of Wady Sudr, where torches were lit and a search for camel tracks made to ascertain whether the party had passed that point. Finding none, Murshed positioned 25 Bedouin in the rocks on one side of the valley and a further 25 on the spur of a small hill on the other side, their greater height reducing the likelihood that they would fire onto the men facing them. Subdeh and his companion, who had joined the attackers, were sent down the valley to cut off any attempt by the Englishmen to retreat. Murshed and his men then waited for their prey.

It was a surprisingly long wait. Given that the party had left Wady Kahalin at 3pm with the intention of reaching Sofieh's camp by nightfall, it should have long passed the place of the attack; that this was not the case suggested to Warren that it must have progressed at an unusually leisurely pace. Finally, the Englishmen appeared. The attackers' account of what occurred next was very different from that of Meter ibu Sofieh and his nephew. Rather than firing a hail of bullets, the Hawetat and Terabin let off five or six shots, gunpowder being in short supply. The nephew's camel was hit, he jumped off, and, when his companions kneeled their own camels and crouched behind them, he ran over to Palmer and a few minutes later threw himself on his camel and raced back down the valley, followed a few seconds later by Sofieh who alternatively stumbled and ran. There was no evidence that Palmer had ordered the nephew to flee, his escape reducing the party's ability to defend itself. Strangely, neither Subdeh nor his companion, positioned to prevent such an event, appear to have fired at the fleeing Bedouin. A rumour that Sofia's nephew and Palmer had been riding the same camel, highly unlikely, and that the former had thrown the latter off as soon as the shooting began and ridden off with the money was not supported by any of the attackers.

The remaining Englishmen and attendant let off at most one

shot; a puzzling lack of resistance that may be related to their paucity of weaponry or could be an indication of Palmer's confidence that the attackers' fear of blood feuds made it unlikely that they would be killed. Dumbfounded at the absence of any significant return fire, the attackers did nothing for five or ten minutes and then rushed the party; a persistent rumour that there was an extended standoff and that the Englishmen were seized in the early morning was not supported by those present and is unlikely given that the baggage was attacked at dawn. The prisoners were immediately stripped off their Arab dress – to deter escape, because the clothes were of value or from anger that non-Bedouins should wear Arab dress – and dragged to a nearby hollow and forced to sit down. Two men were ordered to guard them while the rest of the attackers turned their attention to the captives' camels, which they stripped off all valuables; a number of fights breaking out over who should possess the stolen goods. After peace had been restored, two Bedouin were delegated to remove the dead camel to the Hawetat tents, where it would be cooked and eaten, and three men dispatched to capture Sofieh and his nephew. Murshed and the remaining fighters, meanwhile, rode off to attack the baggage train; followed a few minutes later by one of the guards, disgruntled at being deprived of his share of the likely plunder. The four prisoners were thus guarded for several hours by just one Bedouin, but oddly made no attempt to escape, even though they were unbound and unhurt, perhaps in the expectation of rescue.

Meter ibu Sofieh's account of his attempt to ransom the party was found to be as bogus as his description of the ambush. Those who accompanied him recounted that on arrival at the place of the attack, identified by a pool of blood belonging to the camel that had been shot, they had called out and had been answered by shouts from a nearby gully. Hurrying there, they had found the four prisoners in their undergarments sitting in a row alone; the guard having fled on their approach. Aware that the attackers could return any second and that the guard could have run off to obtain help, Sofieh should have got them away as quickly as possible. Instead, he wasted much valuable time in expressions of pity and placing his coat on Palmer, his headdress on Gill and kissing each of the prisoners in turn. It was thus some time before they were taken back to the rescuers' camels, and, as they were about to mount, Murshed and his fellow fighters were spotted in the distance returning from their plunder of the baggage train. Even then, the group still had a chance of escape. However, instead of immediately riding off, as his companions demanded, Sofieh insisted that they await the arrival of the attackers, and, when his men prepared to defend themselves, ordered their guns to be put away, arguing that the Englishmen's' lives could only be saved through peaceful bargaining.

The actual negotiations between the guide and the attackers lasted less than thirty minutes and were conducted without the support of the other rescuers, who had ridden off, having been threatened with death if they stayed. After informing Murshed that he did not know the whereabouts of his nephew, Sofieh offered the Sheikh thirty camels in return for the release of all the captured men; a derogatory amount, given the number and status of the prisoners and the possibility that under tribal law he could later reclaim the animals. The offer was refused and the funds that the party had been carrying were requested. Sofieh denied their existence at which point Palmer interjected crying out 'Meter has all the money'. Told that the prisoners would be killed if the cash was not produced, the old man again insisted that he did not have the money amid Palmer's cries that this was not the case and that they could have all that he possessed provided that they spared his life. Asked again to produce the gold, Sofieh announced the negotiations to be at an end, walked to his camel and left his former employers to their fate.[5]

After Sofieh's departure, the clothes he had given the prisoners were ripped off, the cook was dragged to join his former companions and the five headmen present held a short discussion over whether the prisoners should be handed over to the nationalists in Cairo or killed, finally deciding that they should die. Why they came to this decision is something of a conundrum. Warren suggested it was disappointment at the non-appearance of the ransom or blood lust, though the latter is unlikely given the time that had elapsed since the ambush. Others theorised that that they were carrying out the Governor of El Arish's and Ali Schwair's order that the party should be killed, or, if the El Arish Governor's instruction had been that the Christians should be captured dead or alive, had chosen the former option, fearing that the British authorities would exact a harsh retribution if they were allowed to live and escaped or Arabi released them. Their men were asked whether they agreed with the decision. None dissented and five fighters were chosen to carry out the deed – three Terabins and two Hawetats; one of the latter, an old man, passing the duty onto a younger fighter, who received a plundered sword in return.

Ordered to rise, the five captives were marched the one mile to a nearby ravine, down which during heavy rains coursed a raging torrent that would obliterate all traces of the crime. Given that it was mid-day and they were clothed only in their underwear with no headdress or boots, they must have rapidly become delirious from the heat of the sun and the pain from their bloodied feet. It also seems likely that to encourage them to walk to their deaths, they were subjected to 'rough treatment'. Nonetheless, it was reported that Palmer remained sufficiently clear headed to repeatedly plead for his life, offering his murderers everything he possessed if they would only release him. Arriving at the ledge along the side of the ravine, the prisoners were lined up facing the precipice. Their murderers stood behind them, aimed rifles at their heads and awaited the order to shoot. Before the command was given, Palmer suddenly began to curse his assassins, calling to heaven to avenge his death. If this was an attempt to terrify and force his killers to reconsider their decision, it did not work. Either out of anger or to silence Palmer, the designated Bedouin shot him in the neck, and, as he appeared to be still alive when he fell, took his sword and slashed open his chest. In the resulting pandemonium, Gill's attendant made a valiant escape bid, dashing down the ledge, pursued by two fighters, who hacked him down with their swords and pushed his body into the gully. The cook, Charrington and Gill, who before he had left for Egypt had told a friend he had a 'horror of old age', meanwhile, either threw themselves or were pushed into the ravine and were shot by their killers from above.[6] To ensure the men were dead, the murderers next climbed down the gorge. Gill was found to be breathing and was finished off with a sword. The cook was dead, but nevertheless again shot. All the bodies were mutilated, either out of bloodlust or to help the vultures in their grisly work. Their job done, the fighters ascended the ravine, retraced their steps and returned to Murshed's tents. According to two witnesses, a Bedouin was dispatched to Marbrook to inform the Governor of Nakhl that the Englishmen were dead, while the remainder rode onto Moses Wells, where they hoped more opportunities for slaughter and plunder awaited them.

Chapter 16

Trial and Guilt

On January 4th 1883 the British government decided that the murder of Palmer's party would be treated as a crime rather than as an act of war. Warren insisted that the suspects had attacked the Englishmen in order to steal the £3,000 they carried and had murdered them to cover up this attempted theft. The decision was understandable. If the deeds of the suspects had been judged to have been part of the armed conflict, the British government would have had no choice but to release them under the amnesty granted on January 1st 1883 to all those involved in the rebellion. Politically, such an outcome would have been extremely damaging to the government. The British public, egged on by the press, were demanding revenge, and it was thought by many that some form of retribution was essential to discourage further insubordination by the Egyptian people and to ensure the safety of future foreign travellers through the region.[1]

Nonetheless, the decision was absurd. The evidence that the murders were an act of war was overwhelming. The attackers clearly stated they were following the orders of Arabi after they had raided the baggage train, when they split the spoils and during the ransom negotiations. The Governor of Nakhl had made a similar pronouncement in his conversation with Sheikh Moussa's messenger and in his letter to his counterpart at El Arish and neither Colonel Kitchener nor Professor Edward Hull of the Royal College of Science, Dublin, who went on an expedition to the area a year after the murders, found a single Arab who believed that the attackers had acted on their own initiative. Bedouin custom also suggested that they were obeying instructions. Tribesmen would shoot intruders in a fair fight, would steal from captives and even beat them up, but they would never take their life in cold blood. By doing so, they would effectively be signing their own death warrants as the relatives of the deceased would be bound by the concept of the blood feud to take their revenge. Instead, captives would be ransomed. In normal circumstances, Meter ibu Sofieh's offer would either have been accepted or the attackers would have captured and ransomed Sofieh or kept the party hostage until a more substantial sum was paid, either by the British government or by the relatives of the men held.[2]

Warren wished the men he had found guilty of murder and incitement to be executed by Khedive decree. He feared that if they were brought to trial they would retract their confessions and believed that as 'savages' they had no right to a defence council. The British government disagreed, and, after much consideration, it was decided that the cases would be heard by the Egyptian court at Tanteh, a town of 60,000 people famous for its great mosque, and the suspects sentenced by a British court marshal. The Tanteh court was unlikely to inquire whether the attack was an act of war or arrive at not guilty verdicts. During the height of the war, 97 Christian, Greek and Levantines had been murdered in the town, a number having locomotives driven over their bound bodies, and there was much resentment towards Arabi supporters among its citizenry. The court marshal, meanwhile, added the sheen of British justice to the proceedings and ensured that the harshest possible sentences would be applied.[3]

Warren and his faithful assistants arrived in Tanteh on February 5th to a frosty reception. The previous day four men had been hanged for inciting and murdering Christians in the days following the Alexandria riots and emotions were high. Stones were thrown at the three English officers as they walked the streets and they were shouted at and cursed by worshippers on a visit to the town's celebrated mosque. Problems emerged almost immediately. The Foreign Office refused to allow Warren to act as Prosecutor, on the grounds that he had conducted the preliminary enquiry. Unwilling to permit the prosecution to be undertaken by someone less convinced of the guilt of the prisoners than himself, he appointed Lieutenant Burton as his replacement, allowing him to direct the case at one remove. The Court President then declined his request that the trial occur immediately, arguing that other cases had already been scheduled and that he and his two fellow judges would need time to read and digest the evidence. Pressure was applied and he agreed to hear the case within two days, but was then recalled to Alexandria. Happy to be rid of a judge so wedded to procedure, Warren accepted the decision, and, when informed that the replacement would not arrive from Cairo for a number of days, dashed to the city to force him to come down the following morning. In the event, the trip was unnecessary – as Warren was boarding his train to Cairo, the judge was getting on one bound for Tanteh.

The trials eventually commenced at 10am on February 8th and were over in three days. To say the least, they were a farrago of justice. The bench comprised the Turkish Court President, who Lieutenant Burton believed to be a 'fool' and seemed to have no knowledge of court procedure or Egyptian law; an Egyptian who hardly spoke during the whole three days; and a 'regular little Frenchman', an Egyptian educated in France, who only appeared on the final day having more urgent business to attend to elsewhere. None of the prisoners had defence councils and witnesses were only called to give evidence against those who had not confessed – those who had admitted the crime heard their confessions read out and were then asked to verbally confirm their guilt three times.[4]

At the end of the proceedings, all the prisoners, plus those who had not yet been captured, were found guilty; a decision greatly influenced by the third judge, who was a close relative of the Khedive. Warren, his assistants and the prisoners immediately travelled to Alexandria for the court marshal, which was as unfair as the trial. Because the evidence collected by Warren and the transcripts of the proceedings at Tanteh failed to arrive in time, the six members of the court had just half a day to read the material. The court marshal itself took 'at most' 45 minutes. After a short prosecution speech given by the Tanteh Court President, the prisoners were asked to confess; four refused, but to no avail. Ignoring their pleas of innocence, a court official announced the sentences.

Five of the suspects received capital punishments, three for actually murdering the party and two head sheikhs for inciting the killings. A further five culprits, not yet caught, were also condemned to death, two for murder and three for incitement; a judgement later retracted when the Foreign Office suggested that sentencing should only occur after they had been arrested and 'tried'. The rest of the prisoners were given custodial sentences. One of the attackers received ten years, four of his accomplices five years each, the Bedouin who had stolen Palmer's camels and had delayed the party three years and Meter ibu Sofieh's nephew fifteen years for the theft of the £2,000, which his family were to repay. The Governor of Nakhl was found guilty of failing to inform his superiors of the attack on the party and being away from his post without permission, Warren having discovered a letter to his superior written the very day he left the fort declining the leave he had been granted. He was discharged from public service and given one years imprisonment with hard labour.

In London, the sentences were received with glee by the popular press, but with deep concern by others. On his return to England, Spencer Charrington had passed his concerns at what he believed had occurred in Egypt to Wilfrid Blunt, who through his connections with the press encouraged a number of journalists to criticise the sentences and persuaded his brother-in-law, Lord Wentworth, to ask a series of questions in the House of Lords. Blunt's main charges, all of which were vehemently denied by Warren and Haynes, were that witness testimony had been extracted through 'the use of duplicity, force or torture' and the evidence against those sentenced to death relied almost wholly on their confessions and that these again had been obtained through unscrupulous means.[5]

Torture was an everyday occurrence in Egypt. A British government report published a year after the rebellion revealed that many prisoners had been kept in underground dungeons for days without either food or water, constantly threatened with death, beaten with slippers and subjected to the thumb screw, flogging and bastinado (the whipping of the soles of feet). There is no evidence that Warren personally descended to these methods of extracting information from witnesses, though he did muse that 'a little delicate manipulation' of the whip may have encouraged Meter ibu Sofieh to become more loquacious. He was not convinced that torture persuaded witnesses to provide accurate information, and, in any case, its use had been specifically outlawed by Sir Edward Malet.[6]

When interrogating witnesses, he adopted a 'soft' and/or 'hard' approach. The former involved friendly chats in his hotel room during which he would offer the witness copious quantities of coffee and cigarettes and persuade them to provide information out of friendship. The 'hard' approach was constant cross-examination. Witnesses would be asked to 'go over their story again and again' until they 'tripped' and contradicted themselves; the interrogators then had 'some hold on them, which makes them confess that they have heard something [and] after perhaps a day or two, what they have heard, we make them confess to have seen, and then finally we get the full account'. Some indication of the harshness of this cross-examination can be elicited from Lieutenant Burton's descriptions of the process; whilst at Suez, he, Haynes and Warren variously 'pound away at the Bedouin', 'hammer out the evidence' and engage in 'persistent hammering'. Interrogations lasted up to fourteen hours per day, continued for days or weeks and were so pitiless that on a number of occasions Robert Gill and Edward Houndle, who were present at most of the interviews, were forced to intervene and demand that the bullying cease. Those who refused to speak remained in Suez jail, which as Lieutenant Burton so rightly commented was 'no joke'. Prisoners shared a single large room, possessed no beds, blankets or sanitary facilities, beyond a communal tub, and were given no food; the lucky ones obtained bread and meat from friends and relatives, which was passed through the barred windows, the rest begged for food through those same bars, stole it from fellow inmates or simply starved.[7]

Those suspected of attacking and murdering the party experienced a more brutal version of this cross-examination. Warren believed that it was crucial that they confessed to their crimes, as Egyptian courts would not convict on witness testimony alone, particularly if both witness and the accused were Moslem; an argument undermined by the enthusiasm with which the Tanteh judges found against both the Governor of Nakhl and Sofieh's nephew, neither of whom had admitted their guilt. Confessions also did away 'with much of the trouble of collecting witnesses'. As regards those who committed capital offences, one, Salim Sheyk, was interrogated at Suez and the rest at Nakhl. In order to encourage Salim Sheyk to admit his guilt, Warren 'hammered' him for six days; placed him in solitary confinement; confronted him with witnesses and the man he believed he had hacked to death, in reality Charrington's brother, who bore a remarkable resemblance to his sibling; and, as discussed, brought him before Salami Shedide. At first Sheyk swore that he had no involvement in the attack, on the fifth day claimed that a friend had divulged to him the identities of the five murderers, the names of whom he passed onto Warren, and, during his interrogation by Salami Shedide, acknowledged that he was present at the murder.[8]

The suspects questioned at Nakhl received far more barbarous treatment, probably because the methods adopted were not observed by Charrington's and Gill's brothers and there was less possibility that they would become widely known.[9] As a result, the prisoners were 'broken' in just four days. During the first interrogation, the brothers Salem and Salami Abu Telhaideh denied that they were related and insisted they were dervishes, who had recently arrived in the district; Merceh el Rashdeh denied any involvement in the affair; and Ali Schwair only admitted that he had taken the message to Sheikh ibu Murshed instructing him to attack the party. On the second day, Salami Shedide was brought into the interrogation rooms and ordered each of the prisoners to confess – none did so. The following day, the interrogators made some progress, the Telhaideh brothers acknowledged that they had attacked the Englishmen and Ali Schwair declared that he was present at the murder, but then retracted the statement.

Warren was woken on the fourth day of interrogations by a strong cold wind, which during the morning developed into a vicious sandstorm so powerful that the party's tents had to be dismantled. At 1pm, at the height of the tumult, the prisoners, who had been questioned since sunrise, were dragged outside the fort, stripped of their clothing and placed in stocks, 'a huge wooden beam with holes for the feet', and informed that they would be left there to die unless they confessed. Impressively, they held out an hour before capitulating. Screaming that they would tell all, they were released, 'shivering and looking most miserable', and brought into the fort, where Ali Schwair and Salami Abu Telhaideh confessed to murder and Salem Abu Telhaideh admitted that he had incited the killings. Merceh el Rashdeh accepted that he was at the murder scene, but denied that he had killed anyone, though the others swore otherwise. Over the following few days, Warren, Haynes and Burton obtained full details of the murders and then wrote the three confessions, 'leaving out all that may be untrue' and any contradictions. These were then translated into Arabic and read to the prisoners, who were asked to sign them in the presence of the new Governor of Nakhl and his Chief Clerk. A few weeks later, Salim Sheyk signed a similar pre-written confession, as did Merceh el Rashdeh, when he confessed to murder during the Tanteh trial.[10]

Whether the five men hanged were guilty of their crimes is debateable. A number of witnesses had named the murderers and the headmen who had incited the killings, but this was only hearsay evidence; none of them had witnessed the decision to kill Palmer and his companions or the actual executions. Moreover, the Bedouin who had been brought to Suez by one of the Mount Sinai monks in early October and the sheikh questioned by Noel Temple Moore at Gaza had named completely different individuals as the murderers. Eyewitness testimony came from the ten-year-old boy, who Warren had interviewed at Nakhl and was subsequently released and therefore did not testify at the trial; one of the attackers, who claimed there were six rather than five murderers and later denied that he was at the scene of the murder; and the five men themselves, who implicated each other in their confessions. Salim Sheyk, however, changed his mind at the trial as to which of the three murder suspects were responsible for the deaths of Gill, Palmer and Gill's attendant and two of the uncaught murderers he identified were named by no other person. Merceh el Rasdeh, meanwhile, accused Sheyk of slaughtering Charrington, but on being told at the trial that the others disagreed, named another man and claimed that Sheyk had only been involved in the decision to kill the party. As regards the validity of the confessions, at the court marshal Salem Abu Telhaideh and Salim Sheyk retracted their admissions of guilt and all the confessions clearly state that the three Englishmen and their two servants were executed together, whereas the blood stain, which was found by Warren on the opposite side of the ravine, the existence of which was omitted from all the official reports, clearly indicates that at least one of the victims was killed later.

As regards the guilt of those not directly involved in the ambush and murder, Warren was convinced that Meter ibu Sofieh was in league with the attackers and created a convoluted account that explained his involvement. On first meeting Palmer, the old man had claimed to be the Chief of the Lehewat and that the tribe controlled the desert between Moses Wells and Misleh's camp in order to ensure that he was employed on the Professor's second foray into the desert and to gain his trust. Informed that this was to go ahead, he then deliberately failed to bring to Moses Wells the escort and camels requested. The group's ability to defend itself was thus lessened and the camels needed for the trip had to be hired, necessitating the diversion to his tents that delayed the progress of the party, giving the assailants more time to prepare themselves, and ensured that the ambush occurred in a locale where it was unlikely to be observed by other travellers, who could come to the Englishmen's aid or raise the alarm. Presented with a sword by Admiral Hewitt, he had given it to Sulieman Zahr's son for safekeeping either because he knew the party was to be attacked and it would be stolen or 'to relieve himself of the responsibilities of gratitude which the gift entailed'.[11]

At the start of the second mission, Sofieh passed the itinerary of the trip onto Salim ibu Subdeh on the beach at Moses Wells or perhaps when he returned to the town on the pretext of hiring another camel driver, and, on the theft of the camels, sent his nephew and others to recover them and allow the thieves to escape whilst the party waited for their return. The resultant delay gave the attackers even more time to organise and enabled him to split the group, further reducing its ability to defend itself. He then conducted the Englishmen to his camp at a leisurely pace so that the ambush occurred in near darkness and to allow Sheikh ibu Murshed to get his men into position. During the actual attack, as planned, he and his nephew escaped. His nephew rode to Marbrook, where he handed the £2,000 to the Governor of Nakhl, who then went to Sofieh's camp to give him his share. Sofieh, in the meantime, returned to the place of the attack. Unexpectedly finding the men unguarded, he deliberately delayed getting them away from the area until Murshed returned from plundering the baggage party or help had been obtained by the guard who had fled on his arrival. During the following conversation he refused to share the stolen money with the attackers, who furious at being double-crossed murdered the party.

At first sight, this theory appears plausible, but crumbles on further examination. Sofieh made no attempt to hide himself after the murders, on the contrary he appears to have toured the region and voluntarily gave himself up. He and his nephew never admitted any involvement in the affair, despite brutal cross-examination, during which they were 'bullied a great deal', and a last minute offer to the nephew that if he implicated his deceased uncle he would face no charges and would not be required to repay the money allegedly stolen. None of the attackers or murderers testified to Sofieh's guilt, and, although there were rumours that he was part of the conspiracy, other gossip exonerated him and Lieutenant Burton strongly believed 'he was straight', and, in an intriguing November entry in his diary, wrote 'things looked very black against old Sofieh as there was £2,000 unaccounted for, but our evidence since has rather cleared him'. The nature of the man also suggests that he was innocent. He possessed no nationalistic sympathies, had no need of £2,000, owning a camel hire business, palm groves and large flocks of camels, sheep and goats, and appears to have been in the early stages of dementia. He behaved extremely oddly during his interrogation and his imprisonment on HMS Carysfort and was judged by those who knew him to be 'light-headed and half-witted'; Richard Burton had heard he was 'almost insane'. His tendency to adopt an exalted status and introduce himself as the Sheikh of the Lehewat was well known and regarded by all as a symptom of his mental disorder.[12]

Moreover, there are glaring holes in Warren's thesis. All the decisions that increased the likelihood of attack that he attributed to Sofieh, would not have been made by a mere guide, but by the leader of the party. Palmer wrote in his diary during his journey to Suez that he made Sofieh and his guards respect him 'by always insisting on having my own way' and it was he who decided to travel to Nakhl via Wady Sudr, to send Bedouin to recover the stolen camels, to split the group and then to ride to his guide's camp at such a leisurely pace.[13] Having travelled through the region just over ten years earlier and an expert of the tribes of the area, it is inconceivable that he did not know that Sofieh was not the Chief of the Lehewat, that the tribe did not control the area between Moses Wells and Misleh's camp/Nakhl and that he was putting his companions at great risk by not employing the true headman of the region as his guide and his tribesmen as camel drivers.

Palmer's other actions are equally incomprehensible. Before leaving England, he alerted Wilfrid Blunt, a well known supporter of Arabi, to his departure for Egypt and revealed every aspect of his mission to Blunt's close friend Walter Besant. On his journey to Alexandria, he befriended a war artist for the *Illustrated London News*, even allowing him to draw his portrait, thus alerting his presence to the press. Rather than discussing a pact with the British with all the sheikhs as he claimed, he intended to make an agreement with just one, Sheikh Suileman, who he was well aware was untrustworthy and did not represent the other Bedouin chiefs. In the event, he made the deal with Suileman's brother, Sheikh Misleh, if possible an even greater scoundrel, who agreed to arrange for the Suez tribes to provide the British with 50,000 fighters, even though both he and Palmer knew that there were not that number of men in the entire desert. Once back in Suez, he divulged details of his first mission to an Arabi spy and his plans for the second mission to Walter Besant; adopted an unbelievable cover story; chose to meet Misleh at Nakhl rather than at his encampment, even though Nakhl was a hotbed of nationalism reached via a well-used route and he and the Sheikh intended to then to travel to the camp; sent a note to Sofieh asking for an escort and camels, well aware that the old man was illiterate and that he would receive neither; decided to forego an escort; packed inadequate weaponry; and, after receiving the £3,000, paraded it around town for all to see. When he and his companions were attacked, he virtually surrendered, and, on their detention, made no attempt to escape, even though they were guarded by just one Bedouin and were unbound and unhurt, and, on the arrival of Sofieh and his fellow rescuers, allowed the old man to waste valuable time fussing over them.

Justifications for Palmer's strange behaviour abounded. Like Warren, Walter Besant believed the main villain to be Meter ibu Sofieh and that Palmer's 'noble spirit' and relationship with the Bedouin had caused him to go along with the guide's decisions. His friend 'could conceive little in humanity to dread and refused to regard the tendency of mankind towards double-dealing and villainy' and was convinced that his Arab acquaintances regarded him as 'one of them' and would never act in any way that harmed him. Richard Burton maintained that he had simply gone mad – that the 'laborious desert march through the fiery heats of July…affected [his]…strong clear brain'. Others suggested he was suffering from a terminal illness and thus cared little about the risks of the expedition – prior to leaving England an asthma attack had caused him to take three weeks off work – or that his actions constituted a bizarre form of suicide.[14]

Another explanation is that Palmer was secretly pro-Arabi and wished his mission to fail in order to increase the chances of a nationalist victory. He was certainly sympathetic to Islam, indeed may have been a secret believer, and, according to Besant, 'spoke as [an Arab] and thought as one…[possessing] that strange sympathy which enables its possessor to feel with as well as for his friends'.[15] However, he never expressed any affinity with the nationalistic cause, Blunt both publicly and privately regarded him as a British stooge and he had a low opinion of the Bedouin, who carried with them 'ruin, violence and neglect'.[16]

A more likely interpretation of his actions is that he always knew that a deal with the Bedouin was an impossibility, but was unwilling to reveal the fact to the Admiralty. On his first journey into the desert, he therefore created a phoney agreement that he knew would never come to fruition, but would lead to the second mission, the delivery of the bribes. On this expedition, he made sure that he would be captured by Bedouin or Arabi forces, which would allow him to steal some of the money he had been given, and, after the goal of the mission had been changed, would enable him to avoid facing the wrath of Sheikh Misleh when he realised that the agreement they had made in the desert was not to be honoured.

To the Admiralty and his friends, Palmer was a wealthy man; earning a high salary as 'Arabic Professor at Cambridge [and]…in receipt of a considerable income from literary work'. In reality, when he agreed to go to Egypt he was close to bankruptcy; the rent on his grand house was twelve months in arrears and he had failed even to pay the undertaker who had buried his first wife.[17] When he died, his second wife and children were destitute, forced to rely on the kindness of friends. The large debts were the result of a series of unfortunate incidents. In 1872, at the age of 57, the aunt who had brought him up after the death of his parents married Samuel Straker, a 64-year-old widower and owner of S. Straker & Sons, a printer of government publications, and had moved to her new husband's palatial house in Peckham. Unable to continue to oversee the operations of the Hoop Hotel, she appointed as its manager her other nephew, William Palmer, who shared with his cousin a restless nature and a tendency to be economical with the truth. Bored with life as a printer's apprentice, at the age of twenty he had supposedly decamped to Italy, where he became an officer in Garibaldi's army and fought at the battle of Calatafimi, before returning to London and working in a series of hotels and restaurants. Newly appointed the Lord Almoner Reader at Cambridge University, Palmer gave his aunt some of his life savings on the understanding that her husband would invest the money and eventually return the capital and the interest. Unfortunately, just three years after her marriage, his aunt died. Palmer, not unreasonably expected the return of his money plus a portion of her estate, his aunt having assured him that her niece and both of her nephews were the main beneficiaries of her will. He received neither. Her assets were left to her husband, who fifteen minutes after his wife's death suffered a fatal heart attack. His estate was left to his son and daughter, who had no intention of sharing their legacy with the relatives of a stepmother they despised. Palmer thus lost both his inheritance and part of his savings.[18]

More bad luck was to follow. Straker's children offered to sell the Hoop Hotel to Palmer's cousin, William Palmer, who lacked the necessary funds to purchase the inn. Seeing an opportunity to recoup his losses and wishing to help the relative who had partly funded his undergraduate education, Palmer lent him the remainder of his savings. Initially, his cousin prospered. The takings of the Hoop Hotel rose and William decided to expand his business empire by buying the Queens Hotel, Aberystwyth. Located on the promenade and offering 63 bedrooms plus a library and coffee, dining, smoking and billiard rooms, it was one of the town's largest hotels. Believing that the fruit and vegetables he purchased were overly expensive, he next bought a market garden just outside Aberystwyth, which supplied all the resort's hotels. As was common in the Victorian era, these acquisitions were purchased with loans from friends and relatives, including Palmer.[19]

Disaster struck in 1877. A number of poor seasons had decimated the number of visitors to Aberystwyth. Like its competitors, the Queens Hotel struggled to attract guests, the demand for fruit and vegetables plummeted, and, in September, William Palmer declared himself bankrupt. Both hotels and the market garden were sold and the proceeds used to pay the creditors.[20] Palmer received nothing. The loss could not have come at a worst time. Desperate for his first wife to live, Palmer employed the best doctors and nurses, booked her into the most luxurious Bournemouth and Paris hotels, the prestigious Hotel du Globe in the French capital, and visited her often, travelling to and from Cambridge. As the costs mounted, his income fell – the commuting and the anxiety resulting from his wife's illness forced him to halt his legal work and curtailed his literary output. Salvation came from his friend John Radclyff Pretyman, who lent him a sum of money sufficient to clear most of his debts. The relief, however, proved short-lived. Two months before Palmer's first wife's demise, Pretyman died. Although Palmer's daughter was a beneficiary of his will to the tune of £1,000, he was left only a painting and a pear pin and Pretyman's heir, his stepbrother Richard, demanded the repayment of the loan.[21]

Given that he was deep in debt, one would have thought that Palmer would have attempted to get his finances in order. In the event, he never even took 'the trouble to ascertain …the amount standing to the credit at the bank and would show you with a smile, as if it was a curious and amusing thing, a cheque of his own which had just been returned with "no effects" stamped upon it'. He continued to socialise with friends with private incomes and lucrative careers, and, not wishing them to be aware of his relative penury, matched their extravagances, staying at the best hotels, hosting grand dinners on his visits to London, dressing in well tailored clothes and giving expensive Christmas and birthday gifts. After his second marriage, his profligacy escalated. Large and luxurious houses in Swiss Cottage and Bloomsbury were rented and holidays taken in France and Germany. Eventually, his debts were such that he was forced to act. In January 1880, he sequestrated some of his income and his life insurance policies; the salaries he obtained from his Cambridge fellowship and readership plus the dividends derived from two £1,000 insurance policies were assigned to a trustee, who held them in trust for the payment of past and future creditors.[22]

Palmer's decision to give up his university career and move into journalism was financial suicide. Expecting to obtain more from his new occupation than from teaching, he actually earned far less, and, on that fateful day in June 1882 when Lieutenant William Gill called on him, he was close to insolvency. The Admiralty, believing him to be independently wealthy, offered no salary for the first mission and the patriotic academic did not request one. It was unbecoming for a gentleman to demand recompense for helping his country in its hour of need and he hoped that the successful completion of his task would result in a permanent appointment or at least a bestselling book describing how he had risked his life for the glory of Empire. He also planned to appropriate some of the money given to him to complete his assignment.

Before departing on his first expedition, Palmer was given expenses of £500. In his report on his time in the desert, he claimed that he had spent almost the whole sum, having given 'exorbitant sums in backshish, payment for escorts etc'. Indeed, his funds were so low towards the end of the mission that he was forced to cancel a meeting with the sheikhs of the Towarah tribe. In reality, he had spent less than half of his expenses, a mere £220. To avoid large expenditure, he had visited only Sheikh Misleh rather than the 27 chiefs he claimed to have called upon and had economised in other ways. Sofieh received no fee for allowing him to pass through his supposed territory and acting as a guide. During his stay in Jaffa, rather than booking into the Jerusalem Hotel, as he later claimed, he lodged with the Reverend Alexander Schapira, who risked his son's life by sending him to Sheikh Suileman with a message requesting a meeting. Generosity that was rewarded with a brief note from the Professor 'conveying his thanks'. Palmer exalted at his cleverness. He wrote in his journal on July 22nd 'I shall save £280 out of this, which is not a bad month's work!' and four days later 'I still have nearly £300 left…that is better than newspaper work, £300 in a month!'. He even considered demanding additional expenses: 'I have been so successful that I shall write for more money saying I have been obliged to spend all mine on presents – a few hundred pounds is a great deal to us and nothing to the government, who would I know have given thousands for what I have already done. Of course I shall make the most of the difficulties'.[23]

Having successfully made a reasonable return from his first expedition, Palmer no doubt intended to make even more from the second mission. His plan was simple. He would exaggerate the number of fighters he could recruit in order to maximise the sum he would be allocated to buy off the sheikhs. Only a small proportion of this money would accompany him into the desert, where it would be stolen by the Bedouin, who given his 'mistakes' were almost certain to attack the party, and, following their own customs and fear of blood feuds, would release its members on obtaining the 'ransom' – the small amount of money the party carried.[24] On Palmer's non-appearance at Nakhl, Misleh would refuse to help the British cause and the Sheikh's ability to act as an intermediary to the other Bedouin tribes would never be tested. The scheme began to falter when the Admiralty at the last minute altered the goals of the mission, which significantly reduced the likely return, but no doubt made

Palmer even more determined to carry it out; the possible reaction of Misleh on discovering that their agreement was not to be fulfilled did not bear thinking about. It collapsed for three reasons: the nephew escaped with the £1,000 he had taken into the desert, Meter ibu Sofieh refused to hand it over when he went to negotiate the Englishmen's release, and the attackers, unbeknown to Palmer, had been given the option of killing the party.

Whether Warren suspected that it was Palmer who stole the £2,000 is not known. Given that he read the journals he recovered, could find no evidence that the £3,000 was taken into the desert, and was well aware that the intrepid academic had done everything in his power to ensure that his party was captured, it seems reasonable to conclude that he did. If so, he failed to share his suspicions – perhaps to protect a fellow freemason or Palmer's wife, at the request of Walter Besant, who he knew slightly, or, more likely, to avoid drawing further attention to a mission that had been unethical from the start.[25]

Warren certainly knew that the attack on the party had been organised by Salami Shedide. A view also held by Lieutenants Haynes and Burton, Charrington's brother, Walter Besant and almost every Bedouin between Suez and Nakhl. Yet he made no attempt to prosecute Salami. His explanation, a lack of evidence, was disingenuous. It was true that all of the apprehended attackers and murderers denied they had received orders from the Sheikh – no doubt out of loyalty or fear of what would happen to themselves and their families if they revealed all – and that Meter ibu Sofieh, who had suggested the Shedides' involvement, was dead. On the other hand, Warren possessed the letter from the Governor of Nakhl to his Akabah counterpart, which implicated the family in the murders and Sheikh Sualem Abu Farag, who had revealed that Salami had ordered him to co-ordinate the attack and had been given immunity from prosecution, was very much alive. Warren, however, had effectively silenced him by placing his son, who he had taken hostage to ensure his co-operation, in the custody of Sard Shedide's uncle, which had given the family a hold over the Sheikh and had later led to his disappearance; Farag agreeing to abscond and thus not testify against the family in return for his son's freedom. Furthermore, Warren would probably have had all the evidence he supposedly so desired had he simply dismissed Sard Shedide from the hunt for the killers on learning that he was attempting to cover up his family's involvement and refused the assistance of Salami and not given him free-reign in the rounding up of the guilty parties in his December 1882 agreement with the Sheikh.

The real reason for Salami's freedom was nothing to do with the absence of proof. It was that neither the Khedive nor the British government wished his involvement to emerge; hence he, his brother's and Farag's recruitment to the search party. The Egyptian administration needed the great Sheikh's continued support – his wealth and influence having given him 'control' of all the Bedouin tribes – and the revelation of his connection to the killings would have confirmed that the deaths were an act of war and prevented the trial and execution of the murderers. He thus went free; continuing to live in Cairo and growing ever richer as his tribe extended their territory into Northern Sinai.[26]

Warren was similarly reluctant to connect the Governor of Nakhl to the murders; the official was found guilty only of leaving his post without permission and failing to report the attack. Again there was probably sufficient evidence to convict – the boast to Moussa's messenger that he had killed the men 'with his own hand' and his presence in the desert when the attack occurred. No charges were brought, as, in doing so, Warren would have implicated the Shedides.

There was far less proof against the Governor of El Arish - only the strong suspicion of Mr Pickard, the man sent to Gaza to cut the telegraph and investigate the disappearance of the party, that Cairo's message to the Hawetat tribe had been relayed through the Governor and that he had altered its contents, informing Sheikh ibu Murshed, via Nakhl's Governor, that the Palmer party should be brought in dead or alive rather than merely apprehended. Warren had discounted the supposition, which Pickard later put in writing, again fearing that the prosecution of the Governor would drag the Shedides into the case. The Foreign Office, however, thought differently. At the conclusion of the court marshal, Warren had expected to be redeployed; it had been suggested that he and his doughty lieutenants would spend their remaining time in Egypt measuring the Great Pyramid. In the event, they were ordered by Sir Edward Malet to travel to El Arish with Pickard to discover evidence that its ex-governor had supported Arabi during the war and/or was connected to the murder of the Palmer party. There was no suggestion that any proof collected would be used to prosecute the Governor, only that Malet believed that the possession of such information against such 'an important man' could prove 'useful'.[27]

On Pickard's arrival in Alexandria, where Warren was now based, the mystery as to why he had delegated the task of cutting the telegraph line to local Bedouin was finally solved. After booking into his hotel, the telegraph engineer became seriously ill, and, on a doctor being called, it was discovered that he had taken an overdose of morphine and that he was a regular user of the drug. Such addiction was not uncommon in Victorian times, though the majority of users were female. Opium was cheap, an ounce of laudanum costing no more than a pint of beer, could easily be purchased over the counter from pharmacists and was regarded as a cure-all for a variety of diseases and the relief of pain.[28] Determined to continue with his mission, Warren decided to travel to El Arish without Pickard, and, three days later, set sail with Haynes and Burton, an interpreter and three servants and the names of three residents who the engineer had assured him had helped the Governor arrange the attack on the Englishmen.

On arrival at the town, which comprised a number of clay houses and a dilapidated fortress situated around a mile from the coast, Warren found himself embroiled in a quite different affair. He rapidly discovered that the new Turkish governor, who was visiting the nearby settlement of El Kantara, was conducting a reign of terror on the local population in revenge for his own rough treatment at the hands of nationalists during the war. Marriage, circumcision and burial ceremonies and meetings at which the Koran was read had all been banned and anyone suspected of harbouring Arabi sympathies had been imprisoned and tortured. Warren immediately telegraphed details of his findings to Cairo, only for the Governor's son, who had taken over his father's role while he was away, to order that he and his companions be confined to their tents, which were surrounded by armed guards. Fearing that the Governor on his return would exact retribution, Warren decided to mount a one-man coup d'art. He and his lieutenants marched to the fort and ordered the commander of the artillery to gather the officials and sheikhs of the municipality. Somewhat surprised, he complied. When they had assembled, Warren waved a sheet of paper, which he claimed to be a proclamation from the Khedive, and announced that he had been sent to the fort by the Egyptian government to depose the existing governor and appoint the artillery commander in his stead. Remarkably, the rouse worked. The governor's son was arrested, and, the following day, a party of soldiers were dispatched to El Kantara to apprehend his father.

Having rid the town of tyranny, Warren turned his attention to the true purpose of the mission. Alas, his efforts to find evidence connecting the old Governor to Arabi or implicating him in the Palmer murders were in vain. None of the three men named by Pickard lived in the town and the new Governor had been ordered by the Khedive to send all of his predecessor's correspondence, including many compromising documents, to Cairo, where they had disappeared. The local Bedouin similarly were reluctant to help, blaming the terrors of the previous few months on the British, though they did disclose that the old Governor, on discovering that Pickard had arranged the cutting of the telegraph line, had offered a reward of £50 to anyone who brought him the engineer's head. Suspecting that Pickard's accusations may have been motivated by animosity, Warren on his return to Alexandria, investigated the three men he had named, discovering that one had supported the British during the war and that the others had not even been in the region when Palmer and his companions were attacked.

Chapter 17

Charles Warren: Post-Search Life

On his return to England from Egypt, Warren was inundated with honours. The Egyptian government awarded him the Khedive's Star and the Turks the insignia of the order of the Madjide. He became a Knight of Justice of the Order of St John of Jerusalem and a Fellow of the Royal Society and received the ultimate accolade of the British establishment – a Knighthood. A rumoured Victoria Cross failed to materialise. The esteem was accepted with a modesty befitting an officer and a gentleman. After a few months leave, during which he recuperated and wrote an article describing the natural features of the landscape he had traversed on his search for Palmer, Warren quietly resumed his duties as Chief Instructor of Surveying at the School of Military Engineering at Chatham. In his spare time, he helped to establish and became the first Master of the Quatur Coronati Freemasons lodge, whose members researched the history of freemasonry.[1]

He soon became bored, and, in early 1884, volunteered to travel to Abyssinia to negotiate the release of Major-General Gordon, who was besieged at Khartoum by the Mahdi. Believing that a military solution was more likely to secure the General's freedom, the War Office turned down his offer. Relief came later in the year when he was made the Commander of a military expedition to Bechuanaland, where six years earlier he had fought the Balaros and Batlapin tribes. Since then, Boers, supported by the Dutch republic of Transvaal, had entered the country and seized from the Tswana tribes large tracts of land that they had named Stellaland and Goshenland. To the British, the land grab contravened an 1884 agreement with the Transvaal government in which its President, Paul Kruger, had accepted that the region was under UK protection, and was a blatant attempt by the Boers to expand their borders, take control of the trade route from Cape Colony to Central Africa and scupper the planned Cape to Cairo railway. The Stellalanders after meeting with Cecil Rhodes, the founder of Rhodesia and the diamond company De Beers, then a member of the Cape Parliament, accepted the region was a British protectorate, though only in return for the recognition of their titles to the stolen land. The Goshenites, however, remained intransigent, and, when the Transvaal annexed the area, clearly breaching the 1884 agreement, the British dispatched a military expedition to eject the Boers by force.[2]

The expedition set off from Hope Town on 19th December 1884. Led by Warren, who was accompanied by Alfred Haynes, newly promoted to Captain, it comprised 4,000 men, three batteries of field artillery and a battery of Gardner machine guns. At the border between the Cape and Goshen, Warren met with Kruger, who refused to back down. The expedition thus marched into the disputed territory, laying down a 220 mile long telegraph line and establishing food stores as it went. Expecting a series of great battles, Warren was disappointed to find nary a single Boer in the entire region; hearing of his arrival all had fled. The expeditionary force thus spent its time patrolling the frontier to ensure that the filibusters did not return, and, for the first time in the field, deployed an observation balloon, enabling the horizon to be scanned over a radius of up to thirty miles. To relieve the monotony, the officers indulged in their passion for shooting and the ordinary soldiers found solace in drink and relationships with local African women.[3]

Having gained control of the territory, Warren turned his attention to its future. Encouraged by John Mackenzie, the ex-Resident Commissioner, he proposed that much of Bechuanaland become a Crown Colony. Rhodes and Hercules Robinson, the Governor of Cape, were appalled. Wishing their own colony to retain some control of the region and claiming that the introduction of colonial government would be costly and impractical, they favoured the creation of a protectorate. A very public argument then ensued that rapidly descended into mutual hatred, particularly between Warren and Rhodes. The two men had first met in 1877 when they had shared a coach from Port Elizabeth to Griqualand West and discussed Man's place in the Universe.[4] Warren had been impressed by the earnest young man, declaring him the 'most fascinating person he had ever met'. Seven years later, his opinion had changed. Appalled by his liking for alcohol and his dress sense, he wore 'the shabbiest and most ragged of coats and a very dirty pair of white flannel trousers with old tennis shoes as his foot gear', he believed the deal with the Stellalands was unfair and profoundly disagreed with Rhodes' belief that the land rights of indigenous Africans should be subordinate to those of white settlers. In the event, the British government acquiesced to the wishes of both sides of the colony/protectorate argument – making the area north of the Molopo river a protectorate and that south of the river the Crown Colony of British Bechuanaland.[5]

Warren was recalled in September 1885 and again proclaimed a hero. The press hailed him 'the Saviour of Bechuanaland' and he was appointed a Knight Grand Cross of the order of St Michael and St George. This was the apex of his career; the following twenty years would be blighted by a series of failures and end in ignominy. His downward trajectory began when the Liberal party asked him to be their Sheffield Hallam candidate in the Autumn 1885 election. Warren accepted with alacrity, though insisted he stand as an independent Liberal, a decision that contributed to his defeat; the Liberal constituents were not prepared to vote for an independent and objected to his somewhat curious manifesto, which laid great stress on Christian morality and Empire.[6]

In standing for Parliament, Warren had incurred the wrath of

General Sir Garnet Wolseley, the commander of the forces that invaded Egypt in 1882 and Adjutant-General of the British army, who had asked him to give up his candidacy on the grounds that he had not received permission to stand and it would be impossible to combine the professions of soldier and politician. Warren had refused, even when warned that he would never be given another military appointment if he did not comply, and, on his defeat, paid the price of his defiance. He was appointed military commander of Suakin, a port in north eastern Sudan, the military equivalent of being sent to outer Siberia. Angry at this snub, he nonetheless embarked for the port, where he proceeded to re-organise the garrison, protect the town from the desert Arabs, who were in the habit of firing into its streets at night, and increasing its trade with the surrounding region. In the event, he was to remain in the Sudan for a mere two months, for in March 1886 he was offered and accepted the post of Chief Commissioner of the London Metropolitan Police. Warren's predecessor as Commissioner, Sir Edmund Henderson, had resigned following criticism of his handling of a Trafalgar Square demonstration.[7] The Home Secretary, Hugh Childers, had cast around for a replacement and chose Warren after considering over 400 other candidates. It had become a tradition to select the Heads of Scotland Yard from the military and Childers, as Secretary of War during the Egyptian campaign, had first-hand experience of the new appointee's organisational and investigation skills.

Warren's period in office was dogged by a number of scandals and was to last just two years. The first embarrassment was the Cass affair. In 1887, a Miss Elizabeth Cass, a young seamstress, was arrested for soliciting in Regent Street. Her employer testified in her favour when the next morning she appeared at Great Marlborough Street Police Court, and the Magistrate found her not guilty. Her false arrest was taken up by the press and Parliament and the reputation of the police was severely damaged, even though a private prosecution against the arresting officer failed and a police investigation into the incident found his actions to be justified. Concerned that the affair had caused the public to lose trust in the force, Warren sought to rectify the situation by prohibiting the arrest of any street walker unless a complaint had been made against her or the constable possessed corroborating evidence. An initiative that only succeeded in further debasing public confidence; 'ladies-of-the-night' became so emboldened that it became impossible to walk down certain streets in broad daylight without being propositioned and the police were criticised for allowing prostitution to get out of control.[8]

A second fiasco was a demonstration that became known as 'Bloody Sunday'. Aware of the fate of his predecessor, Warren had banned all meetings in Trafalgar Square, only to see his decision reversed by the Home Secretary and then by the courts as illegal. On Sunday 13th November 1887, therefore, a march of 20-50,000 men, women and children protesting against unemployment and events in Ireland went ahead. Aware that there could be trouble, Warren positioned 2,000 constables and two squadrons of soldiers around Trafalgar Square, the destination of the march, and a further 3,000 constables and another cavalry squadron in the surrounding streets. The first battles occurred even before the marchers arrived in central London; an incident on Westminster Bridge left 26 demonstrators in hospital. When the protestors finally assembled in the Square, Warren appeared in full uniform and on horseback 'raised his hand to secure silence and for a space of several hundred feet around him there was a pause, a silence so terrible that it seemed like a vacuum in which one could not breathe'. A Magistrate read the riot act, a bugle sounded and the police charged the crowd, supported by 200 mounted cavalrymen. 'Sir Charles looked the picture of dignity and sorrow'. In the ensuing violence, over 200 demonstrators were injured and at least one and perhaps two subsequently died. The following day, the press accused Warren of heavy handedness, the denial of free speech and murder, erroneously claiming that the military had been ordered 'to shoot down the unarmed bread earners of London in cold blood'.[9]

A third blot on Warren's reputation was the murder of six women in Whitechapel by a serial killer who the press christened 'Jack the Ripper'. Critics of the police blamed the lack of progress in discovering the perpetrator on inadequate policing of the area, a new system of deployment whereby constables were moved from district-to-district and the failure to offer a reward and use bloodhounds in the search. Criticisms that were either false – no new system of constable deployment had been introduced, and, after the first murders, Whitechapel was swamped with constables – or misrepresentations. Although Warren was initially against offering a reward, he later changed his mind, but was blocked by the Home Secretary, and bloodhounds had not been used as tests had shown that they were unable to follow trails through crowded city streets.[10]

Ironically, Warren's ultimate downfall was the result not of press criticism, but his failure to form good relations with colleagues and his own vindictive nature. On the defeat of the Liberal party in the 1886 election, Hugh Childers was replaced as Home Secretary by the Conservative Henry Matthews, who had a strong antipathy towards Liberals, possessed a sarcastic and patronising manner that exasperated even the mildest of individuals and rejected his predecessor's view that the Commissioner should be given a free hand in the manner he managed the police. He and Warren clashed over a range of issues, including the prohibition of meetings in Trafalgar Square, the provision of a reward for the capture of the Whitechapel murderer and the finance of the force; Matthews and his staff opposing Warren's proposals for an improved police pension scheme, better control of expenditure and the adoption of a more accurate accounting system.[11]

His relationship with Henry Munro, the Assistant

Commissioner and leader of the Criminal Investigation Division (CID), if possible, was even worse than that with the Home Secretary. Their antagonism arose from Munro's belief that he should have been appointed Commissioner; his millennialism, the belief in the imminent second coming of Christ, which Warren disparaged; and fundamental differences regarding the nature of policing. Whereas Warren believed the force should deter crime through constables pounding the beat, Munro contended that it should solve crimes through detection. An even more damaging bone of contention was the management of the Special Branch, a unit of the metropolitan force formed in 1883 to keep covert surveillance on anarchists, Irish terrorists and possible revolutionaries. Financed from Imperial funds, the department was led by Munro, who was responsible for its actions, not to Warren, but to the Home Secretary.[12]

The collapse of their relationship was largely the result of Warren's determination to seize control of the Special Branch, and, if possible, rid himself of his subordinate. In May 1888, he informed the Home Secretary that the CID was badly administered because Munro devoted too much time to his Special Branch activities. To solve the problem, he proposed that the control of the Branch be transferred to himself. When this request was turned down, he began to interfere in the day-to-day operations of the CID and increased his assistant's workload. The breaking point for Munro was Warren's reorganisation of the command structure of the force. Following the recommendations of the committee established to investigate the riot that had led to the resignation of his predecessor, Warren created three new Assistant Commissioner and two new Chief Constable posts, all of which were filled by ex-army officers. Munro objected to the creation of the new posts, opposed the employment of candidates with no experience of policing and was dismayed when Warren refused to employ as Chief Constable of the CID his close friend Melville Macnaghten on the spurious grounds that he had been 'beaten by hindoos' ie. attacked by land rioters during his service in India.[13]

Announcing that his boss had made his life 'intolerable', Munro offered his resignation to the Home Secretary. Fearful that it would not be accepted, Warren offered his own resignation, making it clear that he would only stay if Munro went. Matthews decided in favour of Warren, fearful of the political consequences of his departure and the press outcry that would result if the officer in charge of the Ripper investigation quit. Warren's victory, however, proved pyrrhic. Munro was made a special advisor to the Home Secretary, given a desk in the Home Office and retained his position as Head of the Special Branch. His replacement, Robert Anderson, who was transferred from the Special Branch and like his old boss was a millennialist, remained loyal to Munro, informing him of his enemy's every move.[14]

Warren's days in the post were now numbered. As criticism of the police mounted and extended to new gripes, such as the rise in the number of burglaries and the enforcement of the law that required the muzzling of dogs, the Home Secretary waited for an excuse to force him out. It appeared in November of that year. An anodyne essay by Warren on the management and discipline of the Metropolitan Police was published in *Murray's Magazine*, one of many such articles he had written over the previous two years. On hearing of the essay from Munro, Matthew wrote Warren a curt letter pointing out that he had broken a Home Office rule that no individual employed by the government should publish any material relating to his official duties without the sanction of the Home Secretary. As intended, Warren took the letter as a direct attack on his independence and character and immediately resigned to be replaced a few weeks later by none other than James Munro.[15]

Warren's swift ejection from the Metropolitan Police threw him back into the arms of General Sir Garnet Wolseley, who had opposed him taking the Commissioner post for the same reason he had been against him becoming an MP. Warren was made the Commandant of the Royal Engineers' depot at Shorncliffe and then appointed Commander of the military garrison at Singapore, a posting as demeaning as his Suakin position three years previously. His new role was doomed before he even arrived in Singapore. There had been a long disagreement between the civil authorities and the military as to who would pay for the construction of the fortifications that the British government insisted were necessary to protect the city's coaling station. The military contended that the scheme should be financed by the colony. The Governor argued that the money should come from the Imperial Treasury, as the 1867 agreement that had conferred Crown Colony status on the region had clearly stated that its government was financially responsible for its own defence, but not for expenses defrayed for the protection of the Empire.

Warren's instructions were to construct the new fortifications, and, on arrival, he drew up extensive plans and asked the local government to provide the necessary finance. The Governor refused on the grounds that the purpose of the works was to protect a coaling station required for the defence of the Empire, the new scheme was too grandiose and the colony simply did not possess the requisite funds, due to a fall in the demand for opium, which had reduced sales and tax revenues. There then followed a fierce disagreement between the two men that led to each writing a series of letters to the Colonial Office and the military authorities protesting at the other's behaviour. Unfortunately for Warren, his military superior was his old enemy Redvers Buller, who tended to blame the situation on the man who had so grievously insulted him in the Southern Cape eleven years previously. In a private letter to his subordinate, Buller wrote 'I am bound to say that you seem to make a good many of the pricks for yourself…[and] I earnestly counsel that you get on better with [the Governor]'.[16] The fortifications eventually were constructed and financed by the local government, though for a time Warren became the most hated man in the colony, ostracised by its polite society. Caring little, he went about his duties, and, in his spare time, helped to form a philosophical society, became the District Grand Master of the Eastern Archipelago of Freemasons and travelled extensively – visiting India, Burma, Ceylon, Siam, Japan, Java and some of the seaports of China.

He was recalled to England in April 1894, returning via Vancouver and the United States, where he spent some weeks exploring the 'wild' west. After a year with no employment, he was made Commander of the Thames District, but almost immediately disgraced himself. He had insisted that during the annual manoeuvres his soldiers carry a heavy kit. On the day of the manoeuvres, a number of men collapsed and his officers remonstrated with him for the kit to be lightened. Warren refused, and, presumably to prove his point, donned the uniform and entire kit of a nearby soldier, which he was still wearing when he took the salute of a nonplussed Duke of Connaught. The incident, plus his tendency to be 'impossible' and 'quarrel with everyone', was reported to the Secretary of State for War, who decided to take no action, despite demands that he be reprimanded or dismissed.[17] Warren thus retained his post, but two years later retired; he and his wife moving to a small house on the seafront at Ramsgate.

In the best of all possible worlds, his retirement would have marked the end of his military and public careers. Unfortunately, the outbreak of the Boer War the following year caused him to be recalled to active service. For some reason, never fully explained, he was given the command of the Fifth Division of the South African Field Force and joined the staff of the commander of the allied army, Redvers Buller. To say the least, Buller was not overjoyed to hear that Warren was about to join him. He regarded his new subordinate as a bad-tempered martinet and was concerned at his relative lack of fighting experience; his staff referring to him as 'the ex-policeman'. He also saw him as a potential rival. Warren had been given a dormant commission and was destined to replace him if he became incapacitated or more ominously relieved of his command. The latter was more than a possibility, as his first battle of the war had been less than successful. Attempting to cross the Tugela river at Colenso to relieve the besieged town of Ladysmith, his men had been cut down by a small number of Boers armed with the latest Mauser rifles and field guns.[18]

The relationship between the two men fractured even before Warren reached South Africa. En route he discovered that Buller had countermanded the order that he was to take command of the campaign to relieve the town of Kimberley. Instead, he was to attempt a second crossing of the Tugela river at Trikhardt's Drift; Buller being loath to lead the mission himself for fear of another defeat. The operation was a catastrophe. When the vanguard of Warren's 13,300 force arrived at the drift, it was guarded by barely 600 Boers, positioned four miles away in the foothills overlooking the river valley. A more experienced commander would have sent his cavalry across the river to over-run the guards or hold them at bay until the infantry arrived, and, in the meantime, got the rest of his men over the Tugela as quickly as possible and then rapidly advanced towards Ladysmith. Warren adopted a different approach. Arriving at the river, he decided that it could only be traversed via pontoon bridges; a conclusion later questioned by his own officers, who insisted that the water was sufficiently shallow for the cavalry, and, if life lines had been used, the infantry to cross. Moreover, he decreed that his force would not advance towards Ladysmith until every last member, including the baggage train, had safely reached the other side. Both decisions were disastrous. The crossing took a remarkable 37 hours, during which time the Boers rushed fighters into the area. Exasperated by the slow progress, the Earl of Dundonald, leader of 1,500 cavalry, on his own initiative advanced, somehow outflanked the enemy and discovered a pass that led directly to Ladysmith. Requesting that infantry should be rapidly brought up and the town taken, Dundonald was dumbfounded when he was ordered to return to the river on the grounds that his men were needed to guard the baggage and the Boers were probably attempting to lead the British into a trap.

Having finally got his column over the Tugela, Warren finally advanced, but on noticing the accumulation of a large number of Boers on Tabanyama Ridge, a crest overlooking his route, returned his men to the bridgehead, fearing that they were too vulnerable to attack. Dismissing the suggestion that he should take a longer route to Ladysmith and thus circumvent the Boer position on the grounds that such a manoeuvre would dangerously extend his supply lines, he decided to make a full frontal attack on the ridge. Thus, the following dawn, several thousand infantry advanced on the Boer trenches, only to be stopped in their tracks by withering fire. As at Trikhardt's Drift, the situation could have been saved by the Earl of Dundonald, who noticed that the British troops were additionally being shot at from a nearby hill, and, again on his own initiative, took some men to the summit, which he found to be unoccupied. Warren was asked to send reinforcements to fire on the Boers lower down the hill and on Tabanyama Ridge, but deigned to reply. The next morning, the attack on the ridge was resumed. Despite accurate rifle fire, the infantry were making good progress when they were suddenly recalled; Warren feared that if the assault continued he would suffer heavy casualties. Ironically, at that very moment, the Boers, short of food and medical supplies, had begun to retreat and had Warren not lost his nerve he would have gained a famous though undeserved victory.

It was Warren's next decision that destroyed his career and reputation. He came to the conclusion that the only way to take Tabanyama Ridge was to first secure a steeply rising hill that overlooked it from the east. Having captured the peak, field guns would be dragged to the summit and would fire down onto the Boer positions on the Ridge. The hill was called Spion Kop and was to be the site of one of the most inglorious defeats in the history of the British army.[19] Rather than immediately carrying out his plan, Warren postponed the action for 24 hours, to allow a reconnoitre of the approaches to the mount and to rest his men; a delay that allowed the Boers to regroup. Finally, shortly after dark on 23rd January, 1,700 troops commanded by Major General Edward Woodgate began the ascent using a handy goat path. At 4am, they were fired upon by a small number Boers. Keeping his head, Woodgate waited until the enemy needed to reload and then charged. One Boer was bayoneted and the rest fled.

It was at this point that the error that lost the battle was made. Woodgate believed that he had reached the crest of the hill. He was mistaken. A mere 200 yards ahead there was a further ascent that led to three mounds, known as the forward crest, Aloe Knoll and conical hill. Warren had failed to reconnoitre the hill itself, merely having a drawing made from ground level, from where it appeared to be topped by a plateau. Believing the sketch to be accurate and failing to notice the three crests in the darkness and mist, Woodgate ordered the digging of trenches. Unfortunately, the ground was hard and the unit had been given just twenty picks and shovels. After three hours, they had thus only managed to excavate a very shallow trench, along the top of which they built an 18 inch wall of stones and soil; Warren having forgotten to provide them with sandbags. Whilst these defences were being constructed, the Boer commanders, alerted to the arrival of the English by their fleeing soldiers, dispatched 400 men up the other side of the hill. Using accurate drawings, they eventually reached the three crests overlooking Woodgate's position.

The battle of Spion Kop began at 7.20am when the Boers opened fire. Reacting quickly to the onslaught, British officers led a series of bayonet charges, but in fierce hand-to-hand fighting were driven back. Warren, ten miles away, at first appeared unconcerned that his men had met resistance; rumour had it that he took his usual morning bathe in his personal tin bath during which he dealt with mundane paperwork. Eventually realising that there was a serious problem, he ordered his artillery to open fire on Aloe Knoll, but rapidly retracted the instruction when it became clear that the shells were hitting the British trenches. He then dispatched reinforcements under the leadership of General John Coke, an odd choice of commander given that Coke had recently broken his leg and found walking difficult. Having done all that he believed was possible, he returned to his tent for a nap.

By this time, the situation on the hill was becoming critical. Woodgate had been hit in the head by a shell splinter and his replacement had also been seriously wounded. Command had thus devolved to a Colonel Malby Croften, who ordered a semaphorer, no telegraph line having been provided, to signal to Warren the message 'General Woodgate dead. Reinforcements urgently required'. The communication actually sent was 'Reinforce at once or all lost. General dead'. Believing Crofton had lost heart, Warren decided to relieve him of his command and replace him with a Lieutenant Alexander Thorneycroft, who Buller through field glasses from his vantage point on a nearby hill had noted had led a brave counterattack on the Boer positions. He thus sent messages to Crofton and Thorneycroft informing them of his decision, but failed to tell Thorneycroft that reinforcements had been dispatched or to give him any instructions as to how he should proceed. He also failed to inform Coke of the change in leadership.

Coke, meanwhile, was proving a reluctant hero. In great pain from his broken leg and disinclined to join the devastation that was occurring above him, he advanced up the hill slowly, taking an hour to reach a ledge 600 yards below the British position.

Having reached this point, he was loath to go on, even after intercepting a runner sent by Thorneycroft with a message for Warren pleading for reinforcements. Instead of immediately going to the assistance of his comrades or informing them of his presence, he and his men remained on the ledge for a further two hours, before he and an advance party ascended to just below the British trenches, from where he spied 'a scene of considerable confusion'. Returning to the ledge, he sent a message to Warren recommending that all the British forces be withdrawn. Rather than ordering the cowardly officer to support Thorneycroft, Warren asked him and his men to return to headquarters to enable him to report on the situation in person.

Thorneycroft's men had now been fighting for over ten hours. Surrounded by the dead and the dying and the stench of 'blood and brains', most of those killed having been shot in the head, they had no food or water and were running out of ammunition. Thorneycroft had received no communication from Warren since he had been informed of his promotion and assuming that he and his troops had been abandoned decided to withdraw. As he made the necessary preparations, Winston Churchill, recently escaped from Boer captivity and commissioned into the South African Light Horse, arrived with a message from Warren promising that during the night 1,400 reinforcements and two navel guns would ascend the hill. The missive was too little too late. Informing Churchill 'better six good battalions safely down the hill than a bloody mop-up in the morning', Thorneycroft and his men left their trenches and returned to headquarters. Ironically, two hours previously the Boer commander had come to a similar decision. Afraid of a night time British counterattack, he had ordered his men to quietly leave their positions one-by-one. By the time the British departed, therefore, the Boer positions were virtually deserted and could easily have been overrun.

Of the 1,700 soldiers that had ascended Spion Kop the

previous evening, 1,250 were either wounded or captured and over 300 dead. The Boers, by comparison, had just 300 casualties, and approximately sixty dead. Warren blamed the whole fiasco on Thorneycroft, recommending that he should be tried and executed for desertion. Unwilling to accept a scintilla of criticism, Buller held Warren solely responsible.[20] In a secret report to the War Office, he described his subordinate as a man 'who cannot command as he can neither use his staff nor subordinates' and threw further opprobrium on him in two articles about the battle published in the *London Gazette*.

Warren only became aware of Buller's report and articles when he returned to England twenty months later. Immediately after Spion Kop, he took part in a number of actions that paved the way for the relief of Ladysmith and was then transferred to his old stamping ground of Griqualand West, where as Military Governor he put down a Boer rebellion. During the latter campaign he was again involved in controversy. At a farm called Faber's Put, his small field force was attacked by Boers with the loss of 23 dead and 32 wounded. Although Warren's unit successfully fought back the raiders, the ability of the attackers to creep to within a few hundred yards of the farm was blamed on his failure to post a sufficient number of sentries; a charge he categorically denied.

On the defeat of the rebellion, he returned to London to discover that his reputation lay in tatters. In an attempt to defend his name, he wrote to the War Office and Field Marshall Frederick Roberts, who had taken over the command of British forces in South Africa from Buller, refuting the allegations made by his former commander and asked that the letters be published. His request was denied. No further postings were forthcoming and he retired for a second time five years later, returning to Ramsgate. Here, he researched the history of the Freemasons, wrote books and articles on military, archaeological and religious topics, helped the Palestine Exploration Fund prepare a map of his Jerusalem excavations, travelled extensively in Europe and devoted himself to good works. Convinced that morality had to be learnt in childhood, he became involved in the Sunday School movement and the Church Lads' Brigade and then helped his childhood friend and fellow soldier Robert Baden Powell to set up the Boy Scouts, establishing Ramsgate's first troop that he modestly named 'Sir Charles Warren's Own'. He died in 1927 of pneumonia at the age of sixty-seven and was buried next to his wife, who had predeceased him, in the pretty graveyard of West Bere, Kent.[21]

Chapter 18

Aftermath

Egypt

On its victory in Egypt, Britain faced two conundrums: what to do with the leaders of the rebellion and how to rule the country. The Khedive and the Europeans living in the main cities, who had seen their friends and relatives slaughtered at Alexandria, demanded that Ahmed Arabi and his co-conspirators hang. The British government favoured leniency. A long trial would disrupt the reorganisation of the country and the UK liberal press and many of the government's supporters strongly opposed execution, regarding Arabi as an African Garibaldi who had been manipulated by the Khedive and the Turkish Sultan for their own ends. More importantly, there was a fear that his death would confer upon him the status of martyr and spark further costly rebellions and the evidence against him was inconclusive. One of the main charges was that he had incited the Alexandria riots of June 11th and ordered the city to be set ablaze. However, although a number of Egyptians had provided damning testimony, this had been extracted through torture and there was no physical proof that was he responsible for either event.[1]

Eventually, the British government, the Khedive and Arabi's barrister came to a compromise. If he pleaded guilty to simple rebellion, all the other charges would be dropped, and, although he would be sentenced to death, the sentence would be immediately commuted to exile from Egypt and the forfeiture of his property and army rank. His court marshal on December 3rd thus lasted a mere six minutes, the commutation of his sentence being met by hisses, boos and cries of 'shame' from the Europeans in the public gallery. A few days later, his six co-conspirators were tried and similarly exiled, and, on December 26th, they, their leader and over sixty family members and servants boarded the train to Suez, from whence they sailed to the British colony of Ceylon.

For the following nineteen years, Arabi lived on the meagre allowance paid to him by the British, supplemented by fees for endorsing Lipton's coffee and chicory essence, and became a minor tourist attraction; a meeting with the great revolutionary being part of the itinerary of most Europeans who visited the island. In 1892, Tewfiq, at just thirty-nine years of age, died of pneumonia, though many suspected poison administered by either the British or the Turks. A pardon was considered and nine years later was finally granted. Half blind and in poor health, Arabi along with the four surviving co-conspirators returned to the country of his birth. Surprisingly, his homecoming was less than celebratory. The new generation of nationalist politicians regarded him a traitor, whose actions had led to the British occupation of the country, and were further angered by his pronouncement that Egypt had benefitted greatly from Britain's presence. He died in obscurity of cancer in 1911, only becoming a nationalist and even a socialist hero after the rise of Nasser in 1952.[2]

An even greater problem for the British government than the fate of Ahmed Arabi was Britain's future relationship with Egypt. A country governed by a pro-British administration was essential for the repayment of its debts, the free operation of the Suez Canal and the maintenance of Britain's political influence over a region that was increasingly coming to the attention of the other great powers. But such an administration was only possible if Britain retained a military presence in the country and controlled the legislature. The war had so undermined the Khedive's authority that the withdrawal of Imperial forces would inevitably lead to his overthrow and the existing regime was incapable of running the country and introducing the necessary economic, political and social reforms. Moreover,

British troops were needed to put down the Islamic rebellion that had flared up in the Sudan and threatened to spread to Egypt and other parts of the Empire. Led by Muhammad Ahmad ibn Abdul, who declared himself the Mahdi or messiah and proclaimed a jihad against Egypt's occupation of his country, the insurrection proved difficult to extinguish. Having annihilated a 10,000 strong Egyptian army led by General Hicks in November 1883, two years later rebel forces laid siege to and then over-ran Khartoum, slaughtering the British army that occupied the town and famously beheading its commander General Charles Gordon.

The government's wish for a rapid withdrawal from the country was therefore never likely to become reality. In November 1882, Lord Dufferin, the Ambassador of Constantinople, was appointed to determine what needed to be done to avoid another rebellion. His report detailed a whole raft of long-term reforms. The man chosen to implement them was Evelyn Baring, who prior to the war had sat on Egypt's Public Debt Commission and later acted as Controller General of Revenues. Viewing the Arab mind as weak and slipshod, he was convinced that Egypt could advance only under Anglo-Saxon rule and enthusiastically set about overhauling the country.

The two most urgent reforms were undertaken before his appointment. To avoid further insubordination, the Khedive was determined that the Egyptian army should be reorganised, and, on the recommendation of the Sultan, chose for the task none other than Valentine Baker with whom William Gill had travelled to Persia and whose career had been destroyed by sexual scandal. The decision was met with undisguised horror by the British, who blocked the appointment on the grounds that the Khedive had made it a condition that the new army was to be officered by the British and no Imperial officer would serve under a convicted rapist. The role thus went to a 'cleaner pair of hands', Sir Evelyn Wood, a recipient of the Victoria Cross, who had fought in India and the Ashanti and Zulu wars. Under his leadership, the army's strength was reduced to 6,000 men, British officers appointed to key positions and British disciplinary standards introduced. As a consolation prize, Baker was made Inspector General of the Egyptian Police and given the task of its reorganisation. Before his death of a heart attack in 1887, he had succeeded in transforming it into a corruption-free professional mounted force with a distinct semi-military character.

Baring's reforms were similarly widescale. A new 'democratic' government framework was introduced. An elected Chamber of Notables of 46 members communicated the national will to a non-elected Legislative Council that passed its decisions to a Council of Ministers, which transformed them into law. The reforms were then implemented by an independent civil service. In reality, the framework was a 'sham', a cloak to conceal British control. The Ministers followed the wishes of the Khedive, who acted on the instructions of Baring, and the higher echelons of the civil service were dominated by British officials and lower level Egyptian administrators 'guided' by British advisers. The resultant reforms thus favoured Imperial interests and were largely designed to balance the budget and create a western style economy that serviced the needs of British industry and the City.[3]

Baring left Egypt in 1907 as a result of his support of the punishments meted out to a group of peasants who had objected to British soldiers indiscriminately shooting their livestock. Awarded £30,000 in recognition of his service, he returned to Britain where he led the Anti-Women's Suffrage Campaign and wrote a number of books on Egypt and the glories of Empire. He was replaced by Sir John Gorst and later Lord Kitchener, who continued his reforms; the country in 1914 officially becoming a British protectorate. Imperial control ceased with the granting of independence in 1922. Troops, however, remained on Egyptian soil until 1956 when they were finally ejected in an eerie replay of the events of 1882. Fearing that the nationalisation of the Suez

Canal by Gamul Abdul Nasser, who had come to power via a military coup four years earlier, would disrupt their use of the waterway, Britain, along with France and Israel, again landed an invasion force. But there was to be no replay of the battle of Tel-el-Kebir. Pressured by the United States and the Soviet Union, the British government was forced into a humiliating withdrawal of its forces and its direct involvement in the country finally came to an end.[4]

Individuals and Organizations

At 9am on February 28th 1883 the five men sentenced to death for the murder of the Palmer party were led to three gallows that had been erected in the market square in the small town of Zagazig. The scaffolds were two-sided wooden frames; two contained two ropes each, beneath which stood four simple stools, and the third, one rope and one stool. Each gibbet was surrounded by soldiers to hold back the hundreds of spectators, 35 of whom were sheikhs, one from every tribe in lower Egypt, who had been ordered to attend the execution in the belief that the horror of the event would act as a punishment and a warning. Around the sides of the square stood 400 armed Egyptian police, their weapons raised in anticipation of trouble, and, in nearby Cairo, two companies of British troops had been placed on alert. The condemned men were ordered to stand on the stools and the ropes placed around their necks. Four submitted quietly, a fifth refused, yelling that he was innocent, and had to be manhandled into place. After a short pause, the stools were kicked away. Four died instantly, the fifth, the culprit who had proclaimed his innocence, appeared to fight death, struggling for several minutes until his body too ceased to move. The crowd met their fellow tribesmen's end in silence, and, after the dreadful deed was done, quietly returned to their homes and workplaces leaving only the mothers, wives and children of the hanged men and paid mourners, who wailed and screamed their grief. The corpses remained hanging for a further four hours – to enable latecomers to discover what happened to those who murdered Englishmen and sought independence.[5]

The other five Bedouin sentenced to death by the Tanteh court were never apprehended, though their relatives, seized as hostages for their recapture, remained in jail and were only released in September 1883 after their plight had been revealed by the *Standard* newspaper and Wilfrid Blunt and questions asked in the House of Commons. Despite his promises to Warren, Salami Shedide refused to fulfil his agreement to arrest the men still at large and was supported by the Khedive, who was unwilling to lose the support of such an important chief. The British government, in turn, was reluctant to put pressure on the Egyptians. It was believed that the Arabs of the region had already been taught a salutary lesson and no further prosecutions were necessary and that forcing the Khedive to act would disrupt British-Egyptian relations. A further man hunt was also doomed to failure. Having seen their fellow tribesmen hanged, the local Bedouin would be loath to give information that would lead five more of their kinsmen to the gallows.[6]

Warren sought to capture a number of the men, rumoured to be holed up at Jebl Helal, a small Terabin village close to El Arish, himself; first via the new Governor of El Arish and then through his own efforts. Both attempts were unsuccessful. The El Arish Governor failed to keep an appointment with his Nakhl counterpart to discuss ways in which the Terabin could be persuaded to relinquish their guests and ignored Warren's request to personally round up the men. His son's claim that his father had travelled to the village only to find the prey had flown was later discovered to be untrue. Warren's attempts to organise an assault on the hamlet when he was at El Arish investigating the connections between the previous pro-Arabi governor and the murders similarly came to nought. The Admiralty insisted the town was in Turkish or Syrian territory and the region's sheikhs refused to provide the necessary fighters, claiming that the attacking force would be grossly outnumbered and would suffer high causalities. Needless to say, Warren refused to admit defeat. On his return to England, he continued to press that the hunt for the culprits continue, demanding that Shedide and his fellow chiefs be called to account for their failure to act and be fined or punished. The Egyptian Minister of the Interior duly arranged a meeting at which Salami and his comrades promised to do all they could before returning to their tents to do nothing.[7]

Of the other Bedouins involved in the Palmer case, the Governor of El Arish was released from Cairo prison in late February 1883 under the amnesty, but was dismissed from public service. On serving his sentence, the Governor of Nakhl eked out a living in Cairo. The five attackers left prison to discover that their livelihoods had disappeared; Salami Shedide having stolen their livestock. Initially, Sofieh's nephew was more fortunate. Although the court marshal had ordered his clan to refund the £2,000 supposedly stolen by his uncle, the family succeeded in hiding their wealth from the Egyptian government and only repaid £100. Pressured by the British to make up the difference from the sale of the property of the three murderers still at large, the Khedive again failed to raise a significant sum, even though Warren estimated the total wealth of the men to be over £4,000. Warren's demands that the Egyptian government be required to repay the £2,000 itself not unexpectedly were ignored. The nephew's luck, however, eventually ran out. A few months after beginning his prison sentence, he was dead, supposedly of natural causes, though many suspected foul play, claiming that he had been killed by the Shedides in order to prevent him revealing their connection to the murders.[8]

In Britain, the Palmer party attained iconic status, particular emphasis being placed on the leader of the expedition. The government wished to create a hero in order to help legitimise a war that many regarded as dishonourable and the press were well aware that descriptions of intrepid acts sold papers. The Admiralty and correspondents thus combined to create a fictionalised view of the expedition; naval officers planting positive stories through leaks and unofficial briefings, which newspapers printed, emphasising the heroic elements. Palmer became 'a scholar whose attainments have been equalled by few and whose work has been surpassed by none...and if spared...might have remedied the confusion of Babel and restored to the human race, after learning all [its] languages, the primitive tongue'. His first mission had succeeded in 'turn[ing] back a Bedouin invasion of the Suez Canal'. Attacked by fierce Arab fighters, he and his party had put up strong resistance, and, at the murder site, on being offered the alternative of being shot or throwing himself over the precipice, Palmer had chosen the noble death, cursing his captors and leaping into legend.[9]

As befitting heroes, the remains of the three Englishmen were interned in the crypt of St Paul's Cathedral; an honour conferred on only nine notables in the twenty years from 1880 to 1900. Attempts to remove the bones of Palmer's cook and Gill's servant from the casket to prevent this bastion of Protestantism housing the remains of a common Muslim and a Jew were abandoned when it was discovered that they were indistinguishable from those of their masters. The internment was an impressive affair, which would have given Palmer paroxysms of joy. At noon on April 7th 1883, 500 mourners assembled in the Cathedral crypt. They included Lord Northbrook, various eminent members of the armed forces, the actor Henry Irving, the officers who had been involved in the search for the party and relatives and friends of the three men, though noticeably Palmer's wife was absent 'being too ill to attend', as was any representative of Cambridge University. Forming a procession, they followed the Union Jack flag-draped coffin that contained the remains of the three gallant men as it was carried to the Chancel Chapel, where it was placed next to the altar table. The funeral service was then read and the procession reformed and moved through the semi-darkness to the party's finally resting place between the tombs of Lord Nelson and the Duke of Wellington. The coffin was lowered into the ground and the cathedral choir sang the hymns 'Thy will be done' and 'Jesus lives no longer now', and as their voices 'echoed among the tombs, there were some present who wept'.[10]

Other honours followed. The three men were posthumously awarded the Egyptian Campaign Medal and the Khedive's Star. A portrait of Palmer in Bedouin dress was commissioned, paid for by past and present Fellows of St John's College, and hung in the college hall, a copy later being displayed in the Assembly Hall of Perse School. William Gill's family gave his alma mater, Brighton College, £1,250 to be used to purchase an alabaster memorial and to fund three College scholarships and presented the Royal Geographical Society with a further £1,000, used to set up a fund in his name to finance exploration. Charrington's life was commemorated in the form of stained windows at St Dunstan's church, Stepney; a plaque and a miniature model of the cairn erected at the murder scene displayed at St Dunstan's Church, Hunsdon, Hertfordshire; and a further wall plaque given to the Holy Trinity Church at Barkingside, Essex. A proposal to carve a gigantic inscription commemorating the three Englishmen on the rock wall above the ravine where they were murdered was only abandoned when the organizers had difficulty finding local workmen prepared to undertake the work and later ran out of money.[11]

The two non-Europeans murdered and those who had searched for the party and brought its murderers to justice were similarly rewarded. At the end of his expedition, Warren arranged a whip-round for the wife, three daughters and parents of the deceased men's cook, who were destitute and close to starvation. He himself donated £5, Haynes and Burton £2 each and Robert Gill and Charrington's brother and sister nothing. Gill, who had inherited approximately £150,000, believed that he had no responsibility for the party's servant, and, when Warren demanded a contribution, volunteered only a few pounds on the understanding that the gift would be anonymous, an offer that was rejected with disgust. Charrington, a large landowner and heir to one of the largest breweries in the country, claimed that he needed the cash he carried to cover his and his sister's living costs and he had unfortunately left his chequebook in England. Thankfully, the British government was more generous, awarding the cook's family a £300 annuity and the seventy-year-old mother of Gill's assistant an annuity of £100.[12]

The interpreters used during the search obtained the Egyptian Campaign Medal and the senior interpreter was allowed to return to Chatham with Warren and remained there until ill-health forced him to leave British service. His request to be allowed to stay in Britain on the grounds that he would almost certainly be murdered on his return home for helping his country's enemy was turned down. Two Bedouin who helped in the search were also rewarded. Sheikh Moussa received a gratuity of £20 and an excellent written testimonial from Warren, who successfully recommended that he be given the lucrative right to conduct travellers through Sinai. A concession he held until his death in 1912 and which was then passed onto his son, Nassir Moussa, but removed along with the sheikhdom when Nassir joined the Turkish cause during the First World War. More curiously, the camel driver who had informed Warren that he had heard that the order to ambush the party had come from the Shedides was made Sheikh of the Aleiqat tribe, having testified at the trial that the existing chief had been involved in the attack on his employers; though there was no other evidence that this was the case and the chief was not prosecuted. The decision was to have far-reaching consequences. The resulting bad feeling between his family and that of his predecessor prompted the latter to support Turkey in the First World War in the hope that they would regain the chieftaincy on an Ottoman victory. In the event, almost all the male members of the clan were killed at the 1915 siege of Tor.[13]

Lieutenants Haynes and Burton were awarded the Egyptian campaign medal, the Khedive's star, and, from the Turkish government, the insignia of the order of the Madjide. Burton, who in early December 1882 had asked his father to persuade his friends to write to Lord Northbrook and demand that Warren and his two assistants be given the highest of decorations, was delighted and wore the medals with pride. His subsequent military career initially was relatively successful. Soon after returning to England, he was struck down with malaria contracted during the search for Palmer and his companions, but soon recovered and went back to Egypt as part of a team that undertook a survey of the port of Suakin and the surrounding countryside. On its completion in October 1883, he was shipped to the Sudan, where he was part of the military expedition that relieved a number of Egyptian garrisons, fighting in the second battle of El Tab, in which the Mahdist forces were defeated with hardly any British casualties, and the battle of Tamai, during which over 4,000 Sudanese soldiers were slaughtered. He then joined the force that relieved Khartoum, commanding a camel/transport company. The remainder of his career was a mundane anti-climax. After two years in Gibraltar helping to build a mono-rail system, he returned to England, where he was stationed variously at Chatham, Colchester, Pembroke and Weymouth as Division Officer and Chief Royal Engineer. On the outbreak of the Boer war, he was sent to South Africa, but spent his time reconstructing infantry barracks in Cape Town and building Prisoner of War Camps. After a long retirement, he died in 1948 at the age of eighty-eight.[14]

Haynes' subsequent life was far briefer. After serving with Warren in Bechuanaland, where he was mentioned in despatches, he became Assistant Instructor of Surveying at the School of Military Engineering, Chatham, where he worked until 1894 when he obtained a post in Mauritius. Landing at Durban on the journey to the island, he discovered that war had broken out in nearby Matabeleland; the Ndebele having risen up against Cecil Rhodes' British South Africa Company that administered the region, which they blamed for the draught, locust plagues and cattle disease that was ravaging the country. Eager to see action, Haynes suggested that he and the company of Royal Engineers that were also onboard the ship bound for Mauritius help put down the rebellion. The High Commissioner concurred and the boat was diverted to Beira, from where Haynes and his men marched to meet their foe. Three weeks later, he was dead; shot whilst leading an attack on a farm occupied by the fighters of a Chief Makoni. To commemorate his death, his commander named a garrison 'Fort Haynes' in his honour and ensured that his killers were brought to justice. Makoni surrendered a few days later, but rather than allowed to go free, as the British had promised, he was immediately 'court-marshaled' and executed by firing squad; his head allegedly hewn from his body and presented to Rhodes as a trophy.[15]

The worship of the Palmer party and those who searched for them was far from universal. As the true facts slowly began to emerge, concerns about the integrity of the mission and Warren's investigation began to appear in the radical press. These were taken up in Parliament by the Conservative opposition, seeking to use the expedition and its aftermath as a stick with which to beat the government. It was claimed that the search party had taken too long to organise, allowing the suspects to escape, and had refused the help of Wilfrid Blunt, whose friendships with the nationalist leaders would have aided their capture. Moreover, there had been the unacceptable use of hostages, generally the wives and children of suspects, who had been held in jail until their husbands/fathers gave themselves up; confessions had been extracted through torture; and the execution of the five most important suspects was little more than 'bloody judicial murder', the attack on the party being a clear act of war. The government rejected each charge. Mr Pickard and Lieutenant Foote had been sent to investigate the disappearance of Palmer and his companions long before the appointment of Warren; Blunt had no connections with the Suez chiefs and would have offered little assistance; in taking hostages, the search party had merely been following Bedouin custom; Warren and his two brave lieutenants had performed their duties with 'good judgment and a perfectly judicial mind'; and there was 'no evidence that the [assailants had] acted under superior orders'.[16]

A far more serious accusation was that the expedition involved such 'double-dyed treason and trickery as was never exceeded in the whole history of tortuous transactions'. The party had not only sought to bribe the Bedouins, but had been intent on cutting the telegraph line used by Turkey, Britain's main ally in the region. The government's response, delivered in the House of Commons by Campbell Bannerman, the Admiralty's Parliamentary Secretary, was to accept that the telegraph had been disabled, but to categorically deny that the purpose of Palmer's two missions was bribery. The Professor had initially been employed to ascertain the disposition of the Bedouins and he had entered the desert a second time to purchase camels for the Indian contingent of Wolseley's army, which was then on its way to Suez.[17]

The explanation, given in late October 1882, silenced the criticism and the government was confident that the controversy had been laid to rest. It was wrong. In March the following year, the *Times* newspaper published a letter from Wilfrid Blunt in which he revealed that he had read and made transcriptions of Palmer's and Gill's journals that had been recovered from the desert and that their contents proved beyond doubt that Bannerman had lied and the Professor had set out to bribe the Bedouin. The letter created a sensation and Lord Wentworth,

Blunt's brother-in-law, raised the affair again in the House of Lords, demanding that the relevant journal entries be made public. The government refused the request, on the grounds that the material was the property of the families of the dead men. Wentworth attempted to read them to the House, but was ordered by the Speaker to desist. Accusing the government of censorship, Blunt thus passed his copies of the journals to the *Daily News*, which published extracts on the morning of March 16th.

The government's response was to weaken the veracity of the accusations by besmirching the character of Wilfrid Blunt and denying everything. Blunt was an ardent supporter of Pasha Arabi, having paid the cost of his defence at his recent trial, and was cynically using the Palmer case to tarnish Britain's well deserved victory over the rebel leader. Moreover, he had lied to both Mrs Palmer and Gill's brother, who had allowed him to read their relatives' journals on the understanding that their contents would never be made public. A charge categorically denied by Blunt, who claimed that both individuals had been well aware that he intended to use extracts in a newspaper article and later asserted that all three families of the dead men had urged him to reveal to the public the true nature of their mission.[18]

As for the actual accusations, Lord Northbrook reiterated that the Professor's first mission was to discover whether the Bedouin of the region supported the nationalist cause and his second to buy camels for which he had been given £3,000. Although the academic had travelled under the name he had adopted when he had first visited the desert in 1870, he had not pretended to be Syrian, informing everyone he met that he was an English gentleman. Gill had not carried the £20,000 to Suez, though he had been a passenger on the boat on which the gold was transported; the money was to meet general expenses and had never been intended to be used as a bribe; and the party had worn Arab dress for comfort rather than disguise. The reasons for Gill and

Palmer's journal entries were a mystery; possible explanations were confusion or that both men had been so infected by 'war fever' that they had fictionalised their roles in the campaign. To ensure the public that the government had nothing to hide, he intended to publish all the Admiralty and Foreign Office correspondence related to the case as soon as it could be collected together. This appeared a few weeks later, and, as Palmer's and Gill's instructions had not been written down, demonstrated that Blunt's claims were baseless. The controversy thus died down. The following year, Lord Northbrook was sent to Egypt as special commissioner to inquire into its finances and then bowed out of politics, opposing his party's policy on Ireland. Blunt turned his attention to Irish home rule and Indian independence and his increasingly complex love life; his wife filed for divorce when he moved one of his many mistresses into the family home. Becoming increasingly addicted to morphine, he died in 1922.[19]

Others not enamoured with Palmer were Cambridge University, the Palestine Exploration Fund and his second wife. Academics at Cambridge University were appalled by the fictions reported in the press and wasted little time in replacing their erstwhile colleague. Of the three possible candidates for his Readership post, William Wright, who had beaten Palmer to the Thomas Adams Chair of Arabic in 1869, preferred his great friend William Roberson Smith, who could not have been more different from Palmer. An asexual pious Christian, he believed rigorous scholarship to be sacrosanct and had little interest in life outside academia. Of the other contenders, Wright regarded Robert Lubbock Bensly as 'horribly slow and unpunctual' and Stanley Lane Poole as 'a very conceited unnameable individual', who only wanted the post 'for the sake of calling himself Professor'.[20]

Wright's problem was that the Readership was the gift of the Lord Almoner, the Dean of Worcester Cathedral, who could 'give it...to my cat Toodles if he pleases', and was 'resolved not to consult the Cambridge men' and was high Church whilst Smith was a dour Protestant.[21] Wright's preferred candidate also had a further drawback – he was a convicted heretic. In 1878, the General Assembly of the Free Church of Scotland charged Smith with heresy for daring to claim in his *Encyclopaedia Britannica* entry on the bible that some of the scriptures were factually inaccurate. Smith challenged the accusation and the case dragged on for three years before the Assembly deemed that he should abstain from expressing 'incautious or incomplete public statements' in the future, to which Smith assented. Unfortunately, almost immediately after the judgement was made, the *Encyclopaedia Britannica* published a further entry by the academic on Hebrew language and literature in which he questioned the origin of the Old Testament. The Assembly went on the attack, again accusing him of heresy, and, more damagingly, of breaking his word, even though its members were well aware that the article had been written well before its previous judgement. Smith was convicted of heresy and dismissed from his Professorial Chair at the Free Church College of Aberdeen, thus making him available for the Cambridge post.

To secure his appointment, Wright launched a letter-writing campaign designed to influence or 'get at' the Lord Almoner. He wrote to the leading Orientalists, most of whom were friends or colleagues or owed him favours, personally requesting that they write to the Lord Almoner recommending Smith for the vacancy. The plan worked. In 1883, Smith was awarded the Readership, and, six years later on William Wright's death, became the Thomas Adams Professor of Arabic. He was to hold the post for just five years, dying in 1894 at the age of just forty-seven from spinal tuberculosis.[22]

For the Palestine Exploration Fund, the disappearance of Palmer's party circumscribed the future operations of the organisation. The questions asked in the House of Commons and the Ministerial replies revealed Palmer's and Warren's former links to the Fund and it became clear to many that its surveys had military, as well as archaeological goals. The Turkish government was thus loath to allow its expeditions to enter its territory and military help was no longer forthcoming. A 1883/4 request for War Office and Royal Engineers assistance was turned down and it was another thirty years before it again received military backing. Orientalists, however, continued to be employed by the intelligence services, both for their knowledge of the region and its people; David George Hogarth, Gertrude Bell, Harry St John Philby and T. E. Lawrence, all at one time or another being employed as gatherers of intelligence.[23]

Palmer's second wife, Auguste, found on his death that she was penniless; her youth and the nature of her marriage suggests that she had previously been ignorant of the state of her former husband's finances. Help initially came from the Royal Literary Fund, which assisted writers in need and awarded her a grant of £200. Even more generous aid came from the government, which had been informed by Besant and the Widnalls that she was in straitened circumstances and was aware that she possessed letters from her husband written in Suez prior to his second journey into the desert that clearly revealed the true purpose of his mission. The Admiralty provided her with a pension of a further £200 per annum, plus a £6,000 lump sum to be used to finance the education and living costs of her four children, unaware that the daughters of Palmer's first wife were actually living in Germany. A petition from her landlord for a share of the £6,000 for unpaid rent was rejected. As was a similar request from the sequestrated creditors, who had not only lost the income from Palmer's Fellowship/Readership but had been refused full payment of his life insurance policies on the grounds that he had failed to inform the insurance company of his change of employment, either because he had forgotten to do so or to avoid the payment of an additional premium. Still short of money, she instructed her solicitors to demand the return of the £100 found in Palmer's Suez hotel room, the £235 in the dispatch box Sofieh's nephew had hidden in the desert and one of the naval swords recovered by Warren. The Admiralty concurred, though refused an appeal for the retrospective payment of a salary and the reimbursement of the cost of the clothes her husband was wearing when he died. A personal request for Lord Northbrook to use his influence to find her brother, Johannes von Langa, suitable employment, however, was granted. The twenty-three-year-old, fresh out of art school, was given a £800 pa post at the Calcutta Mint and promised that after two years service he would be transferred to the London Mint.[24]

In the event, she was not as poverty stricken as she assumed. Despite the fact that her first husband was bankrupt on his death and owned no property or investments, his estate was eventually valued at £2,431. Where this money came from can only be conjectured; £334/17/8 presumably represented the cash found in his hotel room and the hidden despatch box, £100 the repayment of his mysterious loan to Mr Hammond, the P & O ship's captain prior to his trip to Nakhl, and the remainder the missing £2,000, which had somehow been moved back to Britain, perhaps by Mr Hammond. Suddenly relatively wealthy, Auguste and her two sons returned to Germany to live with her parents and step-daughters, where in 1884 she suffered yet another tragedy, the death at the age of two years of her and Palmer's second son, Harold, of scarlet fever and diphtheria. Five years later, she remarried. The lucky man was Horatio Bryan Donkin, twelve years her senior and as eccentric as Edward Palmer. Having trained as a barrister, in 1868 Donkin switched careers and became a doctor, quickly climbing the medical greasy pole. He had a flourishing practice in Harley Street, counting the family of Karl Marx as patients, and lectured at the London School of Medicine for Women and at Westminster Hospital, where in the mid-1880s he became Dean. His specialisms were female hysteria, criminal eugenics and venereal disease. The general view of the time was that women were prone to hysteria, which was both psychological and physical in nature; the symptoms including convulsions, heart palpitations, fainting and sudden and violent mood swings. Donkin believed the condition was related to female manipulative self-regard and unsatisfied sexual drives and could be cured by clitoral massage performed by a physician such as himself. His opinions on criminal eugenics and venereal disease appear similarly wayward, though were widely held at the time. Criminals were drawn to villainy by inherited mental characteristics and when imprisoned should be treated as patients rather than prisoners. The spread of sexual infections, meanwhile, could be halted not by the greater use of condoms, which merely encouraged promiscuity, but by abstinence, and, if this was not possible, the post-intercourse scrubbing of private parts with a strong disinfectant or soap and water.[25]

Away from his work, his main interests were reminiscent of Palmer's. He regularly dined at the Savile Club, eventually serving on its committee, and was an enthusiastic debunker of faith healing, thought reading and spiritualism. With his friend Sir E. Ray Lankester, the zoologist and model for the Professor Challenger character in Conan Doyle's *The Lost World*, he became involved in one of the most famous spiritualist cases of the century. Having attended a séance held by a Dr Henry Slade, a noted American psychic, at which the dead relatives of members of the audience wrote comforting messages on a slate, Donkin and Lankester persuaded the police to prosecute the spiritualist on the charge of obtaining money by false pretences. The action became a cause celebre with both sides producing eminent scientists who variously claimed that Slade's feats were mere conjuring tricks or clear evidence that he had somehow penetrated the fourth dimension. In the event, he was sentenced to three months hard labour, but was freed on a technicality when he appealed and fled the country before a fresh prosecution could be brought.[26]

Donkin married Augusta on the rebound from a previous

relationship with the South African writer and anti-war campaigner, Olive Schreiner, best remembered today for her novel *The Story of an African Farm*. Schreiner was suffering from hysteria and Donkin was recommended to her by Eleanor Marx, the youngest daughter of Karl Marx, whose 'nervous prostration' he had 'cured' several years earlier. The professional association soon developed into friendship, and, for Donkin, love. Unfortunately, Schreiner did not reciprocate his feelings. Although she admired her suitor's 'beautiful child nature' and tried to 'feel sexual' towards him, they had 'irreconcilable differences in [their] views of life' and she could not bear to even kiss him. Moreover, she was in love with Karl Pierson, the founder of the first university statistics department and a distinctly odd choice as an object of romance. Not only was he an anti-Semite, regarding Jews as 'a parasitic race' who were 'inferior physically and mentally to the native population', but he had no romantic interest in her, regarding her only as a friend. Undeterred, Donkin proposed marriage and was turned down. Schreiner declared that her temperament prevented her from ever marrying – 'if I am to live, I must be free' – and that if she did become a wife it would be to a husband 'much stronger than I am…mentally, morally, emotionally, practically'.[27]

Donkin's response to her rejection was to simply ignore it and continue to press his case. When this strategy proved futile, he 'heap[ed] reproaches' on her, asserted that he 'had claims' on her life, and, at one meeting, threw himself to the floor shrieking. Inevitably, his ardour, stalking in modern parlance, caused the return of Schreiner's hysteria, and, in October 1886, she sent him a letter asking him to have no further contact with her and went to live at convents in Kilburn and later Harrow-on-the-Hill, in the belief that she would be safe from his approaches and the peace and quiet would calm her nerves. Two months later, no better, but believing herself safe, she returned to her rooms in London, only to be visited by Donkin, who found her 'utterly smashed' in 'a state of complete temporary madness'. In her delirium, she revealed her love for Pierson. Donkin was devastated, but ever the gentleman wrote to her beloved pleading with him to visit her – 'if you love her as she loves you, go and tell her'. Pearson did indeed call around, but only to repeat that he had no feelings for her. His revelation caused Schriener to contemplate suicide, but gave Donkin hope that their relationship could be resurrected. It was not to be. Schreiner left for Paris, writing to Donkin before her return to London that he was not to visit her and that if he did she would leave the country 'within twenty four hours'. Soon afterwards, she returned to South Africa, and never heard from Donkin again, 'except for a couple of notes when I first left and a beautiful note on his marriage'.[28]

Donkin married Auguste Palmer a year later, adopting her son and the two daughters from Palmer's first marriage. He had been friendly with Palmer whilst the Professor was alive, and, since his death, had met his widow at a number of social occasions. It was a marriage based on convenience rather than love, but like so many such arrangements proved happy. Donkin prospered – becoming HM Commissioner of Prisons and later Medical Advisor to the Prison Commission, sitting on a number of government committees, including the Royal Commission on the Control of the Feeble Minded, and, in 1911, received a well deserved knighthood. On Auguste's death in December 1919 at the age of sixty-two, he remarried an American widow, suffering a fatal heart attack in 1927.[29]

Palmer's children fared less well. On his death, his first wife's father, Thomas Davis, asked Auguste to allow the Widnalls to bring up his two granddaughters, who were still living in Germany. Auguste, aware of her late husband's resentment towards Laura's family and angry at their disapproval of her own marriage, refused, prompting the Widnall's to lodge a claim for guardianship at the Court of Chancery. The request was rejected and the girls stayed in Hamburg, where Walter Besant states they were 'comfortably and happily bestowed and well taught', until Auguste remarried. They were then brought back to London and adopted by Donkin, but had no contact with their mother's relatives until 1889 when Besant persuaded Auguste to allow them to make occasional visits to Grantchester. It was on one such occasion that Ethel, the elder daughter then seventeen years old, made certain accusations against her step-parents. Their nature is unknown, though they were obviously serious and may have been related to Donkin's interest in adolescent sexual hysteria and an attempt to 'cure' Ethel. The local vicar was called to hear the young girl swear on the bible that her allegations were true and to witness her written statement, and the following day, her grandfather contacted his solicitor. Through the mediation of Besant and no doubt the threat of legal action, Auguste was persuaded to allow the Widnalls to become Ethel's legal guardian. Her sister, Laura, and brother, Carl, continued to live with the Donkins until they married, but appear to have had a similarly poor relationship with their stepfather; Carl, two years after his stepfather's death, legally changing his surname from Donkin back to Palmer. Ethel, variously described as 'disturbed' and 'strange', died in 1914 in her early thirties. Carl and Laura lived until the 1950s.[30]

A common trope of horror cinema is that at the end of the movie, the villain, earlier killed in some revolting manner, returns to life. In 1885, it was reported that Palmer was alive and living with the Mahdi tribe. The story was half believed by some of his friends, who somewhat unkindly 'declared that [it proved] he could be thrown from a precipice and still land on his feet'. Others dismissed the news item as a case of mistaken identity or an attempt by a reporter to re-invigorate the Palmer myth. If true, it would have been a fitting end to his story. The image of Palmer in old age sitting around a camp fire amazing his hosts with his conjuring tricks and relating once again how he was once Professor of Arabic at Cambridge University is almost irresistible.[31]

Notes

Introduction

1 Except where stated, the chapters on the disappearance of the Palmer party and Warren's investigation of the mystery are based on Parliamentary Paper (PP) 1883 [C.3494] [C.3761] 'Correspondence respecting the murder of Professor E. H. Palmer, Captain W M. Gill, R.E. and Lieutenant Harold Charrington, R.N.'; National Archives, Kew (NA): ADM 16/45, No. 3; Patrick Maselis (PM): The diaries of Edmund Merceron Burton: Vol. 1 – 1 Sept. to 31 Oct. 1882, Vol. 2 – 1 Nov. to 31 Dec. 1882, Vol. 3 – 1 Jan. to 5 March 1882; Alfred R. Haynes, *Man-Hunting in the Desert, Being a Narrative of the Palmer Search Expedition,* London: Horace Cox, 1894; Walter Besant, *The Life and Achievements of Edward Henry Palmer,* London: John Murray, 1883, pp. 235-330; J. Willis Clark, *Old Friends at Cambridge and Elsewhere* , London: Macmillan & Co., 1909, pp. 255-81; and Watkin W. Williams, *The Life of General Sir Charles Warren*, Oxford: Basil Blackwell, 1941.

Chapter 1

1 Except where stated, the chapter is based on William J. Wright, *A Tidy Little War: The British Invasion of Egypt 1882,* Stroud: History, 2009, pp. 13-71; Charles Royle, *The Egyptian Campaigns, 1882 to 1885,* London: Hurst and Blackett Ltd, 1900, pp. 8-60; Donald Malcolm Reid, 'The Urabi revolution and British conquest' in M. W. Daly and Carl Forbes Petry (eds), *Modern Egypt from 1517 to the End of the Twentieth Century*, Cambridge: Cambridge University Press, 1998, pp. 217-32; David J. Mentiply, 'The British invasion of Egypt, 1882'. Available from: http://www.e-ir.info/2009/03/23/the-british-invasion-of-egypt-1882/ (accessed October 2013); Inari Karsh and Efrain Karsh, *Empires of the Sand: The*

Struggle for Mastery in the Middle East, 1789-1923, Cambridge, MA: Harvard University Press, 1999, pp. 56, 125-9; Juan Ricardo Cole, *Colonialism and Revolution in the Middle East: Social and Cultural Origins of Egypt's Urabi Movement*, Cairo: American University in Cairo Press, 1999, pp. 59, 65, 237-9; Dominic Green, *Three Empires on the Nile: The Victorian Jihad, 1869-1899*, London: Free Press, 2007, pp. 106, 109-118; Karim Zaki-Khalil, 'British Sinai. Its geopolitical significance in the Middle East and its strategic role in British colonial policy', PhD diss., University of Durham, 1998, p. 79; Sean Lyngaas, 'Ahmad Urabi, delegate of the people. Social mobilization in Egypt on the eve of Colonial rule', *Al Nakhlah*, Spring 2011; A. G. Hopkins, 'The Victorians and Africa: A reconsideration of the occupation of Egypt, 1882', *The Journal of African History*, 27 (I986), pp. 363-391; and M. E. Chamberlain, 'The Alexandria massacre of 11 June 1882 and the British occupation of Egypt, *Middle Eastern Studies*, 13 (1) (1977), pp. 14-39.

2 Royle, *The Egyptian*, p. 20.

3 *Ibid.*, p. 53.

4 *Ibid.*, p. 59.

Chapter 2

1 Valeska Huber, *Channelling Mobilities. Migration and Globalisation in the Suez Canal Region and Beyond, 1869–1914*, Cambridge: Cambridge University Press, 2013, p. 157; Charles Warren, *Notes on Arabia Petea and the Country Lying Between Egypt and Palestine*, London: Palestine Exploration Fund, 1887, pp. 40-1; Alexander Schölch, 'The Egyptian Bedouins and the Urābīyūn', *Die Welt des Islams*, 17 (1/4) (1976-77), pp. 47-9. The nationalist government had proposed that tribes should pay the State a certain sum of money in lieu of corvee services, and, in the event of war, form military units (*ibid.*).

2 Katherine Prior, 'Colborne Bradford', *Oxford Dictionary of National Biography*, Oxford: Oxford University Press, 2004; E. Longford, 'Wilfrid Scawen Blunt', *Oxford Dictionary of National Biography*, Oxford: Oxford University Press, 2004; Wilfrid Scawen Blunt, *A Secret*, p. 304. Edward Dicey was unconvinced by Blunt's adherence to the nationalist cause commenting 'I could never take [his] Orientalism seriously after I found out that in order to sustain his character as a denizen of the East, he used, on arrival at Cairo, to be met at the station by his camel and ride to Shepherd's Hotel, a distance of barely five minutes' walk, sooner than take a carriage like a commonplace tourist' (Edward Dicey, *The Story of the Khedivate*, London: Rivingtons, 1902, p. 260).

3 Arthur John Arberry, *Oriental Essays: Portraits of Seven Scholars*, London: George Allen & Unwin, 1960, p. 151.

4 *The Times*, 30 June 1882, p. 10.

5 Besant, *The Life*, pp. 259-60; Palestine Exploration Fund (PEF): PAL (ii), 20, pages found in Wadi Sudr, 7 July 1882.

6 Henry M. Field, *On the Desert: With a Brief Review of Recent Events in Egypt*, New York: C. Scribner's Sons, 1883, p. 274.

7 Schölch, 'The Egyptian', p. 54; Dust'ali Mu'ayyir al-Mamalik, *In the Land of the Pharaohs. A Short History of Egypt from the Fall of Ismail to the Assassination of Boutros Pasha*, London: S. Paul, 1911, p. 116; *The Times*, 18 Oct. 1882, p. 6; Blunt, *A Secret*, p. 87; George W. Murray, *Sons of Ishmael: A Study of the Egyptian Bedouin*, London: George Routledge and Sons, 1935, p. 255; Samuel Colcord Bartlett, *From Egypt to Palestine: Through Sinai, the Wilderness and the South Country*, New York: Harper & Bros., 1879, pp. 331-81, 407. From 1877-1921, the Reverend Samuel Bartlett was President of Dartmouth College.

8 Henry Clay Trumbull, *Kadesh-Barnea. Its Importance and Probable Site*, New York: Charles Scribner & Sons, 1884, p. 245; Edward Henry Palmer, 'The desert of Tih and the

country of Moab' in Edward Henry Palmer and Walter Besant (eds), *Survey of Western Palestine*, London: Palestine Exploration Fund, 1881-3, p. 25.

9 Besant, *The Life*, p. 265, 287; '"ב יניסל רמלאפ תחלשמ לש רמה הלרוג 1882 ורופיסו לש רוכב' at ןוסח". Available from: http://www.boker.org.il/meida/negev/desert_biking/ain_akev/palmer_book/palmer_low.pdf (accessed October 2013).

10 Jamie Fraser, 'Man-hunting in the desert. The mysterious disappearance of the Palmer Sinai Expedition', *Near Eastern Archaeology Foundation Bulletin*, 54 (Oct. 2010), p. 15.

11 Besant, *The Life*, p. 267, 273.

12 Bartlett, *From Egypt*, p. 329. Henry Martyn Field, an American author and clergyman who travelled through the region, described Misleh thus: 'His legs and feet were bare, but he had on a red tunic under his coarse goat's hair cloak and there was a touch of finery in the housing of his saddle. He presented quite a military figure with his gun slung behind his back and his pistol at his belt' (Field, *On the*, p. 237). Henry Clay Trumbell noted that his 'eyesight was failing him, and his lungs were evidently diseased. He had a constant cough' (Trumbull, *Kadesh-Barnea*, p. 250).

13 PP 1893 [C. 3761], Warren's history of the expedition, 21 Feb. 1883.

14 Besant, *The Life*, p. 288. Either seven or twelve sheiks were imprisoned in Jerusalem (*The Times*, 29 May 1883, p. 3; *ibid.*, 18 Oct. 1882, p. 6).

15 Haynes, *Man-Hunting*, p. 157; Palmer, 'The desert of Tih', p. 11.

16 Field, *On the*, p. 239.

17 Bartlett, *From Egypt*, pp. 326, 329-30.

18 Trumbull, *Kadesh-Barnea*, p. 250; George L. Robinson, 'Modern Kadesh or Ein Kadis', *The Biblical World*, 17 (5) (1901), pp. 327-338. During an earlier trip to Egypt, Wilfrid Blunt had also been asked to help release the men,

succeeding in obtaining the freedom of two family members, though he later claimed that he had freed all the prisoners (*The Times*, 18 Oct. 1882, p. 6; Blunt, *A Secret*, pp. 187-9).

19 Haynes, *Man-Hunting*, p. xxi; Besant, *The Life*, p. 288. Unfortunately, the 'marauders got clear off' (*ibid.*).

20 *Ibid.*, p. 272, 278.

21 *Ibid.*, p. 288, 289; Blunt, A *Secret*, p. 307. Palmer wrote to his friend Walter Besant 'I have invented a plan for having all the comforts of an Arabian summer journey at home. You get a huge cucumber frame and walk about under it while blast furnaces are lighted around you. From a number of holes, hot air and fine sand are blown by means of compressed air into your face. After eight hours you sit down to a piece of boiled boot, washed down with warm ditchwater, and there you are - cue for the band!' (Haynes, *Man-Hunting*, p. xxii-xxiii).

22 A wady is the dry bed of a river.

Chapter 3

1 The chapter is based on Green, *Three*, pp. 106-125; Donald Featherstone, *Tel El-Kebir, 1882. Wolseley's Conquest of Egypt*, London: Osprey, 1993, p 45; Wright, *A Tidy*, pp. 69-152; Reid, 'The Urabi', pp. 232-5; Royle, *The Egyptian*, pp. 61-126; Karsh and Karsh, *Empires*, pp. 59-63.

2 Wright, *A Tidy*, p. 75.

3 Hopkins, 'The Victorians', p 374; John S. Galbraith and Afaf Lutfi al-Sayyid-Marsot, 'The British occupation of Egypt: Another view', *International Journal of Middle East Studies*, 9 (4) (1978), p. 485; Zaki-Khalil, 'British', p. 49, 90.

4 Wright, *A Tidy*, p. 117.

Chapter 4

1 H. Yule, 'Memoir of Captain W. Gill' in William John Gill, *The River of Golden Sand: The Narrative of a Journey through*

China and Eastern Tibet to Burmah, London: John Murray, 1884, p. 64.

2 Edward H. Seymour, *My Naval Career and Travels*, London: Smith, Elder & Co., 1911, p. 222.

3 Isabel Burton, *The Life of Captain Sir Richard F. Burton*, New York: D. Appleton & Company, 1893, p. 611.

4 Besant, *The Life*, p. 284, 285. The Governor had fled Suez two days before the assault (NA: FO 78/3462, West to Granville, 7 Aug. 1882).

5 *The Times*, 27 Oct. 1882, p. 8.

6 Tony Hadland, *Glimpses of a Victorian Hero. William Gill - Explorer and Spy*, Coventry: Hadland Books, 2002, p. 74; Schölch, 'The Egyptian', p. 54. According to the geographer George W. Murray, even in the mid-1930s, 'hardly three Bedouins' in Sinai knew how to read and write (Murray, *Sons of*, p. 181, footnote 1).

7 *Illustrated London News*, 4 Nov. 1882; Anon, 'Lieutenant Harold Charrington'. Available from: http://www.findagrave.com/cgi-bin/fg.cgi?page=gr&GRid=42289047 (accessed October 2013). The Charrington family are largely remembered for the activities of Harold's uncle, Frederick Charrington. An ardent member of the temperance movement, for which he gave up his inheritance, he also campaigned for the abolition of music halls and the closure of brothels and founded the Great Assembly Hall in Mile End. He spent his evenings collecting information that could be used against brothel keepers and parading outside East End gin palaces and music halls wearing a sandwich board on which was written 'This Way to the Pit of Hell'. On Sundays, he led his own temperance band through the streets of Stepney and Wapping, drawing large crowds. Repeatedly beaten up by pimps, he rarely turned the other cheek, being once sued for kicking a brothel attendant in the stomach ('Frederick Nicholas Charrington'. Available

from: http://george-powell.co.uk/family/4806.htm (accessed October 2013)).

8 NA: ADM 116/35, Hoskins to Seymour, 28 July 1882; *ibid.*, note, Cartwright, 28 July 1882.

9 Besant, *The Life*, p. 305.

10 Royle, *The Egyptian*, pp. 138-43. De Lesseps was well aware that the British had detailed plans to capture the Canal and that he could and would do nothing to prevent their fulfilment.

11 al-Mamalik, *In the Land*, pp. 113-4; Royle, *The Egyptian*, p. 192; Schölch, 'The Egyptian', p. 54.

12 Bartlett, *From Egypt*, p. 197.

13 Burton, *The Life*, p. 611.

Chapter 5

1 Besant, *The Life*, p. 230.

2 Walter Besant, *Autobiography of Sir Walter Besan*t, London: Dodd, Mead, 1902, pp. 152-5. Peter Linehan, *St John's College Cambridge: A History*, Woodbridge: Boydell Press, 2011, p. 322; Anon, 'Edward Henry Palmer', *The Eagle*, 12, 1883 p. 233; A. G. Temple, *Guildhall Memories*, London: John Murray, 1918, p. 34; Richard Burton, 'The late E. H. Palmer ii. The story of his death', *The Academy*, May 12, 1883 (575), pp. 329-30. Except where stated, the chapter is based on Besant, *The Life*; Arberry, *Oriental*, pp. 122-59; Clark, *Old Friends*, pp. 202-55; and T. G. Bonney, *Memoires of a Long Life*, Cambridge: Metcalfe, 1921, pp. 106-112.

3 British Library (BL): Leland papers, 37173.

4 Linehan, *St John's*, p. 322; Christine Jennings, *Widnall: A Capital Contractor. The Story of a Victorian Household in the Village of Grantchester*, Swavesey: Folly, 2003, p. 59.

5 1841 Census; *Cambridge Independent Press*, 28 Sept. 1839, p. 3; *ibid.*, 11 Jan. 1840, p. 2; *ibid.*, 9 Jan. 1841, p. 2; O. R. McCarthy, 'The key to the sanatoria', *Journal of the Royal Society of*

Medicine, 94 (8) (2001), pp. 413-7.

6 1851 Census; *London Gazette*, April 1850, 1043; John Milner Gray, *A History of the Perse School, Cambridge*, Cambridge: Bowes & Bowes, 1921, pp. 125-8.

7 1861 Census; Gray, *A History*, p. 126; *Cambrian News and Merionthshire Standard*, 25 Oct. 1907, p. 6.

8 BL: Leland 37173, Palmer to Leland, 25 Jan. 1875.

9 Besant, *The Life*, p. 25.

10 Anon, 'Edward Henry'; Laurence Irving, *Henry Irving: The Actor and His World*, London: Faber and Faber, 1951, p. 32.

11 Besant, *The Life*, p. 10.

12 *Ibid.*, p. 19.

13 Besant, *The Life*, p. 21; Francis Cowley Burnand, *The ADC: Personal Reminiscences of the University Amateur Dramatic Club, Cambridge*, London: Chapman and Hall, 1880, pp. 26-7.

14 Edward Henry Palmer, *Ye Hole in ye Walle: A Legende of Walthamstowe Abbey. A Merrie, Metrical and Monastical Romaunce*, Cambridge, 1860.

15 Arberry, *Oriental*, p. 126. 'Palmer's expedition', *Manchester Times*, 4 Nov. 1882. R. L. Bidwell, 'Edward Henry Palmer', *Bulletin (British Society for Middle Eastern Studies)*, 13 (1), (1986), pp. 45-50; 1861 Census. On his return to India, the wealthy Indian gave Palmer £50 to help him in his studies and later sent him a large number of books. The Nawab later described Palmer as 'a young gentleman of very attractive exterior…[he is] the most honourable and gentlemanly of his race: and is, moreover, of such an extremely gentle, polite, obliging, temperate, and moral disposition that he attracts to himself the love and esteem of all hearts. He may be safely denominated "dear as one's life", or rather "the amulet of one's life"; and will be found a most agreeable and trusty companion and the twin brother of sincerity' (Besant, *The Life*, p. 42).

16 Arberry, *Oriental*, p. 126. PEF: PAL (ii), 12-29, Nicholl to

Besant, 18 Dec. 1882. Although a mathematician, Todhunter had an interest in and a facility for languages and could speak Greek, French, German, Spanish, Italian, Russian and Hebrew (Anon, 'Todhunter, Isaac' in *Alumni Cantabrigienses*, Cambridge: Cambridge University Press, 1922).

17 The translation was of 'Lalla Rookh' written by the Irish poet, singer, songwriter and entertainer Thomas Moore. The Persian manuscript was 'Maksad-i-Aksa' byAziz ibn Mohammad Nafasi. Palmer grandly dedicated his English version to Emperor Napoleon III (Bidwell, 'Edward').

18 Anon, 'Besant's life of Palmer', *The Eagle*, 13, 1883, pp. 18-29.

19 Joseph A. Good, 'The Dark Circle: Spiritualism in Victorian and Neo-Victorian Fiction', PhD diss., University of South Florida, 2012, pp. 1-2.

20 The doctor believed he was suffering from tetanus.

21 Besant, *The Life*, p. 115; Jennings, *Widnall*, p, 41; Anon, 'Edward Henry', p. 233; *London Gazette*, 10 March 1863.

22 Jennings, *Widnall*, p. 112, 116. Laura's poetry was published for private circulation in 1876 in a volume entitled *Thoughts in Verse*.

23 *Morning Post*, 5 Nov. 1867, p. 3.

24 Besant, *The Life*, p. 116.

25 *Ibid.*, p. 53; *London Gazette*, 11 Sept. 1866. After the announcement of her engagement, Laura was sent to a Mrs Sharp at Dallington to be 'finished' (Jennings, *Widnall*, p. 116, 139).

26 John James Moscrop, *Measuring Jerusalem: The Palestine Exploration Fund and British Interests*, Leicester: Leicester University Press, 1999, pp. 81, 216-8; Fraser, 'Man-hunting', p.15.

27 Wilson was later to help establish the War Office Intelligence Department and serve as Britain's Turkish Consul General. Both Captain Henry Spencer Palmer and Reverend F. W. Holland were to die relatively young, respectively at the age

fifty-four in Tokyo of typhoid fever and forty-three in a climbing accident in Switzerland.

28 Besant, *The Life*, p. 70. The expedition is described in Edward Henry Palmer, *The Desert of the Exodus: Journeys on Foot in the Wilderness of the Forty Years' Wanderings*, London: Deighton, Bell and Co., 1871.

29 Robert Irwin, *For Lust of Knowing. The Orientalists and their Enemies*, London: Allen Lane, 2006, p. 181; Charles Moore Watson, *The Life of Major-General Sir Charles William Wilson, Royal Engineers*, London: John Murray, 1909, p. 71. Palmer had identified a large number of place names and collected much information on the local Bedouin, though some of his findings are eerily reminiscent of the schoolboy humour to be found in his letters; for example his claim that the severed foreskins of circumcised young boys were placed on the toes of favoured sisters, where they remained until they disintegrated (Charles William Wilson, *Ordnance Survey of the Peninsula of Sinai*, London: Palestine Exploration Fund, 1869, p. 56). The India Office post was awarded to the German Sanskritist, Reinhold Rost.

30 Watson, *The Life*, p. 88-9; Richard F. Burton and Charles F. Tyrwhitt Drake, *Unexplored Syria. Visits to the Libanus, the Tulul el Safa, the Anti-Libanus, the Northern Libanus, and the Alah*, London: Tinsley Bros., 1872, p. 15; Moscrop, *Measuring*, pp. 96-7; Walter Besant (ed.), *The Literary Remains of Charles Frederick Tyrwhitt Drake*, London, 1877, pp. 9-10.

31 Besant (ed.), *The Literary*, p. 11; PEF: PAL/1-9, Palmer to Besant, 31 Dec. 1869; *ibid*, Palmer to Besant, 18 Jan. 1870.

32 *Ibid.*, Palmer to Besant, 31 Dec. 1869. For a full description of the journey, see Palmer, 'The desert of Tih', pp. 1-70.

33 PEF: PAL/1-9, Palmer to Besant, 21 March 1870. It is now generally accepted that Ain el-Qudeirat is the location of Kadesh (Duane A. Garrett and Walter C. Kaiser Jnr., *Archaeological Study Bible: An Illustrated Walk Through Biblical*

History and Culture, Grand Rapids: Zondervan, 2005, p. 14).

34 Besant, *The Life*, p. 185.

35 Mary S. Lovell, *A Rage to Live: A Biography of Richard and Isabel Burton*, New York: W. W. Norton, 1998, p. 260; Besant (ed.), *The Literary*, pp. 14-16; PEF: PAL/1-9, Palmer to Besant, 2 June 1870. In Vienna, Palmer visited the Hungarian orientalist Arminius Vambery and the American mathematician and philosopher Charles Sanders Pierce. Although horrified that the Persian manuscript had been stolen, Leland nonetheless accepted the gift (Charles Godfrey Leland, *The Gypsies*, London: Houghton, Mifflin and Co., 1882, p. 298).

36 Besant (ed.), *The Literary*, pp. 16-21; Moscrop, *Measuring*, pp. 96-7. On being told of Drake's death, Palmer wrote 'just now I am in the dumps for I have heard that Drake, my friend and fellow traveller [has] died' (BL: Leland 37173, Palmer to Leland, 26 June 1874).

37 Walter Besant and Edward Henry Palmer, *Jerusalem. The City of Herod and Saladin*, London: Chatto & Windus, 1899; Andrew Vincent, 'The Jew, the Gipsy and El-Islam: An Examination of Richard Burton's Consulship in Damascus and His Premature Recall, 1868-1871', *Journal of the Royal Asiatic Society*, 2 (1985), pp. 162-5; *The Times*, 7 Nov. 1870, p. 5; *ibid.*, 17 May 1870, p. 6. On visiting tombs described by Palmer as containing a crypt and surrounded by a sacrificial area, the group who went in search of the missing Palmer party were disappointed to find only a few heaps of small stones, prompting one group member to dismiss the *The Desert of the Exodus* as 'twaddle' (PM: Diaries, Vol. 2, 31 Dec. 1882). On this occasion, Burton survived; the Foreign Office merely sending an official to investigate his comments.

38 Henry Grifin Williams had held the Thomas Adams Chair since 1854 and was notoriously unproductive, publishing little of note. In fact, Palmer was not the only Cambridge applicant – Rev. Stanley Leathes also applied for the post.

39 W. Robertson Smith, 'The life and achievements of Edward Henry Palmer', *Nature,* 26 July 1893 (28), pp. 292-3; Anon, 'Wright, William' in *Alumni Cantabrigienses,* Cambridge: Cambridge University Press, 1922. Palmer had received five votes and Leathes one. His only 'academic' publications were Edward Henry Palmer, *Oriental Mysticism. A Treatise on the Sufiistic and Unitarian Theosophy of the Persians, Compiled from Native Sources,* Cambridge: Deighton, Bell & Co., 1867 and Edward Henry Palmer, *A Descriptive Catalogue of the Arabic, Persian, and Turkish Manuscripts in the Library of Trinity College, Cambridge,* Cambridge: Deighton, Bell & Co., 1870.

40 Jennings, *Widnall,* p. 139; Anon, 'Towards understanding of the qur'an. A new translation of the glorious qur'an', *Journal of Muslim Minority Affairs,* 19 (1) (1999), pp. 131-43; *South Australian Register,* 5 June 1884.

41 Donald Paul Nurse, 'An amateur barbarian: the life and career of Sir Richard Francis Burton, 1821 -1890', DPhil diss., University of Toronto, 1999, p. 10; Anon, 'Edward Henry'; BL: Leland 37173, Palmer to Leland, 31 Dec. 1874; Edward Henry Palmer (ed.), *Trübner's Collection of Simplified Grammars of the Principal Asiatic and European Languages, Volumes 1-6,* Trübner & Co.: London; Hertford, 1882.

42 BL: Leland 37173, Palmer to Leland, 24 April 1874; Elizabeth Robins Pennell, *Charles Godfrey Leland: A Biography, Volume Two,* Boston, Mass.: Houghton, Mifflin, 1906, pp. 52-6; Leland, *The Gypsies,* p. 199; E. H. Palmer, 'Mohammed and Mohammedanism', *Quarterly Review,* 143 (1877), p. 237; Edward Henry Palmer, *A Grammar of the Arabic Language,* London, 1874; Edward Henry Palmer, *A Concise Dictionary of the Persian Language,* London: Trübner & Co., 1876; Edward Henry Palmer, *A History of the Jewish Nation From the Earliest Times to the Present Day,* London: Christian Knowledge Society, 1874; Edward Henry Palmer, *Haroun Alraschid, Caliph of Bagdad,* London: Marcus Ward, 1881; Edward Henry

Palmer, *The Qur'ân*, Oxford: Clarendon Press, 1880; Edward Henry Palmer, *The Song of the Reed and Other Pieces,* London: Trübner 1877; Edward Henry Palmer, *The Poetical Works of Behā-ed-Dīn Zoheir,* Cambridge: University Press, 1876-77; Edward Henry Palmer and Eiríkur Magnússon, *L. Runeberg's Lyrical Songs, Idylls and Epigrams,* London, 1878; C. G. Leland, E. H. Palmer and J. Tuckey, *English-Gipsy Songs in Romany with Metrical English Translations,* London, 1875. His co-author of the lyrical songs of the Finnish poet Johann Ludvig Runeberg was Eiríkur Magnússon, the University of Cambridge's Librarian (Andrew Wawn, *The Vikings and the Victorians: Inventing the Old North in Nineteenth-Century Britain,* Cambridge: Brewer, 2000, p. 57). *English-Gypsy Songs* was co-edited by Miss Janet Tuckey and Charles Leland. Commenting on the tsunami of poems Palmer submitted for the book, Tuckey wrote 'Palmer is dreadfully tiresome, but I do envy him his facility. Why he'd soon make a book all by himself!' (BL: Leland 37173, Tuckey to Leland, no date, 1874).

43 Stanley Lane-Poole, *Studies in a Mosque,* London: Allen, 1883, pp. 119-21; Bidwell, 'Edward'; Pennell, *Charles,* pp. 52-6; BL: Leland 37173, Palmer to Leland, 9 Nov. 1874; *ibid.,* 7 Jan. 1875; *ibid.,* 15-18 Jan. 1875; *ibid.,* 25 Jan. 1875; *ibid.,* 9 April 1875; *ibid.,* 6 May 1875; *ibid.,* no date, early June 1875. For a detailed criticism of his translation of the Koran and his other books see Muhammad Sultan Shah, 'A critical study of E. H. Palmer's translation of the Qur'an', *Hamdard Islamicus,* xxxv (2) and A. R. Nykl , 'Notes on E.H. Palmer's 'The Qur'an', *Journal of the American Oriental Society,* 56 (1) (1936), pp. 77-84.

44 BL: Leland 37173, Palmer to Leland, 24 April 1874; *ibid.,* 28 April 1874; *ibid.,* 26 June 1874; *ibid.,* 7 Dec. 1874; *ibid,* 31 Dec. 1874; Besant, *Autobiography,* p. 173; Pennell, *Charles,* pp. 52-6; Charles Godfrey Leland, *Memoirs,* London: D. Appleton,

1893, pp. 392-3. Palmer was determined to achieve high sales for all his books. He promised Leland that he would 'do [his] damnest to make [*English-Gypsy Songs*] go', if necessary resorting to 'a sandwich man with a prospectus on his hat [marching] up and down Regent Street' (BL: Leland 37173, Palmer to Leland, 21 April 1875). The perfect circular he argued would read 'You are earnestly requested to subscribe to the above work; it is the composition of a blind orphan who is deaf and dumb and has no use of his limbs. Unless 50,000 copies at a penny each are taken by a Christian and sympathising public, the book will remain unpublished, and the writer will have no resource but the workhouse or dishonesty' (*ibid.*, Palmer to Leland, 26 June 1874).

45 Anon, *The Savile Club, 1868-1923*, Edinburgh: Neill & Co., 1923, p. 126; Pennell, *Charles*, p. 52; Besant, *Autobiography*, p. 175, 240; Brander Matthews, *These Many Years, Recollections of a New Yorker*, New York: C. Scribner's Sons, 1917, pp. 276-82; Anon, *Recreations of the Rabelais Club, 1880-81*, London: Rabelais Club, 1881. To become a member of the Rabelais Club, candidates had to 'declare on oath that you have diligently read the works of the Master, or else you must make affidavit that you have not read them faithfully. So long as you can make one or the other of these declarations you are eligible' (Matthews, *These*, p, 282). Pretyman owned a boat and the two friends explored the Norfolk Broads together and went fishing for herring off the Yarmouth coast (William Finch-Crisp, *Chronological Retrospect of the History of Yarmouth and Neighbourhood from A.D. 46 to 1884*, London: J. Haddon & Co, 1884, 26 Feb. 1878).

46 On one memorable occasion, possessed by the spirit of a murdered girl, he drew a portrait of her murderer, which he later claimed was the exact likeness of the man later arrested on suspicion of the crime and who he alleged he subsequently bumped into after the individual had been released

due to lack of evidence. On recognising the 'murderer', Palmer claimed he cried out 'You? Why you ought to have been hanged six months ago' (Besant, *The Life*, p. 199).

47 H. Gay, 'Science and Opportunity in London, 1871-85: The Diary of Herbert McLeod', *History of Science*, 41 (2003), pp. 427-458; *London Gazette*, 19 July 1901.

48 BL: Leland 37173, Palmer to Leland, 9 July 1874; Matthews, *These*, pp. 279-80; Jennings, *Widnall*, p. 142. The name Herman Frikell was presumably a play on that of Adalbert Freikl, one of the most famous illusionists of the time.

49 Jennings, *Widnall*, p. 162; BL: Leland 37173, Palmer to Leland, 7 Dec. 1874.

50 Besant, *The Life*, p. 188, 209; Jennings, *Widnall*, p. 167; BL: Leland 37173, Palmer to Leland, 28 Oct. 1876; *ibid.*, Leland 37174, Palmer to Leland, no date (written on the evening of Laura's death); *London Standard*, 25 Sept. 1877; NA: T1/15649, 3528, Admiralty to Treasury, 16 Feb. 1883.

51 Richard Rive (ed.), *Olive Schreiner Letters, Volume 1*, Oxford: Clarendon Press, 1988, p. 177; 1881 Census; *London Standard*, 9 July 1879; *ibid.*, 13 Aug. 1881; Wilfrid Scawen Blunt, *India under Ripon. A Private Diary*, London: T. Fisher Unwin, 1909, p. 15; Jennings, *Widnall*, p. 179; *The Times*, 23 June 1884, p. 1.

52 BL: Leland 37173, Palmer to Leland, 28 April 1874. His decision may also have been influenced by the move from Cambridge University of his close friend William Bonney, who had obtained a Chair in geology at University College, London (David Oldroyd, 'Bonney, Thomas George (1833–1923)' in *Oxford Dictionary of National Biography*, Oxford: Oxford University Press, 2004).

53 Besant, *The Life*, p. 223.

54 Palmer and Besant (eds), *The Survey*; Edward Henry Palmer, *Simplified Grammar of Hindustani, Persian and Arabic*, London: Trübner & Company, 1882.

Chapter 6

1 Murray, *Sons of*, pp. 260-1; Richard F. Burton, *Personal Narrative of a Pilgrimage to El Medinah and Meccah*, London: W. Mullan & Son, 1879, p. 102. After several months imprisonment, Moussa was released on his lawyer proving from ancient manuscripts that the Towarah tribal areas lay beyond the Canal (Warren, *Notes*, p. 42).

2 PM: Correspondence, Burton to Mrs R. Burton, 15 Sept. 1882; *ibid.*, Burton to White, 6 Oct. 1882.

3 St John's College, Cambridge University: W.15 (James 611 and 612); Anon, 'Memoirs. Colonel E. M. Burton', *The Royal Engineers Journal*, 62 (1948); PM: Correspondence, Burton to Mrs R. Burton, 29 Sept. 1882. Kennedy returned to England in early October as his services were no longer required (*ibid.*). Prior to travelling to Egypt, Burton had spent four months in Dresden learning German (PM: Correspondence, Burton to War Office, 1 June 1885).

4 Haynes, *Man-Hunting*, p. 22, 24. It was later discovered that the Bedouin had been the servant of Wilfrid Blunt.

5 Haynes, *Man-Hunting*, p. 45.

Chapter 7

1 The chapter is based on Wright, *A Tidy*, pp. 161-263; Green, *Three*, pp. 125-34; Featherstone, *Tel el-Kebir*, pp. 49-73; Royle, *The Egyptian*, pp. 131-93; Vladimir Borisovich Lutsky, *Modern History of the Arab Countries*, Moscow: Progress Publishers, 1969, chapter xvii; Eric Wood, *The Boy's Book of Battles*, London: Cassell and Company, 1913, pp. 269-74; and 'Tel-El-Kebir'. Available from: http://rhf.org.uk/rhf/index.php?option=com_content&task=view&id=45&Itemid=59 (accessed October 2013).

2 Royle, *The Egyptian*, p. 163.

3 'Tel-El-Kebir'.

4 Brian Thompson, *Imperial Vanities*, London: Harper Collins,

2002, p. 191.

5 The officers obtained £1,000 in gold plus a pension of £12 per month. One ensured that his scouts did not encounter the advancing troops by shifting their position and the other used a lamp to help guide the British to the Tel-el-Kebir defences. In the event, the scouts had insufficient time to raise the alarm and the lantern was not seen.

Chapter 8

1 Haynes, *Man-Hunting*, p. 50.
2 Murray, *Sons of*, p. 248; Schölch, 'The Egyptian', p. 52.
3 Haynes, *Man-Hunting*, p. 55, 57.
4 *Ibid.*, p. 63.
5 *Ibid.*, p. 70.
6 *Ibid.*, p. 91.
7 PM: Diaries, Vol. 1, 15 Oct. 1882.
8 According to Henry Clay Trumbull, Moussa had 'a tall, good figure and his apparent height was increased by a long, narrow woolen robe and a large white turban that surmounted his head. His face, with tolerably good features, had a refined and manly expression; his deportment was easy, grave and dignified and he escorted us with as much suavity as if he had been accustomed to the refinement of civilised life' (Trumbull, *Kadesh-Barnea*, p. 247).

Chapter 10

1 John Ross Macduff, *Early Graves. A Book for the Bereaved*, London, 1883, p. 362; Yule, 'Memoir', p. 62, 64, 65. Except where stated, the chapter is based on Hadland, *Glimpses*, Yule, 'Memoir' and Tony Hadland, 'William Gill, spy and explorer'. Available from: http://www.radleyhistoryclub.org.uk/report_april_2014.pdf (accessed November 2014).
2 Anon, *Selected Papers from the Transactions of the Canadian Military Institute, 1891-92*, Toronto: Royal Canadian Military

Institute, 1892, p. 25; Charles Edwards Buckland, *Dictionary of Indian Biography*, London: Haskell House Publishers, 1906, p. 166; William Rubinstein, 'Jewish Top Wealth-Holders in Britain, 1809-1909', *Jewish Historical Studies*, 37 (2002), p. 141.

3 *The Times*, 16 Nov. 1883, p. 10.

4 The Persian expedition is discussed in Thompson, *Imperial*, pp. 156-8; Dorothy Anderson, *Baker Pasha: Misconduct and Mischance*, Norwich: Michael Russell, 1999, pp. 21-30; Valentine Baker, *Clouds in the East*, London: Chatto & Windus, 1876.

5 Baker, *Clouds*, p. 118.

6 *Ibid.*, p. 130.

7 *Ibid.*, p. 199.

8 *Ibid.*, p.188.

9 Thompson, *Imperial*, pp. 160-6. The attack was responsible for the redesign of train compartments; a window was added to the partitions between compartments and connecting corridors and 'ladies only' carriages introduced.

10 Dicey, *The Story*, pp. 331-2, 348.

11 C. B. E. Reed, *Memoir of Sir Charles Reed*, London: Macmillan, 1883, pp. 131-2.

12 Royal Geographical Society (RGS): WJG 7. Margary's death allowed the British government to put pressure on the Chinese government on a number of unrelated issues. Britain eventually invaded Tibet in 1903/4 (G. C. Boase, 'Margary, Augustus Raymond (1846–1875)' in *Oxford Dictionary of National Biography*, Oxford: Oxford University Press, 2004; Warren W. Smith, *History of Tibet: Nationalism and Self-determination*, Boulder, Colorado: Westview Press, 1996, pp. 154–6).

13 Gill, *The River*, p. 13, 36. The China expedition is described in Gill, *The River* and RGS: WJG 5-6; Journal MSS. China, 1877: Gill, W.J., JMS 10/70. Yule later translated the works of Marco Polo and Frair Jordanus and compiled a dictionary of Anglo-

Indian terms. Von Richtofen is now remembered for coining the term 'the silk road' (Felix Driver, 'Yule, Sir Henry (1820–1889)' in *Oxford Dictionary of National Biography*, Oxford: Oxford University Press; Anon, 'Richthofen, Ferdinand, Baron von' in *Encyclopædia Britannica* (11th ed.), Cambridge: Cambridge University Press, 1911). Wade worked in British embassies in China for over forty years, wrote numerous books on the teaching of Mandarin and campaigned for the discontinuation of 'slicing' executions ('death by a thousand cuts') (Anon, 'Wade, Thomas Francis' in *Alumni Cantabrigienses*, Cambridge: Cambridge University Press, 1922).

14 Anon, 'Edward Colborne Baber', *Dictionary of National Biography. Sup. Volume I*, Oxford: Oxford University Press, 1901.

15 Gill, *The River*, p. 107, 130. Baber remained in China until 1885, making an expedition to the Sichuan highlands in 1877 and the mountains to the north of Chongqing the following year. After acting as Consul General in Formosa (Taiwan), he was transferred to Bhamo, where he died of disease at the age of forty-seven.

16 Hadland, *Glimpses*, p. 20.

17 Keith Stevens, 'A Jersey adventurer in China', *Journal of the Royal Asiatic Society, Hong Kong Branch*, 32 (1992), pp. 1-101.

18 Gill, *The River*, p. 162.

19 *Ibid.*, p. 183, 185, 188, 231. There was a great demand for scarves. Etiquette ordained that each gift had to be accompanied by a scarf, and, on visits to monasteries, they were tied to the rails that protected statues of the Buddha.

20 *Ibid.*, p. 223.

21 *Ibid.*, p. 300, 302, 310, 362. The civil war was between the local populace and the Moslem Hui Hui, identified 'by the white turbans they wear'. 'Acts of frightful cruelty were perpetrated and retaliations still more cruel followed' (*ibid.*,

p. 251, 252).

22 *Ibid.*, p. 313, 316.

23 Stevens, 'A Jersey'. Mesny's skating rink was destroyed by a typhoon.

24 A humorous account of the journey written by Gill later appeared in the weekly magazine *Vanity Fair*.

25 Hadland, *Glimpses*, p. 50. The border was eventually mapped by Edward Hamley, who later fought at the battle of Tel-el-Kebir. During a conversation with a General Sletnitzky, Gill obtained confirmation of Russia's threat to India. The General told him 'we shall get there (India) – we shall creep on and on, for there will always be plenty of fools in England who will believe that we are not doing so; and then some day when you English are unprepared we shall strike the blow' (*ibid.*, p. 45).

26 *Ibid.*, p. 56.

27 The trip to Afghanistan and across Persia is described in RGS: WJG 2: India, Marri Expedition, Persia, Russia – 20th August 1880 to 1st April 1881; Brian Robson, *The Road to Kabul: The Second Afghan War 1878-1881*, Stroud: Spellmount, 2007, p. 239.

28 Hadland, *Glimpses*, p. 62; PM: Diaries, Vol. 2, 5 Dec. 1882. The Tripoli expedition is described in RGS: WJG 4: Tripoli – 18th October 1881 to 16th June 1882.

29 Yule, 'Memoir', p. 48. Gill greatly regretted having to resort to bribery –'it is very immoral...We hold up our hands in pious horror at him who bribes the ignorant voter, and here I am without shame trying to bribe these men to fail in their duty to their government and to go back and tell a pack of lies. It is immoral, there is no doubt about it. We say in England that he who bribes is worse than he who is bribed. Then what a wicked man I must be' (Hadland, *Glimpses*, p. 62).

Chapter 11

1 Williams, *The Life,* p. 146. On occasion, however, Warren acted in a cavalier fashion. For example, he continued to employ his and his colleagues' cook even when he discovered that the Bedouin was the brother of one of the murderers. The cook claimed not to like his sibling or approve of his crime and Warren reasoned that they were less rather than more likely to be poisoned by allowing him to carry on preparing their meals. Aware that he would be blamed if they died, the cook would take every precaution against anyone else contaminating their food.

2 'Professor Palmer's expedition', *Manchester Times,* 4 Nov. 1882.

3 Trumbull, *Kadesh-Barnea,* p. 250; Field, *On the,* p. 215; Bartlett, *From Egypt,* p. 325, 330.

4 Haynes, *Man-Hunting,* p. 138; PM: Diaries, Vol. 1, 30 Oct. 1882. The three Englishmen 'very cold heartedly refused to give [the Bedouin] a drop' of their water, as 'we had very little ourselves and had we given away any we should have had the whole of the camp round us' (*ibid.*).

Chapter 12

1 Charles N. Robinson, *Celebrities of the Army,* London: Publishers' Syndicate 1900, p. 32; Robert I. Rotberg, *The Founder: Cecil Rhodes and the Pursuit of Power,* Oxford: Oxford University Press, 1988 p. 171; Ian F. W. Becket, *Victorians at War,* London: Hambledon and London, 2003, p. 62. Except where stated, the chapter is based on Williams, *The Life*; 'Defender' (pseud.), *Sir Charles Warren and Spion Kop, with a Biographical Sketch,* London: Smith, Elder and Co., 1902, pp. 1-54 and Colin Macdonald, *Warren! The Bond of Brotherhood,* London: Colman Street Books, 2008.

2 His father later commanded the Infantry brigade at Malta, and, on his retirement, was created a Knight Commander of

the Bath.

3 Solomon's Temple was destroyed by the Babylonians in 586 BCE; Zerubbabel Temple was demolished by the Roman Empire in 70 CE. The Jerusalem expedition is described in Charles Warren, *Underground Jerusalem*, London: R. Bentley and Son, 1876.

4 *The Times*, April 5, 1869.

5 David Jacobson, 'Charles Warren vs. James Fergusson. Where Was the Israelite Temple Located?', *Biblical Archaeology Review*, 29 (Sept./Oct. 2003).

6 Williams, *The Life*, p. 45; Anon, 'Sir Charles Warren', *The Geographical Journal*, 69 (4) (1927), p. 383.

7 Jacobson, 'Charles'. The 'Moabite stone' had actually been discovered by a German, the Reverend Frederick Klein (Silberman, *Digging*, p. 110). Coincidentally, one of the goals of Edward Palmer's and Charles Trywhitt Drake's later 1869/70 expedition to the Desert of Tih and Moab was to discover stonework containing inscriptions similar to those found on the 'Moabite stone'.

8 Linda Waldman, *The Griqua Conundrum: Political and Socio-cultural Identity in* the *Northern Cape*, Oxford: Peter Lang, 2007, p. 82, 84. The survey and Warren's time as Griqualand West's Land Claims Commissioner is discussed in Charles Warren, *On the Veldt in the Seventies*, London: Isbister & Co., 1902.

9 Warren, *On the*, p. 40, 48, 54, 90.

10 Those Griqua who successfully held onto their plots were generally persuaded by speculators to sell them at a fraction of their true value, the proceeds of sales often being used to fund a descent into alcoholism.

11 Warren, *On the*, p. 201, 261, 275.

12 *Ibid.*, p. 307.

13 J. Fage and R. Oliver, *The Cambridge History of Africa, Volume 6*, Cambridge: Cambridge University Press, 1985, p. 387; C.

Bundy, *The Rise and Fall of South African Peasantry*, Berkeley: University of California Press, 1979, p. 83; Rotberg, *The Founder*, p. 119. There was also a fear that the continued existence of independent African states increased the likelihood of a general and simultaneous rising of kafirdom against white civilisation.

14 The Diamond Fields Horse had been formed the previous year via the amalgamation of two other volunteer forces (Anon, *A Very Brief Regimental History*, Kimberley: Kimberley Regiment Association, 2010).

15 Williams, *The Life*, p. 75.

16 'So gross was the injustice sustained by these people in the land court', a former Governor told the Cape Parliament, 'that, had I been a Griqua, I too would have rebelled' (Rotberg, *The Founder*, p. 119).

17 After the Griqualand West campaign, the Diamond Fields Horse fought in the 1880/1 Basutoland Gun War and were then disbanded (Anon, *A Very Brief*). Lanyon later fought in the 1882 Anglo-Egyptian war.

18 Situated forty miles North of Kimberley, Warrenton now has a population of 18,000.

Chapter 13

1 Haynes, *Man-Hunting*, p. 144.

2 Burton, 'The late', pp. 329-30.

3 PP 1883 [C.3494], Warren to Seymour, 14 Nov. 1882, Enclosure 1, Evidence of Sofieh, 7 Nov. 1882.

4 Haynes, *Man-Hunting*, p. 147.

5 Hammond later repaid the money to Mrs Palmer.

6 Many Bedouins believed the £2,000 had been buried elsewhere in the Wadi and was never recovered (Larry Roeder Page, *The Bedouin Tribes of the Sinai: Lecture Book*, Self-published, 1988, p. 28).

7 PM: Diaries, Vol. 3, 3 Jan. 1883. He later denied making the

latter statement.

8 Warren had earlier tried to 'break' Sheyk by questioning him in the presence of Sofiah. Unfortunately, the guide had 'got into such a passion' that the interview had to be abandoned (Haynes, *Man-Hunting*, p. 145).

9 'Spencer Calmeyer Charrington'. Available from: http://www.findagrave.com/cgi-bin/fg.cgi?page=gr&GRid=7671817 (accessed October 2013).

10 Joseph Foster, *Men-at-the-Bar: A Biographical Hand-List of the Members of the Various Inns of Court*, London: Reeves and Turner, 1885; *The Times*, 16 Oct. 1882, p. 7; PM: Diaries, Vol. 2, 8 Nov. 1882; *ibid.*, 13 Nov. 1882; PM: Correspondence, Burton to Mrs R. Burton, 18 Dec. 1882. Charrington was so intent on going to Egypt that he pulled out of forthcoming London School Board elections (*The Times*, 21 Oct. 1882, p. 8). Gill and Houndle attended most of the Suez interrogations. Charrington went to one or two, but according to Burton 'read the newspaper the whole time' (PM: Diaries, Vol. 2, 20 Dec. 1882).

11 PM: Diaries, Vol. 2, 14 Nov. 1882; PM: Correspondence, Burton to Mrs R. Burton, 18 Dec. 1882. Neither Gill nor Houndle wished to visit Wady Sudr.

12 PM: Diaries, Vol. 3, 5 Feb. 1882. Trumbull, *Kadesh-Barnea*, p. 246; Bartlett, *From Egypt*, p. 332. According to Samuel Bartlett, who in 1881 employed Suileman as a guide, the Sheikh was 'a fine looking Arab, slender and graceful with a bright countenance, a clear eye and a fine black beard...he was evidently aware of his fine personal appearance and was more picturesquely, expensively and tastefully dressed than any Bedouin I have seen' (*ibid.*, p. 331).

13 George West, the Governor of Suez, suspected a further reason for Salami's refusal to arrest Murshid was that he feared that if the fugitive was subsequently executed his 'vindictive' family would take revenge either on himself or

his relatives (NA: FO 78/3587, West to Granville, 25 June 1883). The theft by sheikhs of the property of nationalist prisoners was a common practice. There is no evidence that it was sanctioned by the Khedive (Thomas Archer, *The War in Egypt and the Soudan. An Episode in the History of the British Empire*, London: Blackie and Son, 1887, p. 150).

Chapter 14

1 Mordechai Eliav, *Britain and the Holy Land, 1838-1914: Selected Documents from the British Consulate in Jerusalem*, Jerusalem: Yad Izhak Ben-Zvi Press, 1997, pp. 81-2; Anon, 'Moore, Noel Temple', *Who Was Who 1897-1915*, London: A. & C. Black, 1920; Graham I. Davies, 'Fresh evidence on E. H. Palmer's travels from Cambridge libraries' in Carmel McCarthy and John F. Healey(eds.), *Biblical and Near Eastern Essays: Studies in Honour of Kevin J. Cathcart*, London: T. & T. Clark International, 2004, pp. 331-40; James Finn, *A View from Jerusalem, 1849-1858: The Consular Diary of James and Elizabeth Anne Finn*, Rutherford: Fairleigh Dickinson, 1980, pp. 315-6. Except where stated, the chapter is based on PP 1883 [C.3494] [C.3761] and NA: FO 78/3416.

2 In 1890, Moore was transferred to Tripoli with the rank of Consul-General. He retired in 1894 and died eleven years later in Hastings.

3 Neil Asher Silberman, *Digging for God and Country: Exploration, Archaeology, and the Secret Struggle for the Holy Land, 1799-1917*, New York: Knopf, 1982, p. 132; Besant (ed.), *The Literary*, pp. 36-7; NA: ADM 16/45, No. 3, Bond to Foreign Office, 13 Dec. 1882.

4 NA: FO 78/3416, Yule to Northbrook, 19 Oct. 1882.

5 NA: ADM 16/45, No. 3, Shapira to Bond, 30 Nov. 1882; *ibid.*, Warren to Hewitt, 16 Feb. 1883.

6 Burton, *The Life*, p. 603.

7 PM: Correspondence, Burton to Mrs R. Burton, 18 Dec. 1882.

8 Silberman, *Digging*, pp. 132-45. The discovery of the Dead Sea scrolls in 1947 in the same area has cast doubt on the original forgery charges. Shapira's Scrolls disappeared, only to re-emerge a couple of years later in a Sotheby's auction, where they were sold for 10 guineas. It seems likely that they were destroyed in 1887 in a fire at the house of their then owner, Sir Charles Nicholson.

9 Burton, *The Life*, p. 242; Lovell, *A Rage*, p 240; Anon, 'Burton, Sir Richard Francis', *Dictionary of National Biography*, Oxford: Oxford University Press, 1901.

10 In fact, the small truss was later identified as belonging to Palmer.

11 PM: Diaries, Vol. 2, 27 Nov. 1882.

12 Jon R. Godsall, *The Tangled Web: A Life of Sir Richard Burton*, Leicester: Matador, 2008, p. 369.

Chapter 15

1 Field, *On the*, p, 239; Alexander Innes Shand, *Days of the Past. A Medley of Memories*, New York: E. P. Button & Co., 1905, p. 239. There is some confusion regarding Sheikh Suileman's allegiences. Although, publicly supporting Arabi and providing him with scouts, there is evidence that he secretly agreed to supply the Khedive with information on the nationalist army's movements and plans (al-Mamalik, *In the Land*, p. 116).

2 PP 1893 [C. 3761], Warren's history of the expedition, 21 Feb. 1883.

3 *South Australian Register*, 5 June 1884; Edward Hull, *Mount Seir, Sinai and Western Palestine*, London: Bentley, 1885, p. 33; *The Standard*, 2 March, 1883, p. 3.

4 ADM 16/45, No. 3, Trial proceedings.

5 Clark, *Old Friends*, p. 276. There were unsubstantiated rumours that Sofieh had replied when asked for the money 'I shall send the money back to its owners' and, after the

negotiations had come to an end, that he was unconditionally offered the prisoners by Murshed, but refused to take them. Both reports appear unlikely.

6 Yule, 'Memoir', p. 64.

Chapter 16

1 Wilfrid Scawen Blunt, *Atrocities of Justice Under British Rule in Egypt,* London: Fisher Unwin, 1907, p. 18. In the short-term, the executions did increase traveller safety. Colonel Kitchener, who subsequently visited the region in late 1883, remarked 'Warren's energetic action in the capture and bringing to justice of the perpetrators…has created a deep impression, and I consider the whole peninsula is now, for foreign travellers, as safe as, if not safer, than it was previously" (Haynes, *Man-Hunting,* p. 272). His optimism proved premature. The Bedouin soon returned to their old ways. In May 1890, a party of English gentlemen were seized and held to ransom, and, five years later, an expedition led by the archaeologist George Robinson was attacked by the Teyahah, who agreed to let them pass on the payment of a 'considerable quantity' of gold after a fire fight lasting twenty minutes (Robinson, 'Modern').

2 Hull, *Mount Seir,* p. 33; Burton, *The Life,* pp. 612-3; Philip Magnus, *Kitchener. Portrait of an Imperialist,* London: Penguin, 1968, p. 39; E. S. Grew, *Lord Kitchener. His Life and Work for the Empire,* London: Gresham, 1916, pp. 87-8.

3 PM: Diaries, Vol. 2, 26 Dec. 1882.

4 PM: Diaries, Vol. 3, 4 Feb. 1883.

5 Haynes, *Man-Hunting,* p. 268.

6 *House of Commons Debates,* 5 April 1883, Vol. 277, cc1477-81; Archer, *The War,* p. 151; Haynes, *Man-Hunting,* p. 149.

7 PM: Correspondence, Burton to Mrs R. Burton, 20 Nov. 1882; *ibid.,* Burton to Mrs R. Burton, 4 Dec. 1882; *ibid.,* Burton to Mrs R. Burton, 18 Dec. 1882; PM: Diaries, Vol. 2, 12/11;

Wilfrid Scawen Blunt, *Gordon at Khartoum. Being a Personal Narrative of Events in Continuation of "A Secret History of the English Occupation of Egypt"*, London: S. Swift & Co., 1911, p. 52.

8 PM: Correspondence, Burton to Mrs R. Burton, 4 Jan. 1883.

9 It would appear that this was the reason Warren decided to question the prisoners at Nakhl, thus breaking his agreement to Shedide not to enter the desert during the 21 days that the Sheikh was searching for suspects and witnesses, rather than arranging for them to be brought to Suez for interrogation.

10 PM: Diaries, Vol. 2, 26 Dec. 1882.

11 *The Times*, 18 Oct. 1882, p. 6.

12 PM: Diaries, Vol. 2, 11 Nov. 1882; *ibid.*, 5 Dec. 1882; *ibid.*, 18 Jan. 1883; NA: ADM 116/ 44, No. 2, Burton to Foreign Office, 11 Dec. 1882; Burton, 'The late'. Sofieh's nephew stated that his uncle had adopted a false identity in order to be employed by Palmer (NA: ADM 16/45, No. 3, Trial proceedings, evidence).

13 Besant, *The Life*, p. 279.

14 Haynes, *Man-Hunting*, p. 161, 173; Burton, *The Life*, p. 611; *The Brisbane Courier*, 19 July 1883.

15 Haynes, *Man-Hunting*, p. 173.

16 Palmer, *The Desert*, p. 297.

17 NA: T1/15649, No. 144, Admiralty to Treasury, 28 Dec. 1882. His friend Thomas Bonney believed that on 'moving to London and journalism he had quickly obtained a large amount of rather lucrative literary work' (Bonney, *Memoires*, p. 111). There were also perhaps financial reasons behind his decision to send his two daughters to be brought up in Germany.

18 'The Straker Family'. Available from: http://homepage.ntlworld.com/andy.kelly/straker/index.htm (accessed October 2013); Besant, *The Life*, pp. 217-18; *Cambrian News and Merionthshire Standard*, 25 Oct. 1907, p. 6; HM Courts &

Tribunals Service: Estate of Mary Ann Straker. No evidence has been found to support William Palmer's claims that he fought in Italy or that became an officer in the army of liberation.

19 London Gazette, 19 May 1874; Archifdy Ceredigion Archives: BRA/7; 'History of Aberystwyth 1850-1900'. Available from: http://www.aberystwythguide.org.uk/history/to1900.shtml (accessed October 2013).

20 Archifdy Ceredigion Archives: BRA/7; W. P. Spalding, *Spalding's Directory of Cambridge 1878*, Cambridge, 1878; Besant, *Autobiography*, p. 153. Ironically, William Palmer later prospered. He repurchased the Queens Hotel, bought the nearby Belle Vue Hotel in 1884, and, the following year, became a major shareholder in the Aberystwyth Pier Co. Ltd, which took over the Promenade Pier. Elected an Alderman and later Mayor of Aberystwyth, he died in 1909, leaving a fortune of £18,445 (Archifdy Ceredigion Archives: [GB 0212] D/LO, 16; *Cambrian News and_Merionthshire Standard*, 20 Oct. 1893, p. 4.; *ibid.*, 25 Oct. 1907, p. 6; *Cardiff Times*, 3 April 1909, p. 7; George Eyre Evans, *Aberystwyth and Its Court Leet*, Aberystwyth: Welsh Gazette, 1902).

21 Clark, *Old Friends*, p. 246; BL: Leland 37173, Palmer to Leland, 28 Oct. 1878; HM Courts & Tribunals Service: Estate of William Edward Pretyman.

22 Besant, *The Life*, p. 217-8; Besant, *Autobiography*, p. 154; ADM 16/45, No. 4, Palmer's solicitors to Admiralty, 29 May 1883.

23 PP 1893 [C. 3761], Palmer to Hewett, 1 Aug. 1882; ADM 16/45, No. 4, Schapiro to Foreign Office, February 1883; Blunt, *A Secret*, p. 306, 307.

24 Palmer writes in the *Desert of the Exodus* 'Thanks to the terrible rigour of the Vendetta or blood feud, homicide is far rarer in the desert than in civilised lands' (Palmer, *The Desert*, p. 80).

25 *South Australian Register*, 5 June 1884; PM: Diaries, Vol. 2, 11

Feb. 1883; PM: Correspondence, Burton to Mrs R. Burton, 20 Feb. 1883. Warren first met Besant in his early twenties when he was stationed at Gibraltar (NA: PRO 30/57/5, Kichener papers, 'Sinai Peninsula Survey and London politics', 1884). Both were Freemasons and helped co-found the Quatur Coronati lodge.

26 Page, *The Bedouin*, p. 245-6; Warren, *Notes*, p. 40; PM: Diaries, Vol. 2, 23 Nov. 1882. Lieutenant Burton suspected Shedide had achieved his freedom through bribery (PM: Correspondence, Burton to Mrs R. Burton, 20 Feb. 1883).

27 PM: Correspondence, Burton to Mrs R. Burton, 20 Feb. 1883.

28 Virginia Berridge and Griffith Edwards, *Opium and the People: Opiate Use in Nineteenth-Century England*, London: Allen Lane, 1981, p. 122; Jessica Rae Henderson, 'Opium use in Victorian England: The works of Gaskell, Eliot and Dickens', PhD thesis, Boise State University, 2009, pp. 1-4.

Chapter 17

1 *House of Commons Debates, 25 October 1882, Vol. 274, cc72-3;* Becket, *Victorians*, p. 60. Except where stated, the chapter is based on Williams, *The Life*; 'Defender' (pseud.), *Sir Charles;* and Macdonald, *Warren!*. Warren had tried to form a similar lodge in 1862 and in 1873 (*ARS Quatuor Coronaturum*, 1, 1886, p. 8).

2 Rotberg, *The Founder*, pp. 170-1, 178, 179; Harry Hamilton Johnson, *A History of the Colonization of Africa by Alien Races*, Cambridge: Cambridge University Press, 1899, p. 87. Garnet Wolseley was appointed to rescue General Gordon. The advance party was led by Captain Charles Wilson, who was an associate of both Edward Palmer, leading the 1868/9 Sinai survey, and Warren. Wilson's Column reached Khartoum in the afternoon of 28th January 1885. It was two days too late. The Mahdi had seized Khartoum and had slaughtered between 5,000 and 10,000 of its residents, including Gordon.

3 Edward M. Spiers, *The Victorian Soldier in Africa*, Manchester: Manchester University Press, 2004, pp. 132-3, 135.

4 Rhodes, who was twenty-four, was holidaying in South Africa prior to returning to his studies at Oriel College, Oxford.

5 Rotberg, *The Founder*, p. 171; *Quarterly Review*, 161 (1885), p. 540.

6 He was also up against a sitting MP and a former Government Minister, who was personally known to the electors.

7 Groups of demonstrators had broken away from the Trafalgar Square protest and rioted in Pall Mall, St James' and Oxford Street. Owing to poor communications, police commanders had sent constables to the Mall rather than Pall Mall.

8 Warren's time as Commissioner is described in Paul Begg, *Jack the Ripper: The Definitive History*, London: Longman/ Pearson Education, 2004, pp. 75-99.

9 'When Sir Charles Warren Rode Down a London Mob', *Daily Northwestern*, 3 Feb. 1900; Edward M. Spiers, *The Late Victorian Army, 1868-1902*, Manchester: Manchester University Press, 1992, p. 213; Bryan Tyson (ed.), *Bernard Shaw's Book Reviews, Volume 2, 1884-1950*, University Park, Pennsylvania: Pennsylvania State University Press, 1996, p. 372.

10 Some modern writers have accused Warren of complicity in the crimes. Knight has claimed that he was involved in a Masonic conspiracy to cover up the involvement of the Duke of Clarence; the key evidence being his decision to wash away the words 'The Jewes are not the men to be blamed for nothing' that had been scrawled in chalk on a wall close to the scene of one of the murders. It is argued that the message was written by the killer and removed because it referred to a Masonic ritual. In reality, Warren believed it to be an

attempt to blame the local Jewish population for the murders and had it washed off for fear that it would provoke riots (Barb Karg and Jon K. Young, *101 Secrets of the Freemasons: The Truth Behind the World's Most Mysterious Society*, London: Adams Media, 2009, p. 201).

Others believe that he was protecting Harold Charrington's uncle, Frederick, who campaigned for the closure of brothels and knew the area well, as the family brewery was close-by, or Colonel Claude Conder, whose presumed guilt is related to the cuts found on the dead women's bodies and the chalk message, both of which were purportedly cryptic messages written in an ancient language. Warren supposedly shielded Federick Charrington out of respect for Harold's father, still grieving the death of his son, and Claude Conder from Masonic loyalty and friendship – both men were Freemasons and had worked together at Woolwich and been employed by the Palestine Exploration Fund in Palestine (John J. Eddleston, *Jack the Ripper: An Encyclopaedia*, Santa Barbara: ABC-Clio, 2001, pp. 204-5; Christopher J. Morley, *Jack the Ripper: A Suspect Guide*, self-published, 2005, chap. 39).

11 'House of Commons Debates', *The Times*, 13 Nov. 1888.

12 An even more preposterous theory as to the identity of 'Jack the Ripper' is that the killer was none other than Henry Munro. He supposedly carried out the murders in order to expose Warren's unsuitability for office. He also had a pathological hatred of women (Robin Odel, *Ripperology: A Study of the World's First Serial Killer and a Literary Phenomenon*, Kent, Ohio: Kent State University Press, 2006, p. 149).

13 Macnaghten became Assistant Commissioner in 1903 and served until 1913 (Douglas G. Browne, *The Rise of Scotland Yard*, London: George G. Harrap & Co., 1956, p. 208).

14 Warren later claimed that Anderson also encouraged members of the CID to brief the press against him.

15 Munro's successor was none other than Edward Bradford, the one-armed Indian army officer who, along with William Gill, in 1882 had been instructed by Lord Northbrook to collect information on the Bedouin tribes bordering the Suez Canal. He served as Commissioner from 1890-1903.

16 Williams, *The Life*, p. 199.

17 Becket, *Victorians*, p. 62.

18 Warren's involvement in the Boer War is described in David Saul, *Military Blunders. The How and Why of Military Failure*, London: Robinson, 1997, pp. 150-80; Byron Farwell, *The Great Boer War*, London: Allen Lane, London, 1976, pp. 159-66; Alan Hunt, 'Charles Warren in Africa', *Journal of the Whitechapel Society*, April 2006; Thomas Pakenham, *The Boer War*, London: Abacus, 1997, pp. 281-319; and 'Defender' (pseud.), *Sir Charles*. Farwell describes the decision to give the command to Warren as an 'enigma' (Farwell, *The Great*, p. 159).

19 The battle is also notable for two other reasons. It gave its name to steep terracing at Liverpool Football Club's ground, which is known as 'the kop', and its participants included Winston Churchill; Lois Botha, the first President of South Africa and the instigator of Apartheid; and Mahatma Ghandi, who later led India to independence (Hunt, 'Charles').

20 Explaining why he failed to over-rule Warren, Buller stated 'I blame myself for not controlling him, but he was sent out after Colenso under such auspices that I did not like to interfere with him' (Lieut.-General the Earl of Dundonald, *My Army Life*, London: E. Arnold & Co., 1926, p. 133).

21 Anon, 'Sir Charles', p. 382. Redvers Buller died in 1908, just eight years after the end of the Boer War.

Chapter 18

1 Giuseppe Garibaldi (1807-82) was the Italian general and

politician responsible for the formation of a unified Italy.

2 Royle, *The Egyptian*, pp. 202-9; Green, *Three*, p. 138; Wright, *A Tidy*, p. 285; Karsh and Karsh, *Empires*, p. 132; Thompson, *Imperial*, p. 199.

3 Green, *Three*, pp. 134-137; Royle, *The Egyptian*, pp. 221-31; Karsh and Karsh, *Empires*, p. 66; Zaki-Khalil, 'British', p. 90; Lyngaas, 'Ahmad', pp. 1-13; Wright, *A Tidy*, p. 282; Thompson, *Imperial*, pp. 192-8; Jessica Watkins, 'British Colonial policies in the Arab region. Sowing the seeds of contemporary Middle Eastern security sectors?', *Arab Reform Initiative*, April 2012; M. W. Daly, 'The British occupation, 1882-1922' in Daly and Petry (eds), *Modern Egypt*, pp. 239-51.The tax code was amended, primary education promoted, agriculture and particularly the cotton sector expanded and the railway and irrigation system extended.

4 Brian Rogers Parkinson, 'Judge Pierre Crabites. A Borbon democrat in Egypt 1877-1943', PhD diss., Florida State University, 2005, pp. 82-3; Lyngaas, 'Ahmad'; Green, *Three*, p. 138; Wright, *A Tidy*, p. 280.

5 'Our Illustrations ', *The Graphic*, 24 March 1883. Warren had wanted the murderers executed at Moses Wells. Another site considered was Tel-el-Kebir.

6 Blunt, *Atrocities*, p. 19; 'The cholera in Egypt', *The Pall Mall Gazette*, 13 Aug. 1883; 'Imperial Parliament', *The Belfast News-Letter*, 17 Aug. 1883; *The Standard*, 17 Aug. 1883, p. 4; NA: ADM 16/45, No. 3, West to Suez Consul, 25 June 1883; *ibid.*, Warren to Admiralty, 15 Aug. 1883.

7 Haynes *Man-Hunting*, pp. 259-60; NA: ADM 16/45, No. 3, Warren to Admiralty, 10 April 1883; *ibid*, Warren to Admiralty, 11 Sept. 1883; *ibid.*, Cairo Consul to Foreign Office, 3 Nov. 1883.

8 *Ibid.*, Mallet to Granville, 13 May 1883; *ibid.*, ADM 16/45, No. 4, Warren to Admiralty, 17 Sept. 1883.

9 Bidwell, 'Edward', p. 49; *Academy*, November 18th 1882.

Walter Besant's poem 'The Death of Sheikh Abdullah' describes Palmer's curse and death:

Yea; like a Hebrew Prophet doth he tell,
Of swift revenge and death and women's moan;
And stricken babes and burning pains of hell.

Then each traitor's heart fell cold as stone.
And through their strong limbs fearful tremblings crept,
And brown cheeks paled and down dropped every head;

Then, with this last fierce prophecy he leaped.
My God! Abdullah Palmer art thou dead?
(Besant, The Life, p. 420).

Besant, ever the opportunist, later rushed out a biography of Palmer. Published in May 1883, just ten months after the Professor's death, the hagiography eventually sold 12,000 copies. It was followed in late 1883 by an edited edition of William Gill's *The River of Golden Sand,* which contained a brief memoir of its author written by Henry Yule.

10 *The Standard,* 7 April 1883, p. 5; Besant, *The Life,* p. 329; Hadland, *Glimpses,* p. 81. Ironically, twenty years later this same chapel became the resting place of T. E. Lawrence, who some regarded as a reincarnation of Palmer. Like his predecessor, Lawrence was physically small, a scholar at Cambridge University, worked for the Palestine Exploration Fund, and, during the First World War, attempted to rally the Bedouin, including the Hawetat, to the British cause, his cover being that he was attempting to fill in the blanks in the maps prepared by Palmer and Drake during the exploration of the desert of Tih. As with Palmer, he also met a violent death at a young age (Basil Henry Liddell Hart, *T. E. Lawrence: In Arabia and After,* London: Jonathan Cape, 1934,

pp. 13-14, 69; Fraser, 'Man-hunting', p. 15).

11 *The Eagle,* 13 (1883), p. 29; *The Standard,* 16 Nov. 1883, p. 2; Anon, 'Lieutenant Harold Charrington'; NA: ADM 16/45, No. 4, Supplementary correspondence; 'General intelligence', *The Star,* 6 March 1883; St John's College: W.3 (part); W. Baker Brown, *The History of the Corps of Royal Engineers. Volume IV,* Chatham: The Institution of Royal Engineers, 1952, p. 63; *Proceedings of the Royal Geographical Society,* 8 (5) (1886), p. 328; Hadland, *Glimpses,* pp. 181-4. Palmer's portrait was by his friend John Collier, who had painted Laura Palmer, the Professor's first wife, shortly before her death – 'a lovely picture, but very sad' (Jennings, *Widnall,* p. 170). Gill was further memoralised through the erection in Rochester Cathedral of a stained glass window and plaque paid for by his army regiment. His Brighton College scholarships are awarded annually to the sons of army officers in reduced circumstances. After Prince Frederick of Prussia visited the site when returning from Mount Sinai in March 1883, the murder scene became a minor tourist attraction.

12 PM: Diaries, Vol. 2, 5 Dec. 1882; NA: ADM 16/45, No. 4, Warren, 22 Feb. 1883; *ibid.* Warren to Admiralty, 20 April 1883.

13 ADM 16/45, No. 3,Warren to Admiralty, 23 Oct. 1883; *ibid.,* interpreter request; PM: Diaries, Vol. 2, 1 Feb. 1883; Murray, *Sons of,* pp. 175-6; Page, *The Bedouin,* p. 76.

14 PM: Correspondence, Burton to War Office, 1 June 1885; *ibid.,* draft letter, no date; NA: MR 1/250/2; Anon, 'Memoirs'.

15 Edwin Alfred Hervey Alderson, *With the Mounted Infantry and the Mashonaland Field Force, 1896,* London: Methuen, 1898; *The Times,* 11 Aug. 1896, p. 9. To mark Haynes' death, his family and friends raised a sum of money that was used to erect a monument in Rochester Cathedral and to fund the award of bronze medals to the best officer and sapper in each batch of recruits that completed the School of Engineering's

fieldwork course.

16 Haynes, *Man-hunting*, p. 268, 270, 269. The description of the Parliamentary investigation of the murder is taken from *House of Commons Debates, vol. 274, 26 Oct. 1882, , cc176-8; ibid., 27 Oct. 1882, c282; ibid.*, 30th Oct. 1882, c368-72; *ibid., vol. 276, 16 Feb. 1883, cc172-3; ibid., vol. 277, 12 March 1883, cc210-2; House of Lords Debates,* 16 March 1883; Haynes, *Man-Hunting*, pp. 268-71. Blunt offered to help rescue the party in a letter to *The Times* (*The Times*, 18 Oct. 1882, p. 6). His offer was not taken up because of his nationalist sympathies.

17 Haynes, *Man-hunting*, p 269.

18 Blunt, *Gordon*, p. 21; Blunt, *A Secret*, p. 311. Arabi's defence cost Blunt £3,500 (*The Bristol Mercury and Daily Post*, 29 March 1883).

19 Elizabeth Longford, *Pilgrimage of Passion. The Life of Wilfrid Scawen Blunt*, London: Tauris Parke, 1979.

20 Bernhard Maier, *William Robertson Smith. His Life, His Work and His Times*, Tübingen: Mohr Siebeck, 2009, p. 216, 218. Smith famously read only one novel per year and then only out of cultural duty. Bensley was a lecturer in Hebrew and Syriac at Gonville and Caius College. Lane-Poole was employed by the British Museum.

21 Maier, *William*, p. 216.

22 *Ibid.*, pp. 216-19; Irwin, *For Lust*, p. 183; John Sutherland Black and George Chrystal, *The Life of William Robertson Smith*, London: A. & C. Black, 1912, pp. 464-5. He was succeeded as the Lord Almoner Reader by Robert Lubbock Bensly.

23 Moscrop, *Measuring*, pp. 141-2; Tania Das Gupta (ed.), *Race and Racialization: Essential Readings*, Toronto: Canadian Scholars' Press, 2007, p. 54. Coincidentally, Hogarth's father, Rev. George Hogarth, was an acquaintance of Palmer's (Bruce Westrate, *The Arab Bureau. British Policy in the Middle East, 1916-1920*, University Park, Pennsylvania: The

Pennsylvania State University Press, 1992, p. 30).

24 Jennings, *Widnall*, p. 195; NA: T1/15649, No. 144, Admiralty to Treasury, 28 Dec. 1882; *ibid.*, No. 1133, Palmer's solicitors to Treasury, 13 Jan. 1883; *ibid.*, No. 3528, Admiralty to Treasury, 16 Feb. 1883; *ibid.*, No. 6823, Palmer's solicitors to Treasury, 10 April 1883; ADM 16/45, No. 4, Palmer's solicitors to Admiralty, 4 Dec. 1882; *ibid.*, Palmer's solicitors to Admiralty, 6 Dec. 1882; *ibid.*, Foreign Office to Admiralty, 24 March 1883; *ibid.*, Palmer's solicitors to Admiralty, 28 March 1883; *ibid.*, Palmer's solicitors to Admiralty, 29 May 1883; *ibid.*, Palmer's solicitors to Admiralty, 30 Nov. 1883; BL: MS 56863, Besant letters to Society of Authors; *The North-Eastern Daily Gazette*, 10 Jan. 1883, p. 4; Parmanand Parashar, *Public Administration in the Developed World*, New Delhi: Sarup, 1997, p. 134; Blunt, *India*, p. 14. Auguste's application to the Society of Authors was supported by Walter Besant and the Editor of the *Evening Standard*. The sequestrated creditors eventually received half the value of Palmer's insurance policies (NA: ADM 16/45, No. 4, solicitors to Admiralty, 29 May 1883). Wilfrid Blunt, who happened to sail to India on the same ship as Mrs Palmer's brother, described him as 'an amiable boy...very like his sister in face and voice' (Blunt, *India*, p. 16). He later achieved some fame for the design of the medal engraved to mark the 25th anniversary of the Conference of German Mennonite congregations ('Commemorative Medals', *Global Anabaptist Mennonite Encyclopaedia Online*. Available from: http://gameo.org/index.php?title=Commemorative_Medals&oldid=94221 (accessed October 2013).

25 HM Courts & Tribunals Service: Estate of Edward Henry Palmer; *The Times*, 23 June 1884, p. 1; Anon, 'Sir Bryan Donkin', *The British Medical Journal*, 6 Aug. 1927, p. 240; Douglas White, 'Society for the Prevention of Venereal Disease', *British Medical Journal*, 29 Nov. 1919, p. 725; *Evening*

Telegraph, 27 July 1927; 'Sex Toys. A History'. Available from: http://pincurlmag.com/tag/vibrators (accessed October 2013); David Garland, 'British criminology before 1935', *The British Journal of Criminology*, 28 (2) (1988); E. Showalter, *The Female Malady. Women, Madness and English Culture 1830-1980*, London: Virago Press, 2007, p, 121, 145. The greater use of condoms would merely encourage sexual promiscuity and the spread of disease.

26 Anon, *The Savile*, p. 117; Horatio Donkin, 'A note on thought-reading', *Popular Science Monthly*, 21 (September 1882), pp. 634-7; Anon, 'Sir Bryan'; *Clarence and Richmond Examiner*, 14 Nov. 1905; *The Sydney Morning Herald*, 12 Dec. 1876; Joseph McCabe, *Spiritualism: A Popular History from 1847*, London: Dodd, Mead and Company, 1920, pp. 160-161.

27 Rive (ed.), *Olive*, pp. 72-3, 116, 123-4, 123, 177; Johannes Meintjes, *Olive Schreiner. Portrait of a South African Woman*, Johannesburg: Hugh Keartland, 1965, pp. 86-7; Ruth First and Ann Scott, *Olive Schreiner*, London: Deutsch, 1980, p 124, 145, 170; T. M. Porter, *Karl Pearson: The Scientific Life in a Statistical Age*, Princeton: Princeton University Press, 2004. Eleanor Marx continued to have problems with her nerves, and, in 1898, on discovering that her partner had secretly married a young actress, she committed suicide by swallowing a phial of poison. She was 41 (Chūshichi Tsuzuki, *The Life of Eleanor Marx, 1855-1898: A Socialist Tragedy*. Oxford: Clarendon Press, 1967).

28 Rive, *Olive*, p. 72, 105, 107, 110, 128, 177; First and Scott, *Olive*, p. 166, 168.

29 Anon, 'Sir Bryan'.

30 NA: T1/15649, 3528, Admiralty to Treasury, 16 Feb. 1883; Jennings, *Widnall*, p. 195, 218, 230, 245; St John's College: W.15 (James 611 and 612); Anon, 'Sir Bryan'; *London Gazette*, 23 Jan. 1929.

31 *Liverpool Mercury*, 18 Feb. 1885.

Bibliography

Archifdy Ceredigion Archive, Aberystwyth

BRA/7; [GB 0212] D/LO, 16.

British Library, London (BL)

Leland Papers: 37173; 37174.
Society of Authors' Papers: MS 56863.

National Archives, Kew, London (NA)

ADM 16/45, No. 3; ADM 16/45, No. 4; ADM 116/35; ADM 116/ 44, No. 2; FO 78/3416; FO 78/3462; FO 78/3587; PRO 30/57/5; T1/15649.

Palestine Exploration Fund, London

PAL/1-9; PAL (ii), 12-29.

Patrick Maselis (PM)

The diaries of Edmund Merceron Burton: Vol. 1 – 1 Sept. to 31 Oct. 1882; Vol. 2 – 1 Nov. to 31 Dec. 1882; Vol. 3 – 1 Jan. to 5 March 1882; Correspondence of Edmund Merceron Burton: To Mrs R. Burton (mother); J. Stokes; War Office.

Royal Geographical Society, London

WJG 2: India, Marri Expedition, Persia, Russia, 20 Aug. 1880 to 1 April 1881; WJG 4: Tripoli, 18 Oct. 1881 to 16 June 1882; WJG 5-6; Journal MSS. China, 1877; Gill, W.J., JMS 10/70.

St John's College Archive, Cambridge

W.3 (part); W.15 (James 611 and 612).

Parliamentary Papers (PP)

PP1883 [C.3494] [C.3761] 'Correspondence respecting the murder of Professor E. H. Palmer, Captain W M. Gill, R.E., and Lieutenant Harold Charrington, R.N.'

Censuses

1851, 1861

HM Courts & Tribunals Service

Estates of Edward Henry Palmer, William Edward Pretyman and Mary Ann Straker.

Periodicals

Academy; ARS Quatuor Coronaturum; Cambrian News and Merionthshire Standard; Cambridge Independent Press; Clarence and Richmond Examiner; Daily Northwestern; Evening Telegraph; Illustrated London News; Liverpool Mercury; London Gazette; London Standard; Manchester Times; Morning Post; Proceedings of the Royal Geographical Society; Quarterly Review; South Australian Register; Spalding's Directory of Cambridge; The Belfast News-Letter; The Brisbane Courier; The Bristol Mercury and Daily Post; The Graphic; The North-Eastern Daily Gazette; The Pall Mall Gazette; The Star; The Sydney Morning Herald; The Times.

Secondary sources

Anon, 'ןוסח רוכב לש ורופיסו 1882 ב יניסל רמלאפ תחלשמ לש רמה הלרוג'. Available from: http://www.boker.org.il/meida/negev/desert_biking/ain_akev/palmer_book/palmer_low.pdf (accessed October 2013).

Anon, *A Very Brief Regimental History*, Kimberley: Kimberley

Regiment Association, 2010.

Anon, 'Baber, Edward Colborne', *Dictionary of National Biography. Sup. Volume I*, Oxford: Oxford University Press, 1901.

Anon, 'Besant's life of Palmer', *The Eagle*, 13 (1883), pp. 18-29.

Anon, 'Burton, Sir Richard Francis', *Dictionary of National Biography*, Oxford: Oxford University Press, 1901.

Anon, 'Commemorative Medals', *Global Anabaptist Mennonite Encyclopaedia Online*. Available from: http://gameo.org/index.php?title=Commemorative_Medals&oldid=94221 (accessed October 2013).

Anon, 'Edward Henry Palmer', *The Eagle*, 12 (1883), pp. 233-40.

Anon, 'Frederick Nicholas Charrington'. Available from: http://george-powell.co.uk/family/4806.htm (accessed October 2013).

Anon, 'History of Aberystwyth'. Available from: http://www.aberystwythguide.org.uk/history/to1900.shtml (accessed October 2013).

Anon, 'Lieutenant Harold Charrington'. Available from: http://www.findagrave.com/cgi-bin/fg.cgi?page=gr&GRid=42289047 (accessed October 2013).

Anon, 'Memoirs. Colonel E. M. Burton', *The Royal Engineers Journal*, 62 (1948).

Anon, 'Moore, Noel Temple', *Who Was Who, 1897-1915*, London: A. & C. Black, 1920.

Anon, *Recreations of the Rabelais Club, 1880-81*, London: Rabelais Club, 1881.

Anon, 'Richthofen, Ferdinand, Baron von' in *Encyclopædia Britannica* (11th ed.), Cambridge: Cambridge University Press, 1911.

Anon, *Selected Papers from the Transactions of the Canadian Military Institute, 1891-92*, Toronto: Royal Canadian Military Institute, 1892.

Anon, 'Sex Toys. A History'. Available from: http://pincurlmag.com/tag/vibrators (accessed October 2013).

Anon, 'Sir Bryan Donkin', *The British Medical Journal*, 6 Aug. 1927.

Anon, 'Spencer Calmeyer Charrington'. Available from: http://www.findagrave.com/cgi-bin/fg.cgi?page=gr&GRid=76718176 (accessed October 2013).

Anon, 'Tel-El-Kebir'. Available from: http://rhf.org.uk/rhf/index.php?option=com_content&task=view&id=45&Itemid=59 (accessed October 2013).

Anon, *The Savile Club, 1868-1923*, Edinburgh: Neill & Co., 1923.

Anon, 'Sir Charles Warren', *The Geographical Journal*, 69 (4) (1927), pp. 382-383.

Anon, 'The Straker Family'. Available from: http://homepage.ntlworld.com/andy.kelly/straker/index.htm (accessed October 2013).

Anon, 'Todhunter, Isaac' in *Alumni Cantabrigienses*, Cambridge: Cambridge University Press, 1922.

Anon, 'Towards understanding of the qur'an. A new translation of the glorious Qur'an', *Journal of Muslim Minority Affairs*, 19 (1) (1999), pp. 131-43.

Anon, 'Wade, Thomas Francis' in *Alumni Cantabrigienses*, Cambridge: Cambridge University Press, 1922.

Anon, 'Wright, William' in *Alumni Cantabrigienses*, Cambridge: Cambridge University Press, 1922.

Al-Mamalik, Dust'ali Mu'ayyir, *In the Land of the Pharaohs. A Short History of Egypt from the Fall of Ismail to the Assassination of Boutros Pasha*, London: S. Paul, 1911.

Alderson, Edwin Alfred Hervey, *With the Mounted Infantry and the Mashonaland Field Force, 1896*, London: Methuen, 1898.

Anderson, Dorothy, *Baker Pasha: Misconduct and Mischance*, Norwich: Michael Russell, 1999.

Arberry, Arthur John, *Oriental Essays: Portraits of Seven Scholars*, London: George Allen & Unwin, 1960.

Archer, Thomas, *The War in Egypt and the Soudan. An Episode in the History of the British Empire*, London: Blackie and Son,

1887.

Baker, Valentine, *Clouds in the East,* London: Chatto & Windus, 1876.

Bartlett, Samuel Colcord, *From Egypt to Palestine: Through Sinai, the Wilderness and the South Country,* New York: Harper & Bros., 1879.

Becket, Ian F. W., *Victorians at War,* London: Hambledon and London, 2003.

Begg, Paul, *Jack the Ripper: The Definitive History,* London: Longman/Pearson Education, 2004.

Berridge, Virginia and Edwards, Griffith, *Opium and the People: Opiate Use in Nineteenth-Century England,* London: Allen Lane, 1981.

Besant, Walter (ed.), *The Literary Remains of Charles Frederick Tyrwhitt Drake,* London, 1877.

Besant, Walter, *The Life and Achievements of Edward Henry Palmer,* London: John Murray, 1883.

Besant, Walter and Palmer, Edward Henry, *Jerusalem. The City of Herod and Saladin*, London: Chatto & Windus, 1899.

Besant, Walter, *Autobiography of Sir Walter Besan*t, London: Dodd, Mead, 1902.

Bidwell, R. L., 'Edward Henry Palmer', *Bulletin (British Society for Middle Eastern Studies),* 13 (1), (1986), pp. 45-50.

Black, John Sutherland and Chrystal, George, *The Life of William Robertson Smith,* London: A. & C. Black, 1912.

Blunt, Wilfrid Scawen, *Atrocities of Justice Under British Rule in Egypt,* London: Fisher Unwin, 1907.

Blunt, Wilfrid Scawen, *A Secret History of the English Occupation of Egypt,* London: Knopf, 1907.

Blunt,_Wilfrid Scawen, *India under Ripon. A Private Diary,* London: T. Fisher Unwin, 1909.

Blunt, Wilfrid Scawen *Gordon at Khartoum. Being a Personal Narrative of Events in Continuation of "A Secret History of the English Occupation of Egypt",* London: S. Swift & Co., 1911.

Boase, G. C., 'Margary, Augustus Raymond (1846–1875)' in *Oxford Dictionary of National Biography*, Oxford: Oxford University Press, 2004.

Bonney, T. G., *Memoires of a Long Life*, Cambridge: Metcalfe, 1921.

Brown, W. Baker, *The History of the Corps of Royal Engineers. Volume IV*, Chatham: The Institution of Royal Engineers, 1952.

Browne, Douglas G., *The Rise of Scotland Yard*, London: George G. Harrap & Co., 1956.

Buckland, Charles Edwards, *Dictionary of Indian Biography*, London: Haskell House Publishers, 1906.

Bundy, C., *The Rise and Fall of South African Peasantry*, Berkeley: University of California Press, 1979.

Burnand, Francis Cowley, *The ADC: Personal Reminiscences of the University Amateur Dramatic Club, Cambridge*, London: Chapman and Hall, 1880.

Burton, Isabel, *The Life of Captain Sir Richard F. Burton*, New York: D. Appleton & Company, 1893.

Burton, Richard F. and Drake, Charles F. Tyrwhitt, *Unexplored Syria. Visits to the Libanus, the Tulul el Safa, the Anti-Libanus, the Northern Libanus and the Alah*, London: Tinsley Bros., 1872.

Burton, Richard F., *Personal Narrative of a Pilgrimage to El Medinah and Meccah*, London: W. Mullan & Son, 1879.

Burton, Richard, 'The late E. H. Palmer ii. The story of his death', *The Academy*, 12 May, 1883 (575), pp. 329-30.

Chamberlain, M. E., 'The Alexandria massacre of 11 June 1882 and the British occupation of Egypt', *Middle Eastern Studies*, 13 (1) (1977), pp. 14-39.

Clark, J. Willis, *Old Friends at Cambridge and Elsewhere*, London: Macmillan & Co., 1909.

Cole, Juan Ricardo, *Colonialism and Revolution in the Middle East: Social and Cultural Origins of Egypt's Urabi Movement*, Cairo: American University in Cairo Press, 1999.

Daly, M. W., 'The British occupation, 1882-1922' in Daly, M. W. and Petry, Carl Forbes (eds), *Modern Egypt from 1517 to the End of the Twentieth Century*, Cambridge: Cambridge University Press, 1998, pp. 239-51.

Das Gupta, Tania (ed.), *Race and Racialization: Essential Readings*, Toronto: Canadian Scholars' Press, 2007.

Davies, Graham I., 'Fresh evidence on E.H. Palmer's travels from Cambridge libraries' in McCarthy, Carmel and Healey, John F. (eds.), *Biblical and Near Eastern Essays: Studies in Honour of Kevin J. Cathcart*, London: T. & T. Clark International, 2004.

'Defender' (pseud.), *Sir Charles Warren and Spion Kop, with a Biographical Sketch*, London: Smith, Elder and Co., 1902.

Dicey, Edward, *The Story of the Khedivate*, London: Rivingtons, 1902.

Donkin, Horatio, 'A note on thought-reading', *Popular Science Monthly*, 21 (September 1882), pp. 634-7.

Driver, Felix, 'Yule, Sir Henry (1820–1889)' in *Oxford Dictionary of National Biography*, Oxford: Oxford University Press, 2004.

Dundonald, Lieut.-General, *My Army Life*, London: E. Arnold & Co., 1926.

Eddleston, John J., *Jack the Ripper: An Encyclopaedia*, Santa Barbara: ABC-Clio, 2001.

Eliav, Mordechai, *Britain and the Holy Land, 1838-1914: Selected Documents from the British Consulate in Jerusalem*, Jerusalem: Yad Izhak Ben-Zvi Press, 1997.

Evans, George Eyre, *Aberystwyth and Its Court Leet*, Aberystwyth: Welsh Gazette, 1902.

Fage, J. and Oliver, R., *The Cambridge History of Africa, Volume 6*, Cambridge: Cambridge University Press, 1985.

Farnie, D, *East and West of Suez: The* Suez Canal *in History, 1854-1956*, Oxford: Clarendon Press, 1969.

Farwell, Byron, *The Great Boer War*, London: Allen Lane, London, 1976.

Featherstone, Donald, *Tel El-Kebir, 1882. Wolseley's Conquest of Egypt*, London: Osprey, 1993.

Field, Henry M., *On the Desert: With a Brief Review of Recent Events in Egypt*, New York: C. Scribner's Sons, 1883.

Finch-Crisp, William, *Chronological Retrospect of the History of Yarmouth and Neighbourhood from A.D. 46 to 1884*, London: J. Haddon & Co, 1884.

Finn, James, *A View from Jerusalem, 1849-1858: The Consular Diary of James and Elizabeth Anne Finn,* Rutherford: Fairleigh Dickinson, 1980.

First, Ruth and Scott, Ann, *Olive Schreiner,* London: Deutsch, 1980.

Foster, Joseph, *Men-at-the-Bar: A Biographical Hand-List of the Members of the Various Inns of Court,* London: Reeves and Turner, 1885.

Fraser, Jamie, 'Man-hunting in the desert. The mysterious disappearance of the Palmer Sinai Expedition', *Near Eastern Archaeology Foundation Bulletin,* 54 (Oct. 2010), pp. 15-19.

Galbraith, John S. and al-Sayyid-Marsot, Afaf Lutfi, 'The British occupation of Egypt: Another view', *International Journal of Middle East Studies,* 9 (4) (1978), pp. 471-88.

Garland, David, 'British criminology before 1935', *The British Journal of Criminology,* 28 (2) (1988).

Garrett, Duane A. and Kaiser Jnr., Walter C., *Archaeological Study Bible: An Illustrated Walk Through Biblical History and Culture,* Grand Rapids: Zondervan, 2005.

Gay, H., 'Science and Opportunity in London, 1871-85: The Diary of Herbert McLeod', *History of Science,* 41 (2003), pp.427-458.

Gill, William, *The River of Golden Sand: The Narrative of a Journey through China and Eastern Tibet to Burmah,* London: John Murray, 1884.

Good, Joseph A., 'The Dark Circle: Spiritualism in Victorian and Neo-Victorian Fiction', PhD diss., University of South Florida, 2012.

Gray, John Milner, *A History of the Perse School, Cambridge,* Cambridge: Bowes & Bowes, 1921.

Green, Dominic, *Three Empires on the Nile: The Victorian Jihad,*

1869-1899, London: Free Press, 2007.

Grew, E. S., *Lord Kitchener. His Life and Work for the Empire*, London: Gresham, 1916.

Hadland, Tony, 'William Gill, spy and explorer'. Available from: http://www.radleyhistoryclub.org.uk/report_april_2014.pdf (accessed November 2014).

Hadland, Tony, *Glimpses of a Victorian Hero. William Gill – Explorer and Spy*, Coventry: Hadland Books, 2002.

Haynes, Alfred R., *Man-Hunting in the Desert. Being a Narrative of the Palmer Search Expedition*, London: Horace Cox, 1894.

Henderson, Jessica Rae, 'Opium Use in Victorian England: The works of Gaskell, Eliot and Dickens', PhD thesis, Boise State University, 2009.

Hopkins, A.G., 'The Victorians and Africa: A Reconsideration of the Occupation of Egypt, 1882', *The Journal of African History*, 27 (1986), pp. 363-391.

House of Commons Debates, London: HMSO.

House of Lords Debates, London: HMSO.

Huber, Valeska, *Channelling Mobilities. Migration and Globalisation in the Suez Canal Region and Beyond, 1869–1914*, Cambridge: Cambridge University Press, 2013.

Hull, Edward, *Mount Seir, Sinai and Western Palestine*, London: Bentley, 1885.

Hunt, Alan, 'Charles Warren in Africa', *Journal of the Whitechapel Society*, April 2006.

Karsh, Inari and Karsh, Efrain, *Empires of the Sand: The Struggle for Mastery in the Middle East, 1789-1923*, Cambridge, MA: Harvard University Press, 1999.

Irving, Laurence, *Henry Irving: The Actor and His World*, London: Faber and Faber, 1951.

Irwin, Robert, *For Lust of Knowing. The Orientalists and their Enemies*, London: Allen Lane, 2006.

Jacobson, David, 'Charles Warren vs. James Fergusson. Where Was the Israelite Temple Located?', *Biblical Archaeology Review*,

29 (Sept/Oct 2003).

Jennings, Christine, *Widnall: A Capital Contractor. The Story of a Victorian Household in the Village of Grantchester*, Swavesey: Folly, 2003.

Johnson, Harry Hamilton, *A History of the Colonization of Africa by Alien Races*, Cambridge: Cambridge University Press, 1899.

Karg, Barb and Young Jon K., *101 Secrets of the Freemasons: The Truth Behind the World's Most Mysterious Society*, London: Adams Media, 2009.

Lane-Poole, Stanley, *Studies in a Mosque*, London: Allen, 1883.

Leland, C. G., Palmer, E. H. and Tuckey, J., *English-Gipsy Songs in Romany with Metrical English Translations*, London, 1875.

Leland, Charles Godfrey, *The Gypsies*, London: Houghton, Mifflin and Co., 1882.

Leland, Charles Godfrey, *Memoirs*, London: D. Appleton, 1893.

Liddell Hart, Basil Henry, *T. E. Lawrence: In Arabia and After*, London: Jonathan Cape, 1934.

Linehan, Peter, *St John's College Cambridge: A History*, Woodbridge: Boydell Press, 2011.

Longford, Elizabeth, *Pilgrimage of Passion. The Life of Wilfrid Scawen Blunt*, London: Tauris Parke, 1979.

Longford, Elizabeth, 'Wilfrid Scawen Blunt', *Oxford Dictionary of National Biography*, Oxford: Oxford University Press, 2004.

Lovell, Mary S., *A Rage to Live: A Biography of Richard and Isabel Burton*, New York: W. W. Norton, 1998.

Lutsky, Vladimir Borisovich, *Modern History of the Arab Countries*, Moscow: Progress Publishers, 1969.

Lyngaas, Sean, 'Ahmad Urabi, delegate of the people. Social mobilization in Egypt on the eve of Colonial rule', *Al Nakhlah*, Spring 2011, pp. 1-13.

Macdonald, Colin, *Warren! The Bond of Brotherhood*, London: Colman Street Books, 2008.

Macduff, John Ross, *Early Graves. A Book for the Bereaved*, London, 1883.

Magnus, Philip, *Kitchener. Portrait of an Imperialist,* London: Penguin, 1968.

Maier, Bernhard, *William Robertson Smith. His life, his Work and his Times,* Tübingen: Mohr Siebeck, 2009.

Matthews, Brander, *These Many Years, Recollections of a New Yorker,* New York: C. Scribner's Sons, 1917.

McCabe, Joseph, *Spiritualism: A Popular History from 1847,* London: Dodd, Mead and Company, 1920.

McCarthy, O. R., 'The key to the sanatoria', *Journal of the Royal Society of Medicine,* 94 (8) (2001), pp. 413-7.

Meintjes, Johannes, *Olive Schreiner. Portrait of a South African Woman,* Johannesburg: Hugh Keartland, 1965.

Mentiply, David J., 'The British invasion of Egypt 1882'. Available from: http://www.e-ir.info/2009/03/23/the-british-invasion-of-egypt-1882/ (accessed October 2013).

Morley, Christopher J., *Jack the Ripper: A Suspect Guide,* self-published, 2005.

Moscrop, John James, *Measuring Jerusalem: The Palestine Exploration Fund and British Interests,* Leicester: Leicester University Press, 1999.

Murray, George W., *Sons of Ishmael: A Study of the Egyptian Bedouin,* London: George Routledge and Sons, 1935.

Nurse, Donald Paul, 'An amateur barbarian. The life and career of Sir Richard Francis Burton, 1821 -1890', DPhil diss., University of Toronto, 1999.

Nykl, A. R., 'Notes on E. H. Palmer's 'The Qur'an', *Journal of the American Oriental Society,* 56 (1) (1936), pp. 77-84.

Odel, Robin, *Ripperology: A Study of the World's First Serial Killer and a Literary Phenomenon,* Kent, Ohio: Kent State University Press, 2006.

Oldroyd, David, 'Bonney, Thomas George (1833–1923)' in *Oxford Dictionary of National Biography,* Oxford: Oxford University Press, 2004.

Page, Larry Roeder, *The Bedouin Tribes of the Sinai: Lecture Book,*

Self-published, 1988.

Pakenham, Thomas, *The Boer War*, London: Abacus, 1997.

Palmer, Edward Henry, *Ye Hole in ye Walle: A Legende of Walthamstowe Abbey. A Merrie, Metrical and Monastical Romaunce*, Cambridge, 1860.

Palmer, Edward Henry, *Oriental Mysticism. A Treatise on the Sufiistic and Unitarian Theosophy of the Persians, Compiled from Native Sources*, Cambridge: Deighton, Bell & Co., 1867.

Palmer, Edward Henry, *A Descriptive Catalogue of the Arabic, Persian, and Turkish Manuscripts in the Library of Trinity College*, Cambridge, Cambridge: Deighton, Bell & Co., 1870.

Palmer, Edward Henry, *The Desert of the Exodus: Journeys on Foot in the Wilderness of the Forty Years' Wanderings*, London: Deighton, Bell and Co., 1871.

Palmer, Edward Henry, *A Grammar of the Arabic Language*, London, 1874.

Palmer, Edward Henry, *A History of the Jewish Nation from the Earliest times to the Present Day*, London: Christian Knowledge Society, 1874.

Palmer, Edward Henry, *A Concise Dictionary of the Persian Language*, London: Trübner & Co., 1876.

Palmer, Edward Henry, *The Poetical Works of Behā-ed-Dīn Zoheir*, Cambridge: University Press, 1876-77.

Palmer, E. H., 'Mohammed and Mohammedanism', *Quarterly Review*, 143 (1877).

Palmer, Edward Henry, *The Song of the Reed and Other Pieces*, London: Trübner, 1877.

Palmer, Edward Henry and Magnússon, Eiríkr, *L. Runeberg's Lyrical Songs, Idylls and Epigrams*, London, 1878.

Palmer, Edward Henry, *The Qur'ân* Oxford: Clarendon Press, 1880.

Palmer, Edward Henry, *Haroun Alraschid, Caliph of Bagdad*, London: Marcus Ward, 1881.

Palmer, Edward Henry, 'The desert of Tih and the country of

Moab' in Palmer, Edward Henry and Besant, Walter (eds), *Survey of Western Palestine,* London: Palestine Exploration Fund, 1881-83.

Palmer, Edward Henry and Besant, Walter (eds), *The Survey of Western Palestine, London: Palestine Exploration Fund,* 1881-83.

Palmer, Edward Henry (ed.), *Trübner's Collection of Simplified Grammars of the Principal Asiatic and European Languages, Volumes 1-6,* Trübner & Co.: London; Hertford, 1882.

Palmer, Edward Henry, *Simplified Grammar of Hindustani, Persian and Arabic,* London: Trübner & Company, 1882.

Parashar, Parmanand, *Public Administration in the Developed World,* New Delhi: Sarup, 1997.

Parkinson,_Brian Rogers, 'Judge Pierre Crabites. A Borbon democrat in Egypt, 1877-1943', PhD diss., Florida State University, 2005.

Pennell, Elizabeth Robins, *Charles Godfrey Leland: A Biography, Volume Two,* Boston, Mass.: Houghton, Mifflin, 1906.

Porter, T. M., *Karl Pearson: The Scientific Life in a Statistical Age,* Princeton: Princeton University Press, 2004.

Prior, Katherine, 'Colborne Bradford', *Oxford Dictionary of National Biography,* Oxford: Oxford University Press, 2004.

Reed, C. B. E., *Memoir of Sir Charles Reed,* London: Macmillan, 1883.

Reid, Donald Malcolm, 'The Urabi revolution and British conquest' in Daly, M. W. and Petry, Carl Forbes (eds), *Modern Egypt from 1517 to the End of the Twentieth Century,* Cambridge: Cambridge University Press, 1998, pp. 217-238.

Rive, Richard (ed.), *Olive Schreiner Letters, Volume 1,* Oxford: Clarendon Press, 1988.

Robinson, Charles N., *Celebrities of the Army,* London: Publishers' Syndicate, 1900.

Robinson, George L., 'Modern Kadesh or Ein Kadis', *The Biblical World,* 17 (5) (1901), pp. 327-338.

Robson, Brian, *The Road to Kabul: The Second Afghan War 1878-*

1881, Stroud: Spellmount, 2007.

Rotberg, Robert I., *The Founder: Cecil Rhodes and the Pursuit of Power*, Oxford: Oxford University Press, 1988.

Royle, Charles, *The Egyptian Campaigns, 1882 to 1885*, London: Hurst and Blackett Ltd, 1900.

Rubinstein, William, 'Jewish Top Wealth-Holders in Britain, 1809-1909', *Jewish Historical Studies*, 37 (2002), pp. 133-161.

Saul, David, *Military Blunders. The How and Why of Military Failure*, London: Robinson, 1997.

Schölch, Alexander, 'The Egyptian Bedouins and the Urābīyūn', *Die Welt des Islams*, 17 (1/4) (1976-77), pp. 44-57.

Seymour, Edward H., *My Naval Career and Travels*, London: Smith, Elder & Co., 1911.

Shah, Muhammad Sultan, 'A critical study of E. H. Palmer's translation of the Qur'an', *Hamdard Islamicus*, xxxv (2).

Shand, Alexander Innes, *Days of the Past. A Medley of Memories*, New York: E. P. Button & Co., 1905.

Showalter, E., *The Female Malady. Women, Madness and English Culture 1830-1980*, London: Virago Press, 2007.

Silberman, Neil Asher, *Digging for God and Country: Exploration, Archaeology, and the Secret Struggle for the Holy Land, 1799-1917*, New York: Knopf, 1982.

Smith, W. Robertson, 'The life and achievements of Edward Henry Palmer', *Nature*, 26 July 1893 (28), pp. 292-3.

Smith, Warren W., *History of Tibet: Nationalism and Self-Determination*, Boulder, Colorado: Westview Press, 1996.

Spalding, W. P., *Spalding's Directory of Cambridge 1878*, Cambridge, 1878.

Spiers, Edward M., *The Late Victorian Army, 1868-1902*, Manchester University Press, 1992.

Spiers, Edward M., *The Victorian Soldier in Africa*, Manchester: Manchester University Press, 2004.

Stevens, Keith, 'A Jersey adventurer in China', *Journal of the Royal Asiatic Society, Hong Kong Branch*, 32 (1992), pp. 1-101.

Temple, A. G., *Guildhall Memories*, London: John Murray, 1918.

Thompson, Brian, *Imperial Vanities*, London: Harper Collins, 2002.

Trumbull, Henry Clay, *Kadesh-Barnea. Its Importance and Probable Site*, New York: Charles Scribner & Sons, 1884.

Tsuzuki, Chūshichi, *The Life of Eleanor Marx, 1855-1898: A Socialist Tragedy*. Oxford: Clarendon Press, 1967.

Tyson, Bryan (ed.), *Bernard Shaw's Book Reviews, Volume 2, 1884-1950*, University Park, Pennsylvania: Pennsylvania State University Press, 1996.

Vincent, Andrew, 'The Jew, the Gipsy and El-Islam: An Examination of Richard Burton's Consulship in Damascus and His Premature Recall, 1868-1871', *Journal of the Royal Asiatic Society*, 2 (1985), pp.155-173.

Waldman, Linda, *The Griqua Conundrum: Political and Socio-cultural Identity in the Northern Cape*, Oxford: Peter Lang, 2007.

Warren, Charles, *Underground Jerusalem*, London: R. Bentley and Son, 1876.

Warren, Charles, *Notes on Arabia Petea and the Country Lying Between Egypt and Palestine*, London: Palestine Exploration Fund, 1887.

Warren, Charles, *On the Veldt in the Seventies*, London: Isbister & Co., 1902.

Watkins, Jessica, 'British Colonial policies in the Arab region. Sowing the seeds of contemporary Middle Eastern security sectors?', *Arab Reform Initiative*, April 2012.

Watson, Charles Moore, *The Life of Major-General Sir Charles William Wilson, Royal Engineers*, London: John Murray, 1909.

Wawn, Andrew, *The Vikings and the Victorians: Inventing the Old North in Nineteenth-Century Britain*, Cambridge: Brewer, 2000.

Westrate, Bruce, *The Arab Bureau. British Policy in the Middle East, 1916-1920*, University Park, Pennsylvania: The Pennsylvania State University Press, 1992.

White, Douglas, 'Society for the Prevention of Venereal Disease', *British Medical Journal*, 29 Nov. 1919 (3074), p. 725.

Williams, Watkin W., *The Life of General Sir Charles Warren,* Oxford: Basil Blackwell, 1941.

Wilson, Charles William, *Ordnance Survey of the Peninsula of Sinai,* London; Palestine Exploration Fund, 1869.

Wood, Eric, *The Boy's Book of Battles,* London: Cassell and Company, 1913.

Wright, William J., *A Tidy Little War: The British Invasion of Egypt 1882,* Stroud: History, 2009.

Yule, H., 'Memoir of Captain W. Gill' in William John Gill, *The River of Golden Sand: The Narrative of a Journey through China and Eastern Tibet to Burmah,* London: John Murray, 1884.

Zaki-Khalil, Karim, 'British Sinai. Its geopolitical significance in the Middle East and its strategic role in British colonial policy', PhD diss., University of Durham, 1998.

Acknowledgements

A great number of libraries and archives were used during the research of this book. I would like to thank the staff of the British Library, London; of the Bodleian Library, Oxford; of the British Library of Political and Economic Science, London; of the National Archives, Kew; of the Archifdy Ceredigion Archive, Aberystwyth; of the Palestine Exploration Fund, London; of the Royal Geographical Society, London; and of St John's College Library, Cambridge. I am also extremely grateful to Patrick Maselis, who kindly gave me access to the diaries and correspondence of Edmund Merceron Burton.

Note. Surnames and place names are spelt as they appear in contemporary documents.

Also by David Sunderland

An Economic History of London, 1800-1914
(co-author Michael Ball)
Managing the British Empire
Managing British Colonial and Post-Colonial Development
Social Capital, Trust and the Industrial Revolution, 1780-1880
Financing the Raj